Marilyn Walton is an
retrace her father's World V
crew, bridges a gap of over s
laced with quick-witted humor, attention to detail and
compassion enabled her to not only bridge the time gap, but also
create new cultural and personal bridges with all those individuals
uniquely involved in her project.

Marilyn takes the reader from the United States and Mexico
to Great Britain, Germany and Poland during the retracing of
these footsteps from the beginning of the B-24 crew training to the
fateful day of "Rhapsody's" demise over Germany in June, 1944.
The ensuing capture of the crew and the mysterious death of Sgt.
Harold Flaugher are meticulously retold along with harrowing tales
of forced winter marches which culminate in the jubilant release of
all the POWs by Patton's forces in April, 1945.

Marilyn's life has undoubtedly changed dramatically through
this endeavor as has the lives of all those she touched during the
course of her travels and the research she undertook in compiling
this interesting story.

Hanns-Claudius Scharff<br>
Son of Hanns Joachim Scharff,<br>
Master Interrogator of Dulag Luft

A tremendous read. In addition to writing an important family
narrative, the author has produced a significant document to
be added to the prisoner of war literature. It will certainly be
a welcomed addition at the Air Force Academy. The book is
an important contribution that offers an objective awareness of
the human condition which is so often lacking in "there I was"
accounts of the experience.

Duane J. Reed<br>
Former Archivist<br>
United States Air Force Academy

Walton helps you discover a group of genuine heroes of WWII, the prisoners of war of Stalag Luft III. Be prepared to shed a tear or two as you accompany the Waltons on their search for what happened to her father and the crew of "Rhapsody in Junk." This is a great read.

John E. Dolibois
Ambassador to Luxembourg
1981-85
Captain, U.S. Army 1942-46
Interrogator of Prisoners of War
Nuremberg War Crimes Commision
Author of *Pattern of Circles*
*An Ambassador's Story*

# Rhapsody in Junk

## A Daughter's Return To Germany To Finish Her Father's Story

by

*Marilyn Jeffers Walton*

AuthorHouse™
1663 Liberty Drive
Bloomington, IN 47403
www.authorhouse.com
Phone: 1-800-839-8640

This book is a work of non-fiction. Unless otherwise noted, the author and the publisher make no explicit guarantees as to the accuracy of the information contained in this book and in some cases, names of people and places have been altered to protect their privacy.

© 2012 Marilyn Jeffers Walton. All rights reserved.

No part of this book may be reproduced, stored in a retrieval system, or transmitted by any means without the written permission of the author.

Published by AuthorHouse 7/31/2012

ISBN: 978-1-4259-7486-2 (sc)

Artwork by Mrs. Diane Stamp
Photography by Mr. Thomas Witte

Because of the dynamic nature of the Internet, any web addresses or links contained in this book may have changed since publication and may no longer be valid. The views expressed in this work are solely those of the author and do not necessarily reflect the views of the publisher, and the publisher hereby disclaims any responsibility for them.

# Contents
★★★

Foreword ............................................................................... i
Acknowledgements ............................................................. iii
Preface ................................................................................ vii

# Chapters

1. Sentimental Mission .................................................... 1
2. Over There... ................................................................. 5
3. Welcome to the 458th ................................................... 9
4. Hell from Heaven Man ................................................ 19
5. Phase Training ............................................................. 25
6. Heading for a Mission ................................................. 31
7. Loss of the Belle .......................................................... 37
8. D-Day ........................................................................... 43
9. Mission to Evreux ........................................................ 47
10. I'll Be Back ................................................................. 51
11. The Pain of War ......................................................... 55
12. Up We Go... ................................................................ 61
13. The Vigil of Sweating It Out ...................................... 75
14. Deadly Black Veil ....................................................... 77
15. A Wing and a Prayer .................................................. 85
16. Death on the Ground ................................................. 93
17. Fuer Dich ist der Krieg vorbei .................................... 99
18. Schloss Gottorf ......................................................... 101
19. Missing in Action ..................................................... 105
20. Come In, I Am Your Interrogator ............................. 111
21. Clipped Wings .......................................................... 125
22. Ferrets and Goons .................................................... 133
23. From a Lonely Bombardier ...................................... 141
24. I'll Be Home for Christmas ...................................... 145
25. The March Is On ...................................................... 149
26. Bash What You Can't Take ...................................... 153
27. Of Historical Significance ........................................ 159

| | |
|---|---|
| 28. Winter's Bitter Lash | 165 |
| 29. Merciful Muskau | 175 |
| 30. Rolling Cells | 179 |
| 31. Center Compound | 183 |
| 32. Train of Misery | 187 |
| 33. Moosburg | 191 |
| 34. Stalag Luft IV | 195 |
| 35. Dean and Gonzales | 201 |
| 36. The First Taste of Freedom | 203 |
| 37. Bavarian Redoubt | 209 |
| 38. Tanks! | 213 |
| 39. Unrestrained Joy | 221 |
| 40. Biding Our Time | 225 |
| 41. A Reversal of Roles | 229 |
| 42. I'll Be Seeing You | 237 |
| 43. Into Waiting Arms | 243 |
| 44. R&R | 249 |
| 45. Fading Away | 251 |
| 46. Still Standing Tall | 255 |
| 47. Now Alone | 261 |
| 48. In Search of the Crew | 265 |
| 49. Worldwide Research | 271 |
| 50. Letters from Matthias | 281 |
| 51. IDPF | 287 |
| 52. Mission Germany | 293 |
| 53. Deutschland | 297 |
| 54. Friends We've Yet to Meet | 301 |
| 55. Into the Woods | 309 |
| 56. With Dignity and Honor | 321 |
| 57. Big Black Gates | 325 |
| 58. Stalag Luft III | 329 |
| 59. In My Father's Footsteps | 341 |
| 60. Spremberg | 345 |
| 61. Munich | 347 |

62. Frankfurt .................................................................... 349
63. Dulag Luft Revisited .................................................... 351
64. Our Hero Stumbles ...................................................... 363
65. Our Hero Falls ............................................................. 371
66. Saying Good-Bye ........................................................ 377
67. Remembering Yesterday ............................................. 383
68. The Good General ....................................................... 389
69. Behind the Wire .......................................................... 395
70. Flight into the Past ..................................................... 399
71. An Unexpected Gift .................................................... 405
72. Dresden ...................................................................... 409
73. A New Family Found .................................................. 421
74. Return to the Woods ................................................... 429
75. Through the Generations ............................................ 435
76. The Missing Documents ............................................. 439
77. Their Legacy ............................................................... 447
Epilogue ............................................................................ 455
Appendix .......................................................................... 469
End Notes ......................................................................... 477
Sources ............................................................................. 479

# Foreword

Marilyn Walton is one of very few people to my knowledge who has immersed themselves in the POW experience to the point where they can write about it as if they had lived the experience themselves. Marilyn's father was a POW himself, and his daughter has told the story of his life as a member of the "World War Two" generation with love, pride and sensitivity. Her research has been thorough and has brought her new friends who sixty years ago were under her father's bombs.

I have had the privilege of watching Marilyn's book grow as she uncovered aspects of her father's experiences as a B-24 bombardier and built them into a rich document that will assist people to better understand our generation's "Great War" for generations to come.

A.P. Clark<br>
Lt. General USAF (Ret)<br>
Superintendent of the United States<br>
Air Force Academy 1970-1974<br>
Author of *"33 Months as a POW in Stalag Luft III-*<br>
*A World War II Airman Tells His Story"*

# Acknowledgements

The completion of this book requires many thank yous. Posthumously, I must thank my father for all the memories of the crew and their missions he kept alive as I was growing up. I knew their names well, long before I actually met them. A big thank you to the men of the crew, Lawrence Dean and Jack Gonzales, whose memories I probed on so many occasions and who were ready with answers to all my questions. It could not have been done without you and the help of your wonderful daughters, Brenda Dean Morea and Linda Gonzales Waddington. My thanks to Alex Cardenas, discovered much later, who regaled us with stories and fascinating recollections and to his daughter, Angelita, who kept us in touch in Mexico via email. Thank you to the late Frank Deimel for reliving those war days with me and to Marian and step-daughter, Anna Taylor. Kay Gamble, daughter of Dee Butler, who shared her late father's journals and pictures, provided an invaluable contribution. Thank you to Jean Brodek for sending her late husband's pictures and letters. Robert Risko, Jr.'s contribution of his father's journal, log book and his collection of pictures filled in many of the gaps. The late Henry Northrop's daughter, Maria Haag, and son, Michael Northrop, sent pictures and stories in memory of their father. Many thanks to Blaine Hill, whose love of his father was so evident--I appreciated sharing your memories. For years, Max Flaugher, brother of Harold "Jack" Flaugher, and my father consoled each other, and I thank Max for his visits to my father and all the mementoes of a lost brother's life he shared. I'm grateful to Max's daughter-in-law,

Tracy Flaugher, for her assistance whenever I called upon her. Thank you to Jack Whetstone for helping to connect all of the crew families and provide information on Stalag Luft IV and to Jim Waddington for photography.

For all the Jeffers' grandsons who loved and honored their grandfather and held him in such high esteem, you have all contributed to his legacy in your own ways. Over the years you showed your interest in his wartime stories and looked through *Clipped Wings* with him from a very early age. To Tim, Alex and Jeremy, your visits gave him much joy. John T., your visits and recorded interviews with your grandfather preserved much history, and your care of him during emergencies gave tremendous comfort. Michael could never write enough about his grandfather's war experiences for school assignments. To Tom and Scott, who provided constant care and kept a vigil at his bedside in his final days, he knew your love. And to his sole granddaughter, Robin, you were the apple of his eye. For Donald Jeffers, Barbara Brooks, Jackie Wright, Denise Payne, Susan Brenner and great grandchildren, Kelsey and Jack, your visits brightened his days. Dave and John, you were the sons he never had. Thank you to my one and only sister, Diane. We shared an outstanding father, and what one of us didn't remember, the other one did.

Thank you to Howard Wilkinson, at the Cincinnati Enquirer, who followed our story and continues to make sure all our World War II vets are remembered.

Thank you to Bob and Mara Zedeker for your timely contact and story of Dresden. My thanks to Trevor and Carol Hewitt, along with Derek and Mabel Hewitt, who showed great interest and provided me with everything English.

This book could never have been completed without the international assistance from my German friends, Hartwig and Ilse Martensen, Gretchen and Juergen Bartel, Wolfgang, Tim and Katie Klaws, Manfred and Angela Gotzke and Claudia, Gerhard, Matthias, Andreas, and Thomas Martensen. You explained to me, you researched for me, you translated conversations and text for me and some of you even dug in the woods with me. You were so gracious to John and to me in your homes and in your country. I owe all of you a great debt of gratitude.

Thank you to Sam Cole, Sam Flynn, Lt. Col. Cathy Cox, Lt. Col. Renita Foster, Arnold Wright, Katharine Petty, Ray Toliver and Dr. Dwight Messimer for their enthusiastic research and individual contributions. I am indebted to Ed Woods, Assistant Chief Pilot, Delta AirElite Business Jets for his astute analysis and to Cliff Leverette for information on the Morley crew. My thanks to Art Durand, Duane Reed, Valerie Burgess, and ex-POW Robert Slane for your knowledgeable contributions and Heike Mitchell and Patxi Ayo for translations. Mary Ruwell and Trudy Pollok of the U.S. Air Force Academy provided their expertise and were indispensable.

Sometimes lives intersect at the right moment as mine did with several very special people. A heartfelt thank you to Darin Scorza, whose dedication to the men of the $458^{th}$ Bomb Group is unequaled. Your help with mission records, interpretations, pictures and technical advice on so many occasions was essential, and your website has reunited many families.

Likewise, to Kevin Pearson, you were so willing to address military/historical issues, the wonders of flight and the interpretation of technical material for me. Your undying respect for our World War II heroes is admirable, and your expertise on the digging out of crash sites and the mechanics of flight is astonishing. You took the complicated and made it easy for me.

My immense thanks to Hanns Claudius Scharff for presenting historical perspective and advising me on everything German. Your contributions have been endless and your enthusiasm unceasing. From historian to translator to editor to friend, you have been unwavering in your dedication to this project, and I thank your wonderful wife, Monika, for your time sacrificed at the computer assisting me. Your hysterical sense of humor buoyed my spirits on many a difficult day.

Nothing could have moved forward without the constant help of Edouard Reniere in Belgium, my European "wizard," pulling answers to the most difficult questions out of your magic hat, often overnight. Your help with archives, data banks, and the tracking of veterans and their families provided me with a wealth of knowledge and information and made the project come to fruition.

An immense measure of appreciation to my son, Scott, whose computer and technical expertise with formatting was timely and invaluable and to son, John T. Walton, and to Aaron Henry, of Great Save Productions, you came in and scored in overtime.

Thank you to my kindred spirits, Jennifer Schwartz and Dr. Tamara Haygood for friendship as well as advice and information. We share a passion for the "Greatest Generation," and your own writings pay a well-deserved tribute to them.

A most heartfelt thank you to my editors and proofreaders, John, Kevin, Claudius, Tamara, Scott, Thomas, Ambassador John Dolibois, and Lt. General A.P. Clark. My work fell into such expert hands.

# *Preface*

When I started to write this book, it was a book about my father and my desire to trace his World War II footsteps through Germany. For nearly sixty years, he sought information on the death of his friend and crewmate, Harold Flaugher. Without the electronic capability available today, he still proceeded with the limited resources available to him to solve the mystery of Flaugher's death. When his health failed, and he could no longer do that, I felt the torch had been passed to me. In addition, my father had been held at two prisoner of war camps, and his experiences there were never greatly discussed. There was much to investigate both for him and about him.

I had intended this book to be for his immediate family who were curious about his past wartime experiences. It became far more. Soon it encompassed several generations of the crew and their families and took me on an odyssey across the United States and through Europe. His story was not an individual one, but a multi-faceted mosaic of lives that intersected with mine and his at critical junctures. It was the completion of that mosaic that presented the full picture with each facet illuminating the darkness of the past. I found that the children of "Rhapsody in Junk," the B-24 we all knew so well, were all as equally dedicated to and passionate about their fathers as I was about mine. They too, sought knowledge to vicariously experience what their fathers had lived during a war which shaped those young men, and, in turn, determined who we were and what we would become.

The odyssey I embarked upon led me not only to the crew and their families, but along my journey to German citizens without whom I could not have finished my father's story. I found the Germans equally passionate about the war, suffering great family losses as they were caught up in the dictates of a madman. Both our side and theirs painted a picture of young men either grown up or blown up—unquestionably touched forever by their exposure to war. And in the end, I found that our basic compassion for each other transcended the brutality of those war-torn times. Intertwined closely with my father's story were their stories, just as ardent, just as haunting and indelibly etched in their minds.

As I conducted my own research looking on message boards, the most sinking feeling came when I read of people my age, many of whom had lost their fathers recently, posing the despairing question, "Did anyone out there know my dad?" There was usually the addition, "He never told me anything, and now he's gone."

The men of the Greatest Generation were not ones to share their experiences. In their humility, they came home from the war and went on with their lives. Caught up in our own lives, so many of us never asked, or else we heard only a few fleeting stories in passing. Now the desire to know is immediate. In my own case, the writing of this book helped me to know my father even better and enabled me to meet the men of his crew. This is their story.

## Dedication

For my husband, John, who willingly dropped what he was doing to run to Germany with me more than once, and who shared the love of my father, caring for him, especially in old age, as a loving son would do. Without your enthusiasm and encouragement, this book would never have been started or finished.

And for my father, the late Lt. Colonel Thomas F. Jeffers–you were the best.

# Chapter 1

# *Sentimental Mission*

Our train pulled into the station and came to a slow stop at the station in Suderbrarup, Germany, on a sunny May morning in 2004. The journey had been a long one, beginning one fateful day, June 18th, 1944. Then it was a journey destined by circumstance and necessity and now, sixty years later, the desire to complete the missing links of ten men who lived and flew a B-24 named "Rhapsody in Junk" during World War II called me to Germany. My father, Thomas F. Jeffers, was one of those men.

My husband, John, and I had passed large fields blanketed with bright yellow rapeseed flowers on that day as our train chugged along through northwest Germany to its final destination. The long arms of modern-day, giant windmills spun lazily in the spring breeze from across the wide-spread farmland of Schleswig-Holstein. It was a peaceful, beautiful, place. It had not always been so serene.

The small train station in Suderbraup, Germany, where our new German friends greeted us

We stepped down off the train onto the nearly-empty platform of the small, picturesque, railway station in Suderbrarup to be greeted by a smiling contingent of local German citizens.

I knew them at once. Tall and thin Matthias Martensen, my fifteen-year-old email friend, was dressed in blue denim and wearing black-framed glasses. He offered a wide, yet cautious smile. Beside him stood his stately white-haired grandfather, Hartwig Martensen, in a light blue sports coat and tie, his tanned face watching us in anticipation. Standing quietly near her husband was Hartwig's wife, and Matthias's Oma, (grandmother) Ilse, in a pretty tan and white print pants suit. Fair and blonde, Frau (Mrs.) Gretchen Bartel, who lived in the home "Rhapsody in Junk" almost hit, was bubbly in her enthusiasm to greet us. She smiled broadly from the platform and was eager to shake our hands. Her animated nature as she pumped our hands up and down required no English translation.

Of the four greeters, only Matthias spoke English. These were all names I knew well, but until this moment I had not been able to put a face with a name. These were the people who would lead me back in time to a horrific war and the destiny that was my father's and his crew's so many years before. They were friends that I had never met, but who knew the intensity of my desire to visit the past and journey through their country on the most sentimental of missions, the retracing of my father's wartime footsteps. His story began six decades before.

## Chapter 2

## *Over There...*

The well-landscaped base at Horsham St. Faith, U.S.A.A.F. 123, in East Anglia, England, was one of the many aerodromes that dotted the landscape in the European Theatre of Operations (ETO) between 1942 and 1945. Historically, Horsham translated to "where horses were kept." Now, it was home to young and eager stallions ready to fight a war. It sat amidst the English fields and hedgerows in a once quiet area of clustered towns. Quaint homes with roofs of slate and thatch sprinkled the countryside and co-mingled with the bustling airfields that had sprung up like mushrooms in East Anglia. The invasion of Americans, bringing the innovation of daylight bombing to the war when General Jimmy Doolittle's 8th Air Force made its presence known in England, brought a piece of the United States to the British countryside.

The aerodromes were typically two miles along each side and criss-crossed by wide concrete runways encircled by a perimeter track and dotted on the track's edge with dispersal areas where the bombers parked. The planes brought over to aid the war effort were grouped into wings, and wings were grouped into air divisions in an orderly and workable organization in a collective effort to defeat the Axis powers.

To live nestled amongst the buzzing aerodromes proved to be exciting and sometimes harrowing for the English citizens. Trevor Hewitt's father and grandfather knew the environs well. Early in the war, the noise was deafening when all the planes went up. The locals learned quickly to differentiate an American Liberator or a Royal Air Force Lancaster, as well as the occasional German Heinkel, each engine having its own distinctive sound.

Early one morning when Derek Hewitt, Trevor's father, walked down a lane in Frettenham with his friend Vic, a plane came out of the fog. The two immediately recognized the shape and sound of it and knew it to be a "Jerry" (German). The pilot manning the machine gun in the nose of the plane took aim and machine gunned the friends. Derek dove into the ditch on the side of the road, and Vic did the same on the other side as the bullets stitched a line down the middle of the road between them before it soared off into the distance. Later, Derek heard that the plane was shot down by a RAF Spitfire from the base at Coltishall a few miles away, and it crashed on the coast near Cromer (North Norfolk). "Sneak attacks" on the English coast at low level happened quite regularly as the war progressed.

Ralph Hewitt, Trevor's grandfather, was not spared the peril of the skies. His house was nearly hit one morning when a Liberator (B-24) from Horsham St. Faith was taking off and could not gain altitude. It flew about fifty feet up just above the trees. The bombardier jettisoned the bombs to lighten the load to gain height, and the salvoed bombs dropped in a line about fifty yards from Ralph's house where the family was asleep. Young Derek saw the tails of the bombs sticking up out of the ground across the field in front of the house. Fortunately, they were not primed. Like so many families, the Hewitts braved the danger and welcomed with open arms the American airmen who answered the call and were sent abroad to join the war effort in Europe. Their loyalty would last for decades.

In ever-increasing numbers, fighting men populated the English countryside, and new bomb groups were added. The first of them, the 458$^{th}$, began arriving at Horsham St. Faith at the end of January, 1944. Four months later a replacement crew headed by Henry Northrop joined them.

# Chapter 3

# *Welcome to the 458th*

Ten men became family as they experienced together the harrowing adventure of wartime Europe. They were ten strangers destined to bond and survive--each life in the hands of the next that spring of 1944.

The pilot, 2nd Lt. Henry "Hank" Northrop who hailed from Batavia, New York, was one of five brothers all serving in the military fighting in Europe. He grew up singing with his brothers in the boys choir in the 1920s, as his father was a minister in Long Island. Northrop had worked at W.T. Grant Company in New York and at Rippey's Diner in Batavia before joining the service. He had trained in Mississippi and Arkansas from February 1943 to October, 1943, earning his pilot's wings.

2nd Lt. Dee J. Butler, a Mormon from Ogden, Utah, served as co-pilot. As a child, he had long been a devotee of model airplanes, building many and marveling at the mechanics of flight. He was the eldest of four siblings and an avid reader. When jobs were scarce after the depression, he took a job as a "gandy dancer" repairing railroad tracks in Reno, Nevada. For three months he slept in double bunks in a box car where fellow workers and bed bugs were his companions. He enrolled in Moench University of Business and worked as a janitor to pay for his education. The first day of school he met Miriam, his future wife. Butler was an excellent stenographer and typist. He was placed in Salmon, Idaho, to work for the Forest Service after completing his studies. Butler enlisted in the Army Air Corps just two months after he married. He was one of three married men on the crew and was expecting his first child.

2nd Lt. Frank C. Deimel, the navigator, son of two German immigrants, was single and came into the service from Chicago, Illinois. He was the old man of the crew at twenty-seven. Deimel had studied in the seminary to become a priest.

2nd Lt. Thomas F. Jeffers, another married man on the crew, served as bombardier. Jeffers, nicknamed, "Jeff," had been raised in New York and spent summers in Massachusetts with his many aunts. He lost his father when he was fifteen and quickly became the man of the house. After graduating from high school in New York, he took a Machinist II job at Wright Field in Dayton, Ohio, later to be called Wright-Patterson Air Force Base. He was also expecting his first child.

Sgt. Alexander Cardenas, the nose gunner, was from Corpus Christi, Texas, and was the nephew of the President of Mexico. He worked for J.C. Penney in Texas selling to the Mexican clientele and later selling beauty accessories to drug stores and small shops until he was drafted. He thought the service would use him as an engineer, but the lieutenant in charge called his name and told him he was going to the Army Air Corps. Cardenas protested saying they had made a mistake as he did not know anything about flying. "We'll, teach you," the lieutenant replied, and passed Cardenas down the line. He was the "pretty face" among the handsome crew, and they teased him about his attractiveness to the young women of England. Cardenas expressed his desire to Jeffers that after the war he would return to Mexico, the native land of his people, and find a blue-eyed senorita.

Sgt. Joe Risko, of Detroit, Michigan, served as armorer waist gunner. He grew up on the east side of Detroit fascinated by

2nd Lt. Henry Northrop – Pilot
Courtesy of Mrs. Marielaina Haag

2nd Lt. Thomas F. Jeffers – Bombardier

2nd Lt. Dee J. Butler – Co-Pilot
Courtesy of Mrs. Kay Gamble

2nd Lt. Frank Deimel – Navigator

Staff Sgt. Harold "Jack" Flaugher – Top Turret Gunner and Flight Engineer
Courtesy of Mrs. Tracy Flaugher

Sgt. Lawrence Dean – Radio Operator
Courtesy of Mrs. Brenda Morea

Sgt. Joe Risko – Armorer Waist Gunner
Courtesy Mr. Robert Risko

Sgt. Alexander Cardenas – Nose Gunner
Courtesy of Mr. Alexander Cardenas

Sgt. Jack Junior Gonzales – Ball Turret Gunner
Courtesy of Mrs. Linda Waddington

Sgt. Charles Clifford – Tail Gunner

the street cars that passed in and out of a housing barn called the "Car Loop." He loved to read and was an excellent actor in high school plays. He loved cars and worked several jobs supporting his parents who worked in factories aiding the war effort. He enlisted with his three best friends, leaving his girlfriend, Jean behind.

Staff Sgt. Harold "Jack" Flaugher, from Bloomdale, Ohio, with grandparents in Germany, flew as top turret gunner and was the flight engineer. In high school, Harold played football, basketball and ran track. With a strong voice, he sang in the church choir and worked for his father at Flaugher's Garage. Harold was the gentle giant of the crew who went to church in Norwich, England, after they arrived rather than go into town with the crew.

"Need any money?" Sgt. Flaugher would often ask, as they left for town for fish and chips and beers.

He looked out for all of them telling them to have a good time but warning them to be careful and come back safely, earning their tremendous respect. He was also working at Wright Field, but his path had not crossed with Jeffers there.

Sgt. Charles Durell Clifford, divorced, was the tail gunner from Fresno, California. Born in Idaho, he was a bit of a loner, the son of a divorced mother. He worked on a ranch breeding horses. When he went into town with the crew, he always left their group and usually remained a bit emotionally distant.

Sgt. Jack Junior Gonzales, the ball turret gunner, was from Los Angeles, California. He was a member of the football and baseball teams and ran track. He graduated from high school and went to work at Douglas Aircraft Company while waiting for his orders to report for duty. When he was eighteen, the call came. He was the second son in the family to go off to war, and his girlfriend threw a farewell party for him. He spent his last day at home swimming at the beach and then left for Florida for basic training at a hotel in St. Petersburg. He had three brothers still serving overseas when he returned home.

Staff/Sgt. Lawrence E. Dean, the radio operator, was from the small town of Kingsport, Tennessee. He was the oldest of eight brothers and five sisters and the son of a soldier who fought in France during World War I. An "A" student at Sullivan High School, he graduated in May, 1941. He worked for Frazier and Brace Construction Company building the Holston Army Ammunition Plant before being called up. He boarded one of eleven buses with Kingsport's young men one morning headed for Ft. Oglethorpe, Georgia, before basic training in Biloxi, Mississippi. No one was left in Kingsport but women and children.

Together, the group of ten, newly-acquainted and richly-diverse, put their lives on hold to fight for their country.

Two months before the Northrop crew arrived in England, "Big Week" had dealt a severe blow to German fighter production. One Sunday, in late February, nearly a thousand American bombers, escorted by fighters, attacked fighter plane factories at Brunswick, Oscherleben, Bernberg and Leipzig in the heaviest assault of the war up to that time. A large part of the force was directed at the Messerschmitt 109 assembly factory and aircraft component plants at Leipzig. Production was stopped at the Leipzig and Bernberg factories, which together had been making thirty percent of all single and twin engined fighters. Output at Brunswick fighter assembly plants had been interrupted by previous attacks, and the bombardment put them out of business for four additional months. Enthusiasm and optimism were running high, and General Jimmy Doolittle decided to increase the pressure on the Luftwaffe with a series of raids aimed at luring the enemy fighters into conflict.

But victory was fleeting, and morale was getting low northwest of the English Channel just before the Northrop crew arrived. Two weeks before, thirteen B-24 Liberators crashed or crash-landed in east Norfolk in one night. Two more were damaged, and thirty-eight men were killed. Another twenty-three men were injured. Fires burned at the base at nearby Seething until past three in the morning. That same day at Horsham St. Faith, one B-24 was lost over Holland. Twenty-four planes returned, but German intruders intercepted them at six-thousand feet, ten miles southeast of the base. Control ordered the formation to fly northeast for twenty minutes before turning back, and an American plane was said to have been brought down by anti-aircraft batteries protecting Norwich.

Besides that, tours were increased from thirty to thirty-five missions, and deep penetration raids ranked equal to short-haul missions. Later, Air Corps Headquarters recognized the great risk of flying into heavily-defended Germany, and a fairer method of assessing missions was implemented.

Having completed training, the Northrop crew, as well as their close friends on the Francis "Red" Morley crew were assigned to the 458th Bomb Group, 754th Squadron, flying over together and arriving in late May of 1944. The crews quickly became oriented to the area. The officers were pleased to find they were assigned to a brick building rather than the standard Quonset huts assigned to officers at the surrounding bases. Two bomber crews were assigned to each brick building. Jeffers and Butler shared an upstairs apartment with four men of the Morley crew--Morley himself, the pilot, Henry "Hank" Hier, the bombardier, Charles Davis, navigator and Bennie Hill, the co-pilot. A simple fireplace with a grate was the only source of heat for the apartment. The crew gave it little thought upon their spring arrival but knew heat would prove challenging during their first English winter.

Officer's Barracks at Horsham St. Faith
Courtesy of Mr. Darin Scorza

The men soon settled into life at the base. The official song of the 458th was the popular, "After the Ball Was Over." The men of the 458th made up many of their own lyrics to it during their stay at Horsham as they learned to live scattered along the narrow streets in the vicinity of Fifer's Lane, Spixworth and Taylor Roads. They traversed the country lanes on purchased bicycles that often disappeared as quickly as they were bought. The crew learned about powdered eggs and morning fog and young, English children who followed and worshipped them like idols. Mostly, they learned what it was like to be a long way from home. Wives, parents, children and sweethearts were all left behind, and men untested in battle nervously anticipated their fates.

Between the terror of scheduled missions and the comparatively calmer "down time" on the ground, the fresh-faced 8th Air Force boys explored Norwich. The Sampson and Hercules Dance Club with its namesakes' statues out front sat opposite the gates leading into the stately Norwich Cathedral whose looming spires towered above. The Lido Club welcomed many a lonesome newcomer. The clubs offered dancing and entertainment, and the American Club which sat in the middle of Norwich proved to be a very popular place for the transplanted Yanks to spend their idle time. The Hippodrome Theatre sat in the center of Norwich and held many a burlesque show. The Black Swan, The White Swan and the Horsham Kings Head were some of the many pubs that served up beer and conversation. The young men's visits into town cast them in the shadow of grey-stoned Norwich Castle, fortress and the site of many battles fought centuries before.

Shows were performed at the Theatre Royal in the center of Norwich and at the Gala Theatre/Dance Hall nearby. St. Andrews Hall, a converted medieval church which held eight-hundred people, was extremely popular with the young men, and the Big Bands came to play there.

Sometimes there was jealousy between the British and American men. The Americans earned more money than the British did. The British would take the local girls to a pub for beer and to play darts, while the Americans could afford to take them to a good restaurant and pay for steak and a bottle of wine. After the dances often arguments broke out and would culminate with the cry of "Yankee, go home!" [1]

At the back of Norwich Cathedral there was a Red Cross Club, one of several in the area of Norwich, but the largest. Within these walls the men could go for rest and recreation. If they had been in the city for the evening and couldn't get back to base, they could spend the night and return to their respective bases in the morning on a truck used for this purpose. Many of the bases were spread a good distance around Norfolk and were quite remote.

Thoughts of music and dancing and dating would all be abandoned when another day at work once more spread fourteen-hundred heavy bombers and eight-hundred fighters across the English skies. Many of the men of the Mighty Eighth lived on borrowed time after harrowing missions where crewmates and friends disappeared, taken by injury, death or German imprisonment. There was a quick turnover of beds and accommodations as new crews came in to replace the crews who never made it back. Cherished possessions were boxed up and sent home to families as quickly as the new replacement crews arrived in this antiseptic world of brief glory and sudden death. The men lived for the moment counting the days until the completion of their ever-increasing assigned missions. Knowing that each mission could be their last, they lived suspended in time from mission to mission walking the narrow tightrope of jubilant success and catastrophic failure. By that time of the war, one in three crews was not expected to return home safely.

## Chapter 4

# *Hell from Heaven Man*

Jeffers' commitment to the war led him to bombardier training. At the age of twenty-one he enlisted with two friends on September 1st, 1942, from his legal address on Walton Street in New York, just one month before he married. He was called up and left for Columbus, Ohio, on January 29th, 1943. From Columbus he was sent to Alva, Oklahoma, as an Aviation Cadet where my mother joined him two months later.

Formal bombardier training was conducted in two phases. Jeffers completed basic training and then twelve weeks of pre-flight training at Ellington Field in Houston, Texas, starting November 13th, 1943. He would have many memories of his training in Texas, including the agonizing job of holding down planes on the field in Houston during a powerful hurricane. Called to the flight line, three cadets were assigned to each wing tip with two in the cockpits. The wind hit at one-hundred-thirty-seven miles per hour. The cadets held the planes down from 2 p.m. until 6 p.m., and then the weary men were relieved to go to the mess hall. Many returned to flooded barracks. The eye of the hurricane passed, and the cadets were once more called to the flight line. They turned all the aircraft around to the changed wind pattern. Rain pelted them like small BBs, and the rubber on their rain coats was beaten off. The episode was one of the most memorable of their training days.

Once a man had completed bombardier preflight training, he was sent to bombardier school, where he was required to take a special oath promising to protect the secret of the Norden bomb sight with his life.

### The Bombardier's Oath

> Mindful of the secret trust about to be placed in me by my Commander in Chief, the President of the United States by whose direction I have been chosen for bombardier training and mindful of the fact that I am to become guardian of one of my country's most priceless military assets, the American bombsight...I do here, in the presence of Almighty God, swear by the Bombardier's Code of Honor to keep inviolate the secrecy of any and all confidential information revealed to me, and further to uphold the honor and integrity of the Army Air Forces, if need be, with my life itself.

Once the oath was taken, the Norden bombsight that had been covered and sitting on a table before the group of men taking the oath was revealed.

For the second phase, advanced bombardier training, Jeffers moved on to Big Spring, Texas. The training was conducted in two phases, a ground school of mostly theoretical subjects with some hands-on training using the Norden or Sperry (or the low/medium altitude D-8) bombsight, and in-flight training using the bombsight to drop practice "bombs" on a target mostly from medium altitudes.

In the first phase, the cadets had a lot of class time interspersed with physical fitness, trainer and flight time. Jeffers learned to locate, identify and bomb assigned targets, but his duties did not end there. He would serve as fire control and armament officer. He would have complete control of the airplane on bombing approaches when the pilot put the plane on auto-pilot. His duties would require a thorough knowledge of operation and maintenance of Norden bombsights, all Allied bombing equipment on all bombers and all types of bombs and fuses. He would have to be proficient in pilotage, dead reckoning, radio navigation and meteorology.

The curriculum was intense. He studied about spinners in the nose of each bomb, which armed it as the bomb free fell after bomb release. He practiced manually releasing a pin which secured the spinner in flight before bomb release. Considerable spinning was necessary to arm the bomb. Unless armed, the bombs would not explode on impact.

Besides the bombs, there was a lot to learn about the plane. B-24s had a reputation for exploding if a shell hit the fuel lines or if the lines just ruptured. Fuel poured onto the extremely hot engine manifolds igniting the fuel. Usually, within thirty seconds, the fuel line fires traveled to the fuel tanks, and the whole ship exploded. There was much harrowing information to learn in bombardier training.

The training culminated in a final test before graduation. The test was feared by all who took it. The setting was a large room where the instructors had placed twenty bombsights. Jeffers and his fellow cadets entered the room one at a time. They were instructed to preflight each bombsight, identify the malfunction and write a paragraph on how to correct the problem. The one thing the instructors did not tell the cadets was that one sight had no malfunction. The men were given limited time to preflight each bombsight. As soon as one cadet finished preflighting the first sighthead and moved to the second, another cadet entered the lab. Waiting cadets were still lined up to go in as the first men exited having left the room mentally exhausted.

Finally, on November 13th, 1943, at 9:30 in the morning, my mother watched her husband graduate along with forty-two other men. He was commissioned a second lieutenant, and she proudly pinned his wings on his olive jacket, sending home a picture for her hometown newspaper in Springfield, Ohio. The newspaper caption read, "Hell from Heaven Man." With the stiffening ritualistically removed from their cadet hats after graduation, the officers converted the familiar hats into "40-mission crush caps." Without the stiffening, the necessary ear phones would conform more easily. The number of missions a man was a veteran of could be seen by the degree of extreme drape evident in his cap.

Mrs. Phyllis Jeffers pinning bombardier wings on her husband, 2nd Lt. Thomas F. Jeffers in 1943

## Chapter 5

# *Phase Training*

Next stop was Salt Lake City, Utah, for phase training. As crews were assigned, Jeffers met the men to whom his life would be entrusted, and they met the man who held their lives in his skillful bombardier hands. The individual crew members reported to the air base at Salt Lake City about December 1$^{st}$, 1943, from their respective training stations for further B-24 training of the pilots, navigators and bombardiers. The gunners who would protect the plane and inflict severe damage on the enemy were assigned to the crew.

After a brief trip with my mother to New York for Christmas, my father returned to Salt Lake on a troop train. My mother joined him a week later after stopping in Ohio, and they moved on to mission training in Casper, Wyoming, the final phase before he would go overseas.

Upon completion of the training in Salt Lake, both the Morley and Northrop crews had been loaded onto troop trains and sent to Casper for mission training. The crews had become the best of friends. Hier, Davis, Jeffers and Deimel spent much time together as two navigators and two bombardiers with a lot to talk about. The Northrop crew, in particular, was very social, and despite the fact the enlisted men and officers were not supposed to fraternize, this crew did. As they trained in Casper, pilot Northrop continually admonished the enlisted men to salute the officers in public. With big grins, they acceded to his request to keep up the appearance of no familiarity between officers and enlisted men, only to spend good social times with Northrop and the other officers shortly thereafter.

Cardenas had trained as a gunner in North Carolina and Florida. He excelled in artillery training as he had much experience shooting on his father's ranch. In training, the gunners started with human silhouettes and progressed to moving targets. Up on the bombers, the trainees shot at a piece of white cloth pulled by another plane. They were given different colored bullets, so the instructors could check the accuracy of their shots. Finally, they learned to shoot at targets while running. Now the gunnery skills of Clifford, Flaugher, Risko, Gonzales and Cardenas would combine with the skills of the officers and radioman, Dean, to ensure a combat-ready crew would transfer to England to make their contribution to the war effort.

Mission training often began at 5:00 a.m. in zero-degree temperatures. Often up at 2:00 a.m., my mother cooked breakfast before sending her husband off into the cold darkness. He had an old jalopy, and he stopped in the darkness to pick up Butler who was crouched on the corner in the cold waiting for his ride. The car had no heater. The air only got colder in the planes as the crew climbed to an altitude where temperatures hovered between minus-twenty to minus-thirty degrees. On a regular basis the heaters froze up. With much practice and training, Jeffers could soon make his hit no more than one-hundred-and-fifty feet from the target from ten to eleven-thousand feet. Gonzales wrapped the camera strap around his waist and strapped his feet to the inside the plane. Then he hung out the open camera hatch from the waist up, buffeted by the numbing wind. When he had filmed the targets and recorded the bomb explosions, Risko took the camera, and they exchanged places for awhile.

They flew simulated bombing missions to Lincoln, Nebraska, to "bomb" the airport. Later, they went to Pierre, South Dakota, returning home exhausted after eight hours in the air. Their simulated missions took them back to Salt Lake and to Denver, Colorado. When not flying, the crew went to meteorology, navigation and aerial gunnery training. Risko and Cardenas became especially close friends during training. It was a good crew.

One frigid morning when the men were getting ready for take off, a snow drift blew across the runway. Gripping the controls, Northrop seesawed down the runway gunning one engine then the other trying to get out of the snowdrift. No matter how hard he tried, the reluctant plane would not break free. When the mission was finally canceled due to weather, Jeffers told him they had used fifty-gallons of fuel and never got off the ground.

Finally, phase training was complete. Phyllis Jeffers and Miriam Butler, who had followed their husbands through training, returned home to wait out the war and wait for their babies. The crew left by train in April for Topeka, Kansas, to pick up their new plane and fly it to Europe.

The Northrop crew arrived in Topeka on Easter Sunday, 1944, and remained there for two weeks. They were briefed on their trip overseas and given their combat gear. Standing in front of their shiny B-24, #106, the men had their official crew picture taken on April 28th, 1944. Ten youthful faces smiled broadly as the officers and enlisted men posed. They were crew #2400 and ready for action.

"Red" Morley would fly #168, another new unnamed plane.

Picture of the crew taken in Topeka, Kansas, in 1944 just before leaving for England Front Row: Deimel - N, Northrop - P, Butler - CP, Jeffers - B Back Row: Clifford - TG, Risko - G, Cardenas – NG, Flaugher - TT/E, Dean - RO, Gonzales - BTG

Before they left for Europe, Hank Northrop held a party for the entire crew at the famous Jayhawk Hotel in Topeka. The next day they all flew east. Northrop flew over his home in Batavia, New York, on the way. Down below was the girl he had once planned to marry. More recently, he had met Billie Conners, a student at the University of Utah, when he trained in Salt Lake. He would have much time to think about the women in his life as a new pilot in the ETO.

The first stop was overnight in Manchester, New Hampshire, where they stayed for three days while the plane was fitted with auxiliary gas tanks to fly the longer distance. From Manchester on, Jeffers kept a journal.

### Undated

> "We left Topeka, Kansas, the morning of April 27$^{th}$ arriving in Manchester, New Hampshire, at Grenier Field that night. Visited Brockton next night and then flew out of Grenier the morning of the twenty-ninth arriving at Goose Bay, Labrador, that afternoon."

What Jeffers failed to mention in his journal was that his trip to Brockton, Massachusetts, along with one of his buddies, was the one time in his life when he went AWOL (Absent Without Leave). Seeing his aunts and mother not far from Manchester one more time before going off to war was a top priority with him, and he decided to take the risk. The next day, April 29$^{th}$, the crew flew off to war. That date would prove to be a meaningful date for him and his fellow officers, as they would find out much later.

## Chapter 6

# *Heading for a Mission*

The crew flew through a thick fog into Goose Bay and then on to Iceland.

In Iceland, Jeffers continued his journal.

**Undated**

"Stayed overnight at Goose Bay and left next night for Meeks Field, Iceland. Had a nice trip flying over an overcast almost all the way."

While in Goose Bay, the crew had further training with several of the other crews, including Morley's crew, which had been with the Northrop crew since their departure from Utah. The scenery of Meeks Field in Reykjavik, Iceland, and Goose Bay, Labrador, was all new to Tennessee and California boys like Lawrence Dean and Jack Gonzales. The first thing they noticed was there were no women to be seen in Goose Bay. With two days to kill there, Dean and Gonzales wandered out to explore the isolated area. On one of their walks, they heard music coming from the day room. Eagerly, they followed the music and found a WAC (Women's Army Corps) singing "Shoo Shoo Baby." Years later, they remembered the moment and thinking she was gorgeous only because she wore a skirt. But their entertainment was short lived, and they flew out very soon.

### Undated

"Had to stay in Iceland for two and one half days due to weather but managed to leave finally & again flew over an overcast most of the way landing in Nutts Corner on Lough Neagh in Northern Ireland on May 3, 1944. It was on this leg of our trip that a crew went down, and I lost one of my friends from Big Spring, Bill Carpenter of Marshall, Texas. He went down just short of our goal & within sight of Scotland.

It seemed strange in Ireland to have daylight up until about one o'clock in the morning and darkness for only a few hours. One loses all semblance of time in such a place. We stayed overnight in Nutts Corner and were robbed blind losing even our airplane among many other things. Went to Lorne above Belfast & the next day spent the night in a British camp & took the ferry across the Irish Sea to Stranraer, Scotland, and then took a train to Stone, England, just North of Birmingham & Coventry."

(Author's note - Research into the loss of Bill Carpenter's plane is indicated below.)

"Killed with 9 other crew members of their B-24 when the defrosters failed, and it crashed into a frozen mountain near Goose Bay, Labrador, on May 1, 1944. The crew was en route to England on tour of duty."

After they arrived in Iceland, the crew flew on to The Combat Crew Replacement Center #235 in Nutts Corner, Ireland, for more training. Once in Ireland, both the Northrop and Morley crews lost their new planes there. They, like many other crews who passed through Nutts Corner, lost many of their personal possessions as theft was rampant there. The new planes were reserved for more seasoned crews in England, so C-47s flew the crews in transit to England from Ireland, and the Northrop crew arrived in England on May 3rd.

## Undated

"We stayed about a week in Stowe in which time I managed to go flat broke shooting craps & playing Black Jack. I have now given up gambling.

After getting a shot of tetanus at Stowe we made the same trip back through Stranraer & Lorne back to Northern Ireland. Seemed pretty damn silly to us.

We went to a combat crew replacement center on the other side of Lough Neagh only a few miles from Nutts Corner. Tried to visit Tom's sister in Londonderry while I was there but could get no farther than Cookstown, so I had to give up & call her from there. We had quite a pleasant conversation on the phone & I promised to write to her.

After taking a training course in Northern Ireland we were flown back to England & are now assigned to the 754th Bomb Squadron of the 458th Bomb Group 96th Wing and Second Division of the A.A.F in the European Theatre of Operations.

We are now stationed at Horsham-St. Faith, a former RAF base just outside of Norwich, England.

We haven't been assigned to an operational mission for some reason or other as yet. We have been here nine days now. I hope I can soon get started so I may be home before my baby is born."

After leaving Ireland and arriving in England, the crew was ordered to Air Operations the next day at 10:00 a.m. There were eighty air crews of ten members each, eight-hundred men that had just crossed the Atlantic. In the big operations room they met the Commander, "Big Jim" Isbell, and the Assistant Commander, 1st Lt. Robert H. Hinckley. Isbell was assigned as the group's second Commanding Officer in November, 1943, and he remained in that position until March of 1944 – the longest tenure of one commanding officer in the 2nd Air Division, if not the entire 8th Air Force.

In an undercurrent of idle chatter, the colonel entered the room.

"Attention!"

Everyone stood very still in the sudden silence.

"At ease!" he said.

A low murmur filled the room.

"Today you will be incorporated into this squadron and group of which I am the commander. Most of you believe that you are the best aviators of all, right? Well I want to inform you that as to flying in combat, you guys are a bunch of incompetents, and all of us are sorry about that."

After welcoming the new men and informing them of the number of squadron losses, and teaching them the different attack strategies of the Luftwaffe, he ordered the men to show up with all their equipment at Air Operations. There, each crew was assigned a plane. The men left Air Operations mad and grumbling as they headed towards the barracks. Once there, they put on their flight suits, and afterwards trucks carried them to the runway.

The first plane took off and flew around the base until all of the planes were in the air. Isbell ordered the pilots to form a "V" shape, and for two hours he kept yelling trying to get the "V" perfectly open with a distance of about ten meters between each plane.

"Number three, bring your wing closer to mine, number six, get closer, number ten get that wing closer!" he ordered.

Afterwards, he ordered the crews to return to the base and to Air Operations. Once there, he explained the reason for flying so close in formation saying that when the formation was close, the enemy planes couldn't penetrate, and the powerful force of the machine guns of twenty-five planes of a squadron would hit directly into the enemy, disintegrating them in the air. At the same time, the bombs would be released at once covering a big area and destroying everything in it.

Practice missions continued. Again and again, Isbell ordered the crews to show up at Operations with all their equipment ready to fly. A truck carried the men to the assigned runway and plane. Northrop ordered the flight engineers to haul eight-hundred gallons of fuel, so Flaugher and Cardenas made sure that is what they had. Flaugher checked the engines on the right side, and Cardenas checked the ones on the left. They checked the oil and added more as needed. Finally, they checked the machine guns and loaded them with ammunition clips of fifty bullets each.

"Get in your positions," called Northrop to the crew.

Cardenas scrambled up into the nose turret, always awed by the panoramic view. He saw the first flare that came from the control tower signaling Northrop to start the first two engines in the middle of each wing--numbers two and three. Then the plane moved towards the runway.

"Let's go!" ordered Isbell, and they took off.

Twenty-five planes spiraled into the air. Once in the air, they again practiced the close "V" formation keeping only two meters from plane to plane. Soon they would get it right.[2]

## Chapter 7

# Loss of the Belle

The Northrop crew had been in England only five days when tragedy struck at Horsham St. Faith. The misty countryside was just awakening at 6:15 a.m. There was still a morning frost on the grass. The Hewitt family had become accustomed to the roar of B-24s from Horsham St. Faith flying at low level over their home as the massive planes pulled to the left on take off heading north to either fly a circuit or head straight out. Often, the family slept right through the heavy and constant drone.

But, this morning was different. A bomber from Northrop's squadron crashed on take off. A terrifying thundering crash and multiple deafening bangs caused great alarm. Ralph Hewitt and his son, fourteen-year old Derek Hewitt, leapt out of bed to investigate. Ralph peered out the window and was horrified to see crackling orange flames licking upward and swirls of smoke clouds rising from a crashed plane just a short distance down the road from their home.

"I'm going down the road to see what I can do. There are some poor devils in there, and they might need help," he called over his shoulder to his wife, Grace.

Dressed in his long johns, shirt and heavy work boots, Ralph bolted out the door, and it slammed behind him. He had told Derek to stay behind, but the boy raced after him with his father's trousers and suspenders in hand. Ralph tried to send him back to no avail.

Ralph and Derek Hewitt who ran to the crash site of the "Belle of Boston"
Courtesy of Mr. Trevor Hewitt

Soon, they were both crawling along the hedgerow towards the shattered plane. As they got closer, they ducked exploding bullets that zinged off the road and ricocheted from the trees in every direction. Ferocious fires flared in every direction. Moving low and trying to protect themselves, the Hewitts edged slowly towards the burning, disintegrated hulk which had once been the proud "Belle of Boston." They crept closer, and the intense heat reddened their faces. Bits of the plane and debris were strewn across the road and the adjoining field. They could see the ghostly remains of the engines enshrouded by the snapping flames. The fuselage and a bit of the tail stuck up in the air. The glow of flames reflected off the olive-drab fuselage. The distinctive blue K on a white circle was still emblazoned on the tail. It designated the broken plane as belonging to the 458th Bomb Group. The fuselage and broken tail stood juxtaposed incongruously on the smoky grass field.

In and about the wreckage, they saw airmen lying on the ground, scattered about the bomber's remains like rag dolls. Some were crying, some were shouting and others were ominously silent. The inferno raged as the Hewitts worked quickly to remove the men from further danger. First, they found the navigator, John Rogenmuser. The dark-haired man was slipping in and out of consciousness. When he was alert, he chewed a piece of gum as hard as he could.

"My back, oh, my back hurts," he groaned.

The Hewitts carried him carefully to the side of the road and braced his back with a parachute.

A ghostly blond figure carrying his helmet emerged from the wreckage. Sherman Cassidy, the top turret gunner, had been thrown clear of the wreck. He was the only crew member uninjured. Shocked and dazed, he viewed the devastation around him in disbelief. He had just talked to and joked with these men. This was his crew. These were his friends. Only minutes before, they had climbed aboard the Belle to bomb an aircraft factory in Brunswick, Germany. Now the broken bodies of his crew were twisted grotesquely in the debris. Many would fight the war no more.

As the fires raged on, the Hewitt's neighbor, Albert Sydell, arrived to offer help. The plane's wing had landed on the roof of his bungalow just missing Albert as he stood in his garden.

Ralph and Albert found Albert Nix, the ball turret gunner, with his legs pinned under a massive Pratt and Whitney engine. They dashed through the crackling fires that surrounded the injured man and rolled the heavy engine off of him. Then, they dragged him to safety. By this time, Albert had to run back to his bungalow and get two pairs of boots for Ralph and himself, as their boots were melting in the intense heat.

Next, they turned to Arthur Doyle, the bombardier, who was badly injured, and quickly pulled him to safety. Then they assessed the shattered wreckage once more. Much to their dismay, they found they could do no more. The rest of the men, Homer Ausman, Patrick Cook, Wayne Danielson, Raymond Hunter, Paul Kingsley and Ben Wishinski had all perished far from home. On what was to be a fine English spring morning, fate had dealt a different hand, and "Belle of Boston" lay in broken pieces.

More neighbors arrived to help, and then Jeeps arrived. The injured were placed upon the hoods their heads propped against the windshields and were whisked away.

For many years, the Hewitts wondered what became of the survivors, but in the throes of wartime England knew they would probably never find out.

## The ill-fated crew of the "Belle of Boston"

Back Row: Raymond Hunter - E, John Rogenmuser - N, Homer Ausman - CP, Paul Kingsley - P, Arthur Doyle - B
Front Row: Albert Nix - G, Sherman Cassidy - G, Wayne Danielson - G, Ben Wishinski - RO, Arthur Neubacher - NTG
Arthur Neubacher was replaced by Patrick Cook around the crew's 5th mission.

Courtesy of AFHRA

## Chapter 8

# D-Day

Tension mounted for the crews as rumors spread about the Allied invasion of France. Crews sat tight, biding their time waiting for the word to go.

**June 4, 1944**

"I received fourteen letters today mostly from Phil, which made me very happy. She claims she is feeling fine for which I am very glad. Also had several letters from mom, Lorraine, Bob Glaudino & Gene also one from Donald, which amused me very much. We had a practice mission scheduled this afternoon, but it was scrubbed due to an operation coming up. That made me very happy as I don't have a lot to do on these practice missions but go along for the ride. Wrote several letters tonight. Wrote up my log, played checkers with Dee for awhile & am now going to hit the sack. Hope my wife is feeling okay tonight. I sure miss her."

## June 5, 1944

"Not much doing today. We weren't even scheduled for a practice mission. Went to ground school for awhile & had the enlisted men a little sore because I didn't show up to take them out to shoot skeet. I'm not the only officer on the crew, and I needed a haircut badly. First one since Iceland. Went to a movie tonight and there are all kinds of rumors that tomorrow will be D Day. May be, who knows. Had to wash some long handles last night (by hand) and they aren't dry yet. It's a rough life. Wrote my honey, Lorraine & Don & so to bed."

All crews were confined to base before and during D-Day. The Allies put five-thousand-one-hundred-twelve bombers in the air on D-Day, and Horsham St. Faith had added a third mission that day in addition to the normal two. Eager to get in the action, Flaugher, Gonzales and Risko, despite Northrop's protestations, flew with other crews on D-Day watching the spectacular sight over the invasion coast. With bad weather, they ended up bringing their bombs back to England and dropping them off the coast in what was designated the "wash." The men marveled at the sight of the D-Day landings with more ships than they could ever imagine floating in the troubled waters there.

## June 6, 1944

"It looks like the rumors were true. Today was D Day after all and for some unexplained reason our crew and a couple of the other crews in our squadron, Red Morley's and Hank Newell's spent the day on the ground. In the years to come, we can tell our children that we spent D Day sitting on our butts getting fat while other men were out fighting and dying. The weather has set in now and if it doesn't clear up over night, the boys in France are going to have a rough time tomorrow without any heavy bomber air support. Jerry has been sending over all kinds of propaganda all day and it is really good. I guess it is designed to get on our nerves. They have beyond a doubt the best program over here. Hank spent the day on his hands & knees begging for a ship, without results. We have lots of rumors today, chiefly that the 30 mission tour is canceled & we are all indefinitely restricted. It is hard to believe but is okay with us if we can attain some results that way. J.P., L.R. Dee & I went to the movies tonight. Spring Fever. Very Good."

After the excitement of D-Day, the base settled back down into its normal routine.

### June 7, 1944

"No mail from my honey today, but then no one on the crew got any. I read in the paper that Major Clark Gable has completed his military mission and is to return to civilian life. Wonder how that was arranged. Dee & I went into Norwich tonight & went to a British Vaudeville Theatre. Boy, it was strictly corn. The chorus is the original beef trust, also went to a dance at the Lido & stayed maybe fifteen minutes. Didn't even bother to dance, & left fast. Probably this was our first & last visit to town."

### June 8, 1944

"No mission again today but Hank is scheduled for one tomorrow so maybe we'll get something soon. Heard on the news that the Luftwaffe is getting a little more active over France, so may be we'll begin to get some rough opposition soon. Seems like they are getting mad about the invasion now. Have to hit the sack soon as I'm keeping everyone awake with the light on. I sure miss my honey tonight. Love, I guess. G'nite honey."

### June 9, 1944

"Not a damn thing today & nothing scheduled for tomorrow either. I'm getting pretty tired of sitting on the ground. I guess it would make Phil happy if she knew. Hank Hier bought a bike yesterday. It was stolen today. Nice fellas here."

### June 10, 1944

"Not a damn thing today. Didn't even go to a movie. Saturday night too. I can't see these English towns, no entertainment possibilities at all. Just dry as hell."

On June 11th bombers from the 458th hit an important railway bridge at Blois-Saint Denis in France cutting a German supply line to the front and relieving the pressure on the Allied Armies pinned down on the Normandy bridgehead.

### June 11, 1944

"Scheduled for a mission today but were scrubbed. I expect we'll get off tomorrow okay though and it's about time J.P. and Les went yesterday & passed the outskirts of Paris on the way back. They could have landed on the Flak. Going down to the Pub with Frank tonight & throw darts. Oh joy, what fun. No movie again today."

## Chapter 9

## *Mission to Evreux*

In mid-June, the Morley and Northrop crews started flying missions out of Norwich and left the safety of the European coast. The Northrop crew had "Downwind Leg" assigned to them and flew it to Evreux-Fauville, France, on June 12th carrying fragmentation bombs. Downwind Leg would later go down with another crew and would appear on the pages of Der Spiegel, a German magazine. But it served the Northrop crew well for their first mission, and within its rattling frame they were part of the longest formation to date.

Through the clear nose, Jeffers had a broad view of the steep majestic White Cliffs of Dover as the crew soared beyond the surf out over the English Channel to Evreux. Those same cliffs would be a welcome sight on the return. Many a pilot sighed with relief upon seeing the chalky expanse beckoning to him as the slosh of white caps lapped at its base. It was the feeling of going home.

The shortest distance from Norwich was twenty minutes across the English Channel. On a clear day in Dover, on England's southern coast, one could see the hills above Calais, France, the area that Adolf Hitler had been convinced was going to be the location of the D-

Day landings. With binoculars in hand, plane spotters defending Dover could see the flash of guns firing in Calais, and from the castle in Dover, guns and tanks were visible across the Channel. Fifty-nine seconds passed from the sighting of a flash in Calais for a lobbed shell to explode in Dover. With a deep BARROOM, the shells came every twenty minutes.

Crossing the English Channel, the crew could see the remains of the D-Day landings. Thousands of ships were floating like matchsticks in the Channel, and the sight filled each man with awe.

But that day, eyes turned toward Evreux, and Jeffers watched for the glowing red flare from the lead ship that signaled the bombardiers to open their bomb bay doors. With eager anticipation, he removed the heated cover blanket from the bombsight, checked his gyroscope's stabilizations and made sure all bombing switches were on.

Deimel cross-checked with the lead crew navigator, and a re-check of compass heading and reference points assured the target was dead ahead.

Cardenas's oxygen mask filled with ice crystals. He pulled it off his face to dry the sweat that caused the crystals to form. The tiny ice crystals fell onto his chest and bounced off his flight suit. He unhooked his electric jacket. With tension and fear, he sweated profusely, and he did not want to freeze any part of his dampened body that was exposed to the cold air.

Within minutes, the lead bombardier's voice crackled over the interphone.

"I've got the target."

Northrop checked his flight instruments for precise eighteen-thousand feet altitude and one-hundred-and-sixty miles per hour indicated airspeed and carefully leveled the aircraft on auto-pilot. Over the target, the burden fell to Jeffers to line up the cross hairs of the bombsight and make adjustments as Northrop turned over the flying of the plane to him.

"On airspeed, on altitude," he called to Jeffers calmly, "You've got the aircraft."

Jeffers made a final level of his bombsight and took over steering the aircraft with it. At minus-forty degrees, his eager fingers operated the azimuth and range controls. Later in the war, the lead bombardier would have a switch that could simultaneously release all the bombs of the other aircraft in the formation. But on this day, the individual bombardiers were on their own. Bright-colored lights blinked on the bomb panel where Jeffers had set up how the bombs were to be released on the bomb run. The bombs could be set for salvo with all bombs dropping at the same time, or they could be set to drop one at a time at intervals which were measured in microseconds. From the ground, the sight of bombs falling in clusters indicated they were salvoed. A straight line of bombs falling toward earth at "bombs away" meant they were timed in precise intervals. The type and size of target to be hit determined how Jeffers would set the panel. Each light on the panel had a corresponding bomb in the bomb bay. Once the bomb was released, its light went out indicating that the bomb had fallen.

B-24 Bombardier's Panel
Courtesy of Mr. Darin Scorza

The navigator in the lead plane was sweating out his check points to stay on course. All eyes were on the formation leader. When the lead bombardier released his bombs, Jeffers would drop his. Visual inspection by Dean and sometimes Flaugher would verify the status of the bombs after "bombs away." Plumes of flame shot up from the ground, and the formation would turn to pass over the flattened targets of the doomed and bloodied earth far below. After bombs away, the camera would record the impact.

One mission under their belts, the crew found that flight combat in the ETO (European Theatre of Operations) bore little resemblance to the training flights undertaken back home in much kinder conditions. Besides heavy flak, six rockets were shot at the bombers. The crew had bombed Evreux, and thankfully, they had returned safely. Three aircraft had aborted, but the rest bombed with good results. Flak damaged three planes in the formation. On their return, they were debriefed, and they were offered cognac and warm cookies.

### June 12, 1944

"Went on our first mission today to Evreux, France, just west of Paris. We were unable to find our group at assembly point so went over with the 466th. After hitting the target, our own group went over just below us so we peeled off & joined them for the trip back. We dropped 24 250 lb. demolition bombs, and the three groups really plastered that field. Flak was pretty rough & had us jumping around a little on the way back. The lads that aim those guns are pretty sharp. We were low on gas coming back & I sweated out the landing more than the mission."

### June 13

"Scheduled for a mission today but it was scrubbed. Just as well too because it was a hell of a long one. Scheduled tomorrow too so am hitting the old bed a little early. Did my laundry, took a bath & talked about Ohio with Red Morley the rest of the evening. Rumor has us flying close to Berlin tomorrow."

## Chapter 10

## *I'll Be Back*

On June 14th, Northrop piloted B-24, "I'll Be Back," to the region of Maison Ponthren, France, to bomb the Rocket Coast rather than the expected Berlin. Loose formations on missions to Abbeville, France, at that location cost the Second Air Division dearly, as the Germans dug in to defend the Rocket Coast. This was the area held by the Germans at Pas de Calais, which continued to remain troublesome to the English coast, being the closest point to England across the Channel. It was here where the Germans developed robot bombs to fire across the Channel. The German's development of longer-range rockets posed a severe threat to Britain. For that reason, the mission target, the village of Domleger near Abbeville, was a top priority. Some of the Lufwaffe's best pilots were assigned to the area flying their yellow-nosed Messerschmitts and Focke-Wulf 190s. The official Luftwaffe name for them was Jagdgeschwader (JG) 26, and they were known as either "The Abbeville Boys" or "The Abbeville Kids" by both the British and Americans who flew against them.

The second mission started early. Shortly after take-off, waist gunner, Joe Risko, developed a problem with his flight suit. Northrop gave him the choice of parachuting back down over Norwich or going on with the crew. Without hesitation, he chose to go on. Many years after the war, Jeffers recalled Risko had lost his glove. An old letter that Cardenas's mother wrote to my grandmother indicated Risko's suit caught fire at high altitude when it was twenty-seven degrees-below zero, and his ears and right hand were frostbitten. Other crew members said the suit shorted out. Whatever the cause, as the plane gained altitude, the crew wrapped Risko in blankets and tried to keep him warm. The temperature had dropped to fifty-below zero, and Risko was practically paralyzed with cold. Flak was heavy, and three rockets were shot upward, but there was no fighter opposition. Risko struggled heroically and in much pain to complete the mission. Upon his return to Norwich, he was taken to the hospital for medical care. Once again on the ground, Risko wrote in a journal he kept.

> "My heated suit went out on me, and I froze both my ears, right hand, and my left shoe had a short which slightly burned my foot. I was put in a hospital ward and grounded for six days."

Jeffers recorded the day's activities in his journal.

### June 14, 1944

> "Didn't go to Berlin today but hit the Rocket coast. Dropped 500 lb. G.P.s (author's note – general purpose) on a supply dump for the New Rockets at the Village of Domleger near Abbeville. The flak was terrific on the bomb run & it seemed Jerry didn't want us to pound that dump. The Germans fired one rocket last night across the channel, and as a result the whole second division hit them today. I'll bet they are sorry. Colonel said the projectile fired weighed 12,000 pounds. That's as big as one of our railway tank cars & it is claimed it left a crater 200 feet across where it hit. We were scheduled for another mission this afternoon but it was scrubbed while we were being briefed. I

was very happy about that too, as it was to a Paris airfield and the Flak would have been terrific. Also Jerry is known to have 350 fighters in that area. We got a little dent in the nose from Flak today, but it was Newell's first mission & he got seven holes. Risko got frostbitten today when he lost his right glove. I fixed him up as best I could with Sulfa-diozene ointment & it did pretty good I guess, because he'll only be in the hospital for a couple of days. We went over to see him & he calls me "Mr. Hero." Gee. Dee to go on a big one tomorrow. France again I guess.

### June 15, 1944

Went to see Risko today & his hand is okay. He'll be out tomorrow. Had another mission scheduled but it was scrubbed again. Not much today.

### June 16, 1944

Scheduled and scrubbed again today. Sure having a rough job getting some missions in. Risko is out of the hospital today and will be ready to fly tomorrow. Red's plane got a hole in the wing over Paris yesterday & did he scream. All we've had so far is a dent in the nose turret and that's enough for me. Flak is pretty accurate in France. Luckily there isn't much of it. Got a mission scheduled tomorrow hope it's not scrubbed."

By mid-June, "Red" Morley had the original plane he had flown over from the United States, #168, assigned to him again, but he had lost it again June 16th due to battle damage. Another crew had flown it to France that day, and over the invasion coast it received a flak hit through the outer wing. The pilot managed to fly it back to England but left it at another base.

The Northrop crew's third mission sent them into the heart of Germany, but originally they were scheduled for France. On June 17th, Northrop's crew, flying #106, "Miss Pat," was scheduled for an early morning raid on Bourges, France. Red-headed Armament Officer, 1st Lt. William Brodek, a quiet serious math student, decided to fly along as a gunner substituting for the frostbitten Risko. Although he was a first lieutenant, and the highest ranking man on the crew, he served as a gunner. This was a point not lost on the Germans later.

Armament Officer 1st Lt. William Brodek, substituted at the last minute for frostbitten Sgt. Joe Risko
Courtesy of Mr. Bill Brodek and Mrs. Jean Brodek

The crew awoke early and prepared for the morning flight. While taxiing out, the mission was scrubbed due to bad weather, and all crews returned to barracks. When the mission was called again later that day, Brodek decided he didn't want to go. Normally, another gunner would be chosen, but for some unknown reason, the whole crew was changed, and instead, Morley flew "Miss Pat" off to France in the plane that bore his wife's name.

Jeffers went to Mass on the base and served as an altar "boy" as he awaited the return of the Morley crew, knowing he would be uneasy until his roommates returned.

# Chapter 11

# The Pain of War

But the Morley crew did not return. As flak hit the plane in three sections, co-pilot Hill jumped from his seat and ran to the bomb bay. Fuel from the damaged wing had spilled into the area and caught fire, and crackling flames licked menacingly at the fuselage. In seconds, the whole section, including the bombs, was ignited. He could do nothing. He raced back to the cockpit and slid into his seat to tell Morley. Within minutes, the plane exploded, blowing Hill free of the fireball.

The flames burned the covering off his parachute, but the chute popped out and blossomed. Above him, he could see it was on fire, and the fire was inching down the shroud lines. Just as he approached the ground, the parachute burned completely, dumping him on the ground. He struggled out of his harness and slowly peeled each glove from his hands. The gloves had melted, and with each removal, the skin on his hands came off. In terrific pain, he reached for his oxygen mask with his raw burned hands and pulled it from is face. The skin on his face came with it. Hill slumped to the ground in excruciating pain. Then the Germans arrived.

The men who surrounded him splashed dirty water on his burns to try to get him to talk. He could not. They turned him over to Catholic nuns who took care of him in a hospital where German doctors performed many skin grafts on the prisoner of war, taking skin from inside his upper legs and grafting it onto his face and hands. As American troops got closer, the area was bombed quite regularly, but no shells ever hit the hospital.

When "Miss Pat" was blown out of the sky, the crew was making its way to Tours, France. Flak hit the bomb bay, and the plane took a bad blow at its left wing root while over Caen. Witnesses would later report that they saw the entire fuselage burst into flames, and the aircraft nosed down. In its death spiral, the tail twisted off during the spin, and the aircraft was seen to crash. Only one chute was reported, that of horribly burned co-pilot Bennie Hill.

Scriptwriter and author, Jackson Granholm, who was a navigator on an adjacent plane, would write of the fate of the Morley crew fifty-six years later in his popular book, "*The Day We Bombed Switzerland.*"

> "Our lead navigator of the day was a bit off course and took us directly over Caen. The city was full of panzer units, and they opened fire. As I was to learn with time, the anti-aircraft fire of German tanks was highly accurate. They laid their first shells right to the middle of our formation, and for the first time I got the full impact of flak fire.
>
> Gniewkowski was down in the nose with me. Though he was only to toggle on the drop of the lead ship this day, he always liked to practice at his bombsight, preparing for the day when he would lead the attack — performing the essential sighting himself — in the nose of the foremost bomber of the formation. When the intense sounds of the bursting flak shells hit our ears, I looked at Eddie Gniewkowski. His face was as white and bloodless as I'm sure mine must have been.

The Morley crew that had only one survivor, Bennie Hill
Standing: Paul Dulmage - RO, Jerome Caffey, - TG, William Rickert, - TT/E, Wesley Darden, - BTG, Earl Dunaway, - RWG, Max Detty, - LWG.

Kneeling: Henry Hier - B, Bennie Hill - CP, Frank "Red" Morley, - P, Charles Davis, - N.

The sound of accurate flak aimed at your bomber is unforgettable. To this day I can remember it, and hear it, and have bad dreams about it. There is the loud crunch of the shell explosion, followed by the sharp rip of those fragments which penetrate the fuselage, and the rattle of those which bounce off. It sounds a bit like someone throwing big fistfuls of gravel down a huge tin pipe.

At about the tenth loud crunch a bomber of the 754th Squadron, flying formation to our right, suddenly pulled up and out of formation. This was the aeroplane of Lieutenant Morley's crew, in bad trouble. The ship made a 180-degree turn, heading back for England, and feathering the right inboard engine. I watched this turning back with fascination from my side blister window. About the time our neighbour had finished his turn and was northbound, headed noticeably downhill, the bomber burst into flame. The whole ship lit up in a giant, blinding flash of fire.

There was a great fire in the sky where the bomber had been the instant before. The whole tail section fell off, and one parachute dropped out of the wreckage. The rest of the aeroplane, burning fiercely, fell spinning into the countryside of France below.

I fought off the urge to vomit in my oxygen mask. But the facts were made plain to me: one could die suddenly flying combat with the Eighth Air Force over Europe. I'd just watched some people do it. My knees were still shaking when we got back to Horsham St. Faith four hours later." [3]

All of the other eleven crews returned to Horsham St. Faith that day.

Incoming crews told what they saw. Finally, word of the tragedy was passed along to the Northrop crew. Overnight, Jeffers' and Butler's roommates, Davis, Morley and Hier were killed in action. The six others on the crew also perished. Jerome T. Caffey, tail gunner, from Duck Hill, Mississippi was locally known as Talmadge, and was the son of a soldier gassed during World War I, who later died from lung ailments when Jerome was ten-years-old. The hand of war had now reached down to the next generation. Sgt. William Rickert, top turret gunner and engineer, Sgt. Earl Dunaway, right wing gunner, Sgt. Paul Dulmage, radio operator, Sgt. Wesley Darden, ball turret gunner and Max Detty, left wing gunner were all casualties in those fateful seconds over France.

In later years, when I traveled to London, my father handed me a paper with the men's names on it--names I vaguely remembered hearing growing up. He asked me to look for the names in the Books of Remembrance at St. Paul's Cathedral and the RAF Chapel, St. Clement Danes in London. Each name was there, written in stark black letters against the cream-colored paper. The pages were turned daily with much respect and honor.

As he awaited the return of the Morley crew that day, Jeffers wrote in his journal:

### June 17, 1944

"Supposed to go to airfield at Bourges with some 500 (illegible) but as usual it was scrubbed. This time just as we started to taxi. Going to try again tomorrow. Red & the rest of the boys went somewhere this afternoon & aren't back yet. We weren't scheduled for that one. All we get are those that are to be scrubbed I guess. Maybe we'll get off tomorrow. Oh yes, we can now wear a bronze star on our ETO ribbon."

## Chapter 12

# Up We Go...

With the sting of death following them, the crew flew out the next morning on June 18th. There was little time for grief in the war. Deep in the recesses of each man's mind, he knew with all his heart that he very well could meet the same fate handed out randomly by the enemy below. Each man had the friendship of his crewmates to sustain him that warm summer day, and the crew consoled each other over the tragic loss of most of the Morley crew. Then they concentrated on the mission ahead.

Now, with their plane lost over France, they had no plane of their own, so the crew was assigned the B-24, #733, "Rhapsody in Junk," serial number 41-28733. She was a Douglas Tulsa B24H-10-DT Liberator, part of Contract 18722 of May 20, 1941, for four-hundred-thirty-three aircraft, serial numbers 41-28754 to 41-29006 undertaken by the Douglas Aircraft Company and manufactured at their Tulsa Aircraft Assembly Plant Number Three in Oklahoma. Rhapsody had been one of the original ships to come over in January of 1944 and was showing her battle fatigue. Records indicate that she had flown sixty-seven missions to date. She was one of the "war wearies" with too many miles and too little rest.

War-weary B-24 "Rhapsody in Junk"

Ground crews in baseball caps and coveralls worked feverishly through the night preparing the planes for battle. The ground crews were emotionally close with their air crews and took pride in maintaining the ships whose preparedness would figure greatly in their safe return. The area around the bombers was a hub of activity through the early morning hours. Ordinance snapped into action loading ammunition, and bomb-laden trailers moved from the dumps to the waiting planes. Mechanics pre-flighted the planes, and gas trucks bumped busily over the tarmac. The drivers jumped out to fill the massive wings with fuel. In the morning, "Rhapsody in Junk" would embark on the 458$^{th}$'s first major mission to strategic targets since D-Day.

The mission, dubbed an "all available aircraft" mission, started early after Bomber Command waited for the weather report the day before. The weather was predicted to be warm and clear with a few clouds. With a positive weather report, the target had been picked, and like a line of balanced dominoes, the movement of one unit of command triggered the actions of the next. Teleprinter messages clacked and hummed as decisions were transmitted from Bomber Command to divisions. The alerted divisions next alerted the wings and the wings alerted the groups. Awakening stations surrounding Norwich would soon be at full alert. Five hours after take off would climax weeks of planning and determine the failure or success of each mission.

Olive-drab "Rhapsody" stood at its hardstand poised to strike. The June sun came up very early out of the North Sea to warm the awakening English countryside that day. Long before its first rays shone through, the crews were awakened in darkness at 2 a.m. by the squeak of the operation jeep's brake wheels outside their door. The groggy crew, eager and anxious for their third combat mission, stumbled from their beds to their lockers where they kept their flight gear and donned their flight suits.

Barely awake, they made their way to the equipment hut in the dark and deposited their personal possessions to be left behind as they readied themselves physically and mentally for the mission. The men picked up their escape kits. Small enough to fit in a shirt pocket, they were clear square packets containing money of the countries near the target, concentrated food and greatly detailed maps printed on silk. The square held a compass and some Halazine pills for purifying water. The men slipped the kits into the pockets below the knee of their coveralls. For those who wanted them, electric flight suits, heated bootees that plugged into the suit legs to avoid frostbite, and heated gloves were gathered up to be worn on the plane. Men who did not have to move too far from their position on the plane preferred the suits that they could plug in. Dean was one who preferred the electric suit. Some preferred long johns and layers of clothing. Over the olive drabs went a summer flak suit and leather jacket. Each man wore a bright yellow Mae West life vest over his flak suit.

By 3:30 a.m., the officers joined others in the officer's mess hall for a breakfast of fresh eggs and brownish/grey English bread. They washed it down with coffee. The enlisted men, in a separate mess hall, even at such an early hour were calling out to the cooks how they wanted their eggs prepared.

Afterward, the crews came together and sat on the hard seats in the briefing room at a Quonset hut to learn the "Target for Today." The Second Air Division briefing for that day detailed the assignment of bombing. So late in the war, the chance of flying to "Big B" was increased. The hopes of the crew were up, and just maybe their target would be Berlin, the most heavily defended city in Europe.

But Berlin would not be their mission on the 18th. At the end of the platform, a large map of North Western Europe hung on the wall. The map was covered by a green curtain. The mission briefing was conducted by the always smiling and charming Major Charles Booth, who would later become a prisoner of war. Anxious crews focused to see where the red route ribbon on the map would lead. Audible reaction always followed the revelation of the target. When the curtain was pulled back, the map showed Fassberg, an airfield near Hamburg. Oil refineries at Hamburg and Misburg would be taken care of by the B-17s of the First and Third Bomb Divisions. Oil refineries at Bremen and Luftwaffe control centers at Fassberg and Stade were the responsibility of the 458th crews.

The strategically important Luftwaffe Control Centers at Stade and Fassberg in the Lueneburger Heide between Hamburg and Hanover were clearly marked on the map. The airfields lay halfway between the cities of Muenster and Celle in Northern Germany. The target was a rocket research station, barracks and an airfield. The Fassberg airfield had been used by fighter groups before the war, but during the current conflict there were also bombers based there, principally *Kampfgeschwader 4* (Combat Squadron 4) with Heinkel He 111 aircraft. Further, in 1942 the Luftwaffe's Technical Flight School Two had been transferred to Fassberg.

The men listened and studied the map. Yellow push-pins marked anti-aircraft guns. Reconnaissance cameras had recorded the target, and the weatherman showed where the clouds would be. Instructions were given on the correct way to taxi out, and the formations were drawn on a blackboard. Flak areas were indicated, and the rendezvous points of fighter escorts were revealed. Jeffers and the other bombardiers were briefed in order to pre-set information into the bombsights. They took notes on the target details, aiming point, bomb loading, fuse settings, bombing altitude, bomb ballistics and intervalometer setting for the spacing of the bombs on the target. Deimel and Jeffers ironed out and coordinated all the details, since bombardiers and navigators worked closely side by side. Then a chaplain appeared and closed the briefing with a prayer.

Afterward, the crews went to their lockers to get their parachutes and harnesses. Their helmets were on the plane as were the interphone transmitters and receivers enabling them to talk to each other after take-off. The transmitter was a throat microphone strapped around the neck and was placed over the larynx. Because the air was so thin at high altitude, the vocal cords did not make much noise. The receiver, or headset, was worn in the leather flying helmets or on a headset with the receivers worn over the ears suspended by wire and cloth on the top of the head.

Gonzales took the parachute from his locker and double checked the harness.

"I'm not going to jump out of NO plane!" he said to his fellow crewmen.

But, the thought of not returning to England was implanted early. Evasion briefings educated the men regarding avoiding capture and the possibility of being shot as they parachuted down.

Fully equipped, the men checked for Pepsin gum to keep ear pressure equal. Everything accounted for, they were ready to go.

Out on the tarmac Flaugher viewed the battered plane, patched and showing newer paint to cosmetically hide its many repairs. He checked the tires that were nearly devoid of tread. He double checked everything on the plane making sure the tanks were full, caps were wired down and bomb racks were loaded satisfactorily. He made sure there were no oil leaks anywhere. He wanted safety for his crew. Soon, upon his own inspection, Jeffers pronounced the plane aptly named.

By 4:50 a.m., the gunners piled aboard the jeeps and 6x6 trucks for the short, bumpy ride through the grass to the dispersal points. Walking out in their bulky flak suits would have caused the crew to perspire too much had they gone on foot to the plane, and their wet skin would have frozen more quickly flying at high altitude where the temperature dropped down to fifty and sixty-below zero. They were grateful for the ride.

The field that warm summer morning lay in darkness. The eastern sky showed faint hints of dawn fingering through the clouds penetrating the haze of ground fog as the nervous men gathered about the deadly brooding, yet hauntingly beautiful, plane. Her slick wheels were still chocked as she sat in the English morning ground fog. The aroma of rich earth and sweet-smelling grass, remnants of pre-war England, competed with clouds of choking exhaust. The acrid smell of burnt-engine oil and hi-octane aviation fuel increasingly replaced the earthen traces of summer.

"Hey, lieutenant," called the crew chief jocularly to Jeffers as he started to swing up through the bomb bay, "Don't bring this one back."

Loaded with equipment, the crew swung up through the open doors of the bomb bay and took their places inside. They found their helmets with attached earphones and squeezed through the narrow fuselage to their places, brushing against each other in the tight quarters. Clifford, quiet as usual, was terrified. On each previous mission he had become so petrified, he was physically sick. The crew wondered if they would have to replace him if he could not perform his duties as he lay isolated away from the crew in the empty tail of the plane. Brodek and Cardenas stood in position near the open waist hatches preparing for the mission. Long cartridge belts snaked down to the floor standing ready for a ferocious fight. Gunners loaded and situated their guns, swiveling them into position and lashing them down for take-off. Before too long a cold wind would blast through the open hatches for the remainder of the mission. Cardenas checked for his gun, but most of the men did not carry their regulation issued .45s that day. Upon capture it was more likely they would be shot on the ground if they carried the guns, yet many wanted them for self-protection.

"We don't need them," said Dean. "We'll be back."

After Dean pulled himself aboard, he moved toward the radio table on the flight deck directly behind the co-pilot. He sat atop his radio table and looked out the small blister window next to him. From his vantage point he had often watched in the past as daredevil pilots flying during formation purposely touched wing tips imagining in a flight of fancy that they could create sparks. He gazed into the first light of dawn and wondered what the mission that day would bring.

Jeffers, Cardenas and Deimel took their seats on the narrow-cushioned bench behind the flight deck for take-off and clicked the ends of the heavy metal seat belts together. They waited for Northrop to start the sequence. The Liberators were never quite free of petrol fumes, and the crew became accustomed to the smell.

A red flare burst from the control tower balcony signaled them to taxi out. With great anticipation, yet still heavy hearts, the Northrop crew left for Germany. It was 5:40 a.m. when from high up in the cockpit, Northrop signaled with a wave to the two ground crew members. They ran up and pulled out the chocks from in front of and behind the wheels. Two green flares arched over the field as the planes coughed and choked to life at their dispersal points. The deafening roar escalated as each pilot ran up his engines, and the airfield came alive like a swarm of angry hornets urged from the safety of their hives, all capable of vicious stings when provoked. A specially-equipped PFF (Pathfinder Force) plane led the pack in case its pathfinder capabilities were needed in uncooperative weather rendering poor visibility. With checks complete, the hulking aluminum frames lined up nose to tail on the taxiway.

The full bomb load of M-44, blunt-nosed, one-thousand-pound GP demolition bombs and M-12 incendiary clusters lay cold, silent and deadly resting in the racks of the bomb bay. Packed in tightly, the dark green and yellow payload narrowed the passageway of the one-foot catwalk that lay between the bombs.

The bomb bay doors could be opened by either an electrical switch by the bombardier, or by the pilot using a second switch. A manual handle also served the same purpose. The manual handle was preferred. If the electrical switch did not open the doors all the way, the bombs would not drop. Because Dean was closest to the handle, he would pull it up to ensure the doors were fully opened, so Jeffers could initiate the drop once they were over the target.

Brakes screeched in a symphony as pilots systematically released them. Planes lurched, and pungent clouds of blue smoke belched from their engines billowing forth to hover over the taxiway. The engines caught, and sputtering graduated to thunder. "Rhapsody in Junk's" four weary engines bellowed as she lined up with the others behind the polka-dotted assembly plane which led the PFF plane upward.

Initially, PFF ships were the lead planes in the lead element of the lead (middle) Squadron of a Group and led the Group. When the PFF ship dropped its bombs, all the rest of the bombardiers in the Group toggled theirs. The Luftwaffe soon caught on to this tactic because of the radar dome extending from the ball or the chin turret. They began focusing attacks on these lead ships. In response, Command started assigning PFF ships to other positions in the Group, usually as Deputy Lead of the lead or high Squadron of a Group, since all ships could see the high Squadron lead pretty well.[4]

In contrast, the assembly planes were the clowns of the airfield painted white over olive drab in places and covered with colored polka dots to be easily seen. They were the traffic cops of the air, and for each mission a different crew flew them, returning to the base after the planes were all in formation.

Assembly was often as dangerous as the mission. Every pilot knew the dangers of jockeying for position in a formation. Wing tips and planes collided, and men had been lost during formation assembly without ever getting close to enemy territory. One in seven aircraft lost in the ETO was due to formation accidents either going to, or coming from, Germany.

The assembly plane sat at the top of the concrete T on the ground. Once the planes were assembled on the east and west top of the T, they alternated feeding into the shaft behind the assembly plane for take off. Depending on the size of the formation, the assembly plane, a large ungainly duck with goslings following obediently behind, could be airborne for half an hour to more than an hour making sure every aircraft was in the correct position.

All the planes from Horsham St. Faith that day were B-24s, designated as "heavies." The darkness lifted by 4:30 a.m., and a partly cloudy morning shone through for take-off. By 7:32. a.m. the lead bomber of the 96th Combat Wing moved out. The hulking "Rhapsody in Junk" waited to swing around off the tarmac and onto the runway. She was eighth to take off in section one.

In turn, the plane pulled into position. In minutes, under Northrop's control, the battered green plane would make the transition from bouncing all over the runway to drifting into the orderly formation where planes were staggered side to side and top to bottom. Once there, he would be alert to other planes in the wrong place in the formation. He would have to concentrate hard to keep his own plane from drifting, and like the squadron leaders, correct his position, which was made all the more difficult as he battled the prop wash of the other planes.

The frame shook as her slick tires, worn from far too many take-offs, clicked rapidly over the expansion joints of the runway past the red and blue marker lamps. With building speed vibrating her rivets against the ever-strengthening force of the wind, Northrop heaved the heavy into the sky. With an upward thrust, she was in the air lifting thirty tons of bombs, plane and men from the earth. Passing the control tower, "Rhapsody in Junk" was on her way. Behind her, twelve more planes in section two took their position in the macabre dance.

Flaugher squeezed tightly past the outer side of the bombs as he passed through the bomb bay. He refused to walk on the catwalk, fearing it would not hold his weight. He was a large man, and he didn't trust it. Jeffers, Cardenas and Deimel, bulky in Mae Wests, inched along the catwalk between the bombs to get to the nose turret where Deimel's fold-up desk was stored under the flight deck. There was no seat for the navigator. When Deimel was not standing, he sat on the front metal ridge of his table which kept his equipment from sliding off in turbulence. Under flight overalls, navigators bore the red creases of the ridge marked deeply into their backsides. Jeffers would kneel, leaning into the bombsight, as he focused on the cross hairs. The nose turret on the B-24 was the equivalent of a wind tunnel with freezing wind from leaky nose turret doors whistling through. It became very cramped with ammo cans, belt loads and a mounted pair of 50-caliber guns.

Northrop knew his job well, but it did not make it any easier. "Rhapsody" had seen too much combat action, and her engines had been revved up to their maximum peak so many times there was not much emergency power left in them. They would just barely permit Northrop to keep up with the formation as he kept them on maximum power.

The first plane leaving Horsham St. Faith that morning circled the field. Others fell in behind. Three at a time, planes moved off, and the pattern repeated itself as the continual line of planes corkscrewed upward into formation.

Each bomb group formed up on a Splasher homing beacon over their own station. As soon as the Group departed the Splasher beacon, they headed for a Buncher beacon where the combat wing would form. Once the combat wing was in formation, the wing headed to a designated point on the English coast for division assembly. Each assembly was supposed to proceed on-schedule, and each group was assigned a color of flare to use for assembly. With weather and other factors, the groups sometimes got separated, especially if they had to "shuffle the deck," when two groups flew towards each other, and they had to separate to avoid collision. Flares and aircraft markings were the only way to re-form.

Northrop eased into position, as others in the formation spiraled in the sky like vultures drifting lazily in the breeze searching for a victim below. By 8:00 a.m. the loud drone overhead in Norwich was deafening. The Hewitts and their neighbors paused to look to the skies and follow the cacophonous spectacle. Like a flock of war birds, as forbidding as giant black ravens flying east in a fading formation, the roaring planes eclipsed into pencil points against the early morning sky.

Northrop climbed to about ten-thousand feet, standard altitude before crossing "landfall out" at the English coast. After crossing the English Coast, he climbed to his assigned operational altitude over the North Sea. On a cooler day, when the air was thicker, it was easier to climb, and planes often would continue to climb over the continent after take off, but the warming summer day dictated that his climbing pattern that morning would be more gradual. Higher altitude offered more protection from flak, but that day routing the formations around known flak corridors would prove more helpful.

Climbing higher, electric flying suits were turned on, and at twelve-thousand feet the crew went on oxygen. Each crew member had snapped the oxygen mask onto the right side of his helmet before take-off. When Northrop announced they were at twelve-thousand feet, the crew snapped the other side of the mask into the plug-in outlets in the wall at each station. Each connected hose reached two feet. If for any reason they had to move from one place to another, they moved quickly. Gonzales's mask had become unplugged on the prior flight to France, and in a very short time someone noticed it wasn't plugged in and motioned to him. He tried in vain to plug it in but kept missing the outlet due to his rapid disorientation. Lack of sufficient oxygen at higher altitudes could be as dangerous as flak. The oxygen that flowed through the narrow green hose from the tank to the oxygen masks meant the difference between life and death.

Once in their positions, the crew communicated through the interphone system.

Every ten minutes, Jeffers called for oxygen checks. The crew was assigned a number from front to back.

"One, o.k."

"Two, o.k.," and so forth until all men and their steady oxygen supply were accounted for.

Northrop climbed higher to catch up with the assembly plane up above at fourteen-thousand feet, which was circling slowly waiting for the B-24s that followed to pop through the cloud layer hiding her. Climbing up for five miles, the ice blue of the sky provided sharp contrast with the muted patchwork of brown and green earth below. Shrieking winds buffeted the Plexiglas sphere of the nose section as Jeffers scanned the quilted ground below. Oxygen checks, muffled against the plane's drone, continued for hours as the men prepared to make their way deep into the Third Reich.

The formation had to be tight. The tighter the formation, the less chance of German fighter penetration. A tight formation lessened the chance of guns on the ground picking off stragglers when determined enemy pilots swept through the hazardous skies. While the bombers joined up in their formations to fly to target, they used up fuel, but the necessary tightening up of the formation justified the fuel consumption, as it decreased the planes' vulnerability to German fighter aircraft. A bomber that fell out of formation could be attacked simultaneously by several fighters. Bombers in a tight formation could combine their firepower to limit fighters largely to frontal attacks. While attacks from the front could particularly endanger the pilot, navigator and bombardier, they were less effective than the combined efforts of multiple fighters in bringing down the entire ship. Northrop would do what he could to maintain his place in the formation as the squadron flew on to Germany.

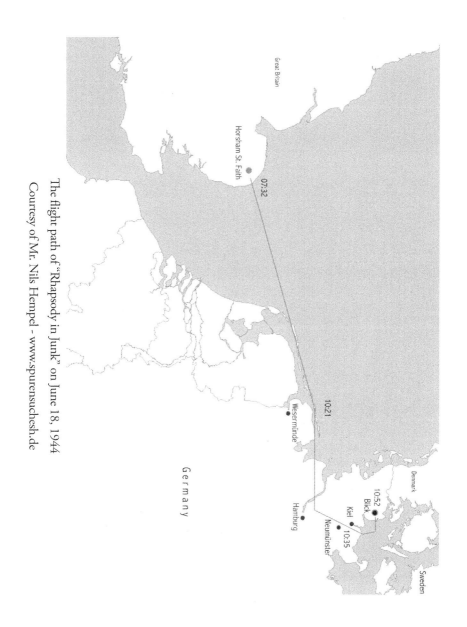

The flight path of "Rhapsody in Junk" on June 18, 1944
Courtesy of Mr. Nils Hempel - www.spurensuchesh.de

Chapter 13

# The Vigil of Sweating It Out

Once the planes were airborne, the vigil for those left behind began. After the formation disappeared in a sea of vapor trails, the ground crews looked wistfully off into the wide patch of leaden sky. They returned to their beds, having worked all night, and collapsed to sleep a restless sleep until their planes returned. The flight crews left behind occupied themselves as best they could for the remainder of the day, until they formed up again hours after a take-off to collectively await the planes' return.

Some sitting on bicycles, some leaning on the walls of the block tower and many standing or sitting on the grassy ground, scanned the skies searching for a small black dot that would become a larger black circle and then silhouette a battle-fatigued warplane. Contrails were a fact of life at Horsham St. Faith, and the men knew their patterns well as they studied the skies "sweating out" the return of their friends. Upon return, Northrop would once again peel off wide from the formation and come in for a landing. It was a well-rehearsed, choreographed dance in the sky.

Some missions were "milk runs," with little or no resistance. Others were life-threatening battles so intense that the shot-up planes, magnets for flak, barely made it back. Flak was the German abbreviation for Flugzeugabwehrkanone, meaning anti-aircraft gun. The 88mm flak guns were the most feared of the German anti-aircraft weapons. It took only twenty seconds for a shell to appear at twenty-five thousand feet. So the thinking prevailed, if the crew could see flak, it was close. If they could hear it, it was very close, and if they could feel it, the pieces of lead were within forty feet of the plane. Luftwaffe gun crews were able to place large sections of simultaneous fire at a specific altitude leading to the expression, "flak so thick you could walk on it." It took four-thousand shells to knock one plane down, and the Germans fired sixteen flak guns at the same time. To maximize their damage and use, the Germans loaded flak guns on railroad cars and moved them around to wherever they were needed.

Bullets from enemy fighters hitting the planes rattled like hail on a tin roof. Bullet holes and gaping flak damage perforated the thin aluminum skin of the planes. Often, damaged planes crashed on their approach killing those aboard. Red flares sent up from returning planes on approach signaled wounded aboard, and ambulances, nick-named "meat wagons," sped out to greet them.

The men on the ground watched and waited early that summery afternoon and prepared to count them as the planes came in.

## Chapter 14

## *Deadly Black Veil*

The crew would need all the help they could get on June 18th. Fighter escorts would provide some protection to the bomber stream as it flew closer to the target that day. The fighters had proved their worthiness many times over. In 1943, with the stunning loss of sixty of two-hundred-and-eleven planes on the Schweinfurt raid on ball bearing plants, deep penetrations into Germany were halted. By February of 1944, with the help of fighter escorts, key Luftwaffe factories were once again fair game. To the men in formations the fighter planes were called "little friends," protecting the heavies until they were in close proximity of their target. Then the P-51s would peel off and fly low to strafe targets of opportunity such as marshalling yards or aerodromes.

The route to target on June 18th over the North Sea would bring the bombers in over Holland. It took two hours to assemble and fly across the North Sea to reach the coast, each minute moving them closer to danger. The bomber stream flew low at nine-thousand feet to eliminate the use of oxygen masks. Behind Jeffers' right shoulder, Deimel sat at his folded-out wooden navigator's desk and plotted their course. Deimel's maps and calculations would keep the crew on course. Crammed in tight behind the bombsight, Jeffers' eyes scanned the choppy waters. The two men were wedged in so tightly, neither could move.

In the nose section above Jeffers, Cardenas could barely move with all his equipment on but stood ready to man his guns. Like black flies in the distance, the enemy fighters could appear at any moment. In anticipation, he envisioned the lights flashing from their wings. Then he would hear the burst of Flaugher's top turret guns and Clifford's tail guns and feel the whole plane shake. Gonzales would fire at them from the ball turret. In his mind, he could picture the brilliant flash of planes exploding, battered and broken above the Third Reich, and soon the odor of pungent gun powder would swirl around him. In the loud roar of the nose turret, Cardenas reviewed his training. He would have to remember to calculate "Rhapsody's" speed and deflection angle before snapping the triggers of his machine guns, and he hoped his aim would be good. But for now, he waited. He listened to the comforting periodic crackle of his crewmates' voices over the interphone. The action would come soon enough.

"What am I doing here instead of lying safely on the beaches of Acapulco?" he asked himself.

Cardenas's thoughts were interrupted. It was time to prepare for action and break the monotony. Flaugher fired from the top turret, and Clifford manned the tail guns. With loud bursts, the gunners tested their guns out over the water before approaching the European coast.

Soon, "Rhapsody" passed the Friesen Islands on the Dutch coast. Once the formation approached the varicolored patchwork past the coast of Europe, it flew southeast into the heart of Germany.

Their eyes scoured the skies watching for Focke-Wulfs coming out of the red-gold sun and ME 109s sweeping through the clean skies. They watched for dull, blinking-yellow flashes of flak generated by steel-helmeted Germans manning the massive stuttering guns of the 88 mm and 105 mm flak batteries. Soon, those counterparts on the ground would be engaged in the battle. The eyes of the German soldiers manning the flak batteries would watch for chutes falling from crippled planes in an angry smoke-stained sky.

The flight was long and cold, but the droning monotony could quickly be replaced by sheer terror. Their routine flight became anything but, as they approached their target.

Closer in, the bomber stream increased its altitude to twenty-one-thousand feet to confuse the flak batteries. Frigid air permeated the rubber oxygen masks reddening the skin of the youthful faces. The plane hummed on toward the IP (Initial Point) where the bomb run would commence.

"IP," called Deimel calmly from his navigator's desk.

They were only twenty miles from their destination when Jeffers would take the controls and find the target in his bombsight.

Cardenas turned off his electric flight suit, since he was soaked from the fear sweat he knew so well. He looked into the troubled skies, and his heart was pounding.

"Control yourself," he told himself, as he shook his head to clear it.

Northrop followed the lead ship, but the lead pilot had trouble locating the target in the undercast. Attacks by the other Bomb Groups had to be made by PFF. At that point in the war, many ships had the ball turret or chin turret removed, and in its place was a white H2S radar dome. The dome contained the most advanced radar equipment of the day and was used when undercast conditions were present as a navigational aid for the bombers to reach their target and for blind bombing. The radar navigation officer aboard operated the special equipment. The radar officer, or "Mickey Operator," as they were sometimes called, was positioned on the flight deck with the radio operator on B-24s. Through his scope, he could see the outline of the terrain through the clouds.

Still hoping to see the target, Northrop completed his turn at 10:10 a.m. and headed east to Wesermunde. At 10:21 a.m., the formation passed right by Hamburg. Towering cumulous formations around Hamburg diverted the mission. Hamburg was a smoldering ashen cinder by the time the RAF got done with it, and it had been pounded so many times that crews knew the danger of bailing out there. Civilians on the ground had killed men who had the misfortune of falling into an angry mob.

There would be no bright sun glinting off the wing and glaring into Northrop's and Butler's eyes that day as they penetrated the cloud cover. Up above in the top turret, Flaugher was watching for enemy fighters. With his three-hundred-sixty-degree view, the sky was immense, and they could come from any angle.

The enemy below was waiting. The battle was on. Flak batteries fired upward, and the crew could see the puffs of black smoke all around as the shells exploded with fury around them. The Liberators dove through flak, reeling and shaking from the hits. Then the number one and four engines failed.

As the bomber stream tried to locate the target, oil and smoke streamed from the two malfunctioning engines. Northrop made a wide circle. Sick and shaking, Clifford watched as they made a second pass with little success. He became more anxious as the superchargers started overspeeding on the damaged engines as a result of lower engine rpms. A shell hit the same engines, rendering them totally useless. Still crammed in the ball turret, Gonzales rocked violently to one side as the plane jerked to the right. Northrop got it back and broke formation and told the men to lighten the ship.

Jeffers raced from the nose to the back and opened the bomb bay doors. He took a screwdriver and unfastened the bombs for salvo hoping to lighten the ship. With the engines failing, he could no longer release them with the toggle.

The plane became momentarily buoyant at the bombs' release, and the salvoed bombs fell to the earth below. But one bomb was stuck. As Jeffers stood by the open bomb bay, a piece of flak tore through "Rhapsody's" thin skin and whistled by his head, just barely missing it.

Dee Butler, as co-pilot, would write of the stuck bomb almost fifty years later, as he reminisced in a letter written to Jeffers on his 50th wedding anniversary:

> "Next came a struggle for our lives for Jeff and me and for the lives of our entire crew while on a combat mission over Germany. Our B-24 was scheduled to

drop incendiary bombs, and in the process, one of the bombs stuck in the bomb bay. The bomb was armed and ready to explode anytime. The entire B-24 could have exploded too. Jeff and I didn't have time to calmly think out a solution. He and I located a rope, and Jeff was lowered to kicking distance of the bomb. A lifetime passed while he kicked time and time again, and these efforts successfully dislodged the threatening bomb. Our B-24 crew didn't know this was going on."

There were sheet metal "walls" on each side of the catwalk in the bomb bay. To kick the bomb loose, Jeffers had to climb over the wall four feet from the catwalk to the top of wall to be lowered down to the bomb shackle holding the hung-up bomb. It was with great relief that Jeffers and Butler saw the bomb dislodge from its shackle and fall to the clouded earth below.

Thinking the plane might go down, Gonzales used the hydraulic switch and brought the ball turret up. As the plane shook after each flak burst, he climbed out.

The crew grabbed everything they could find and threw what they could out the open bomb bay to further lighten the ship. First to go were their flak suits, and Gonzales dumped them in quick succession out the open hatches. The gunners, Cardenas, Brodek, Gonzales and Clifford, threw their guns out. Up above in the top turret, Flaugher struggled to loosen his gun to throw it out the hatch, but he could not pull it loose. In desperation, he turned and pulled Dean's radio off the radio table. In a moment of dark humor, Dean snatched it back from him.

"Let ME throw that out!" cracked Dean. "I've been waiting to throw that damned thing out."

But Flaugher remained somber.

Then the number three engine failed, whether a victim of flak or poor maintenance, is unknown. With oil pressure dropping, Northrop saw the propeller spinning faster and faster out of control. He hit the feathering button to shut down the engine and feather the propeller, turning the edge into the air stream to stop the windmilling. He hit the fuel shut-off switch. He closed the mixture control, cut the throttle and pulled off the rpms, hoping the propeller would feather. Simultaneously, Flaugher worked on the other engines, now hit with flak, reallocating fuel to keep them going.

After losing two engines near Hamburg, the loss of a third one sealed their fate. The third engine was the main engine containing the vacuum controls, and all controls for the other three engines were tied to the third. The plane was losing altitude at five-hundred-feet per minute. They had dropped from twenty-one-thousand feet to eighteen-thousand feet, and the plane kept steadily descending. Dean stood behind Northrop watching the altimeter drop from nine-thousand to eight-thousand feet. Airspeed was at one-hundred-twenty miles per hour. Northrop further considered their options.

"Alex, Jack—come to the cabin," Northrop called through the interphone.

Cardenas climbed out of the nose turret and crawled through the narrow tunnel and squeezed by Jeffers and Deimel. He could see the cockpit control panel where the oil pressure and cylinder head temperatures were approaching the red zone on the gauges. Flaugher followed behind him. They both agreed that the plane could not fly much longer, or it would blow up.

"Bring the manifold pressure down from thirty-two inches to thirty to keep the cylinder heads cool," advised Flaugher.

Cardenas told him to bring the revolutions of the engines down as well from 2400 to 2000 rpms. Then Northrop opened the cowl cooling flaps to lower the temperature of the cylinder heads.

"This plane won't fly on just one engine," Northrop said.

Sweden, Switzerland, Spain and Portugal were neutral countries where crews could be interred for the duration of the war. As the crippled bullet-riddled plane struggled, Northrop called for a heading to Sweden. He doubted they would ever make it. Jeffers took the heading to Sweden from Deimel who worked feverishly at the navigator's desk. Deimel knew they could not make it to Sweden on the remaining number two engine. Besides, the route to Sweden was fraught with danger, as Deimel indicated they would have to fly over Kiel and the heavily defended submarine pens there. They had been briefed on Kiel and were aware of the danger there. Despite Northrop's best efforts, the plane continued to lose altitude. Denmark would have to do with the hopes they could take a boat to Sweden with the help of the Danish underground. But, their refigured route would still take them over Kiel.

From the moment "Rhapsody" took off, navigator Deimel had kept meticulous records. He carefully recorded their diversion towards Kiel after they had left formation.

> "0732 - 10,000 feet, and -2 degrees. 0909 - Kiel smoke screen. At 0921 over enemy coast at 23,000 feet and -20. At 0930 from 21,000 feet, 88 mm shells set to explode at the plane's altitude, peppered the air bomber stream. "Rhapsody" passed Kiel at 0937 a.m., and Northrop turned near Lubeck at 0945. Flak was intense and accurate over Lubeck at 1000 a.m. on the approach. At 1010, it was -22 degrees."

As a stray from the formation, the crippled plane approached Kiel, having regained a few thousand feet. There was intense fire from the ground as it limped through the air. The ship was riddled with holes.

Northrop wracked up the wing tip on one side and then the other in evasive action. But the opposition was too strong. Flak bursts tore huge holes in the fuselage, and the beleaguered plane swung violently from side to side. The damaged B-24 struggled on, traversing the sparkling blue estuary at Kiel, as one-hundred-fifty anti-aircraft guns obscured by a smoke screen protecting the submarine pens defended their positions. The clatter of flak slammed against the aluminum skin of "Rhapsody" in a deafening staccato. Puffs of oily black and brown smoke spread across the sky in a dirty and deceptive veil. The plane flew on through the flak bursts rattling with greater intensity.

The men of "Rhapsody" had seen and heard of many a crew that had fallen victim to the unrelenting guns. Centrifugal force had pinned many a desperate and helpless man against the plane's interior. As his crippled plane spun in a slow-motion death spiral, the helpless airman rode to his death. They prayed it would not be them.

This is the flak battery in Barkelsby, Germany, that shot down "Rhapsody in Junk."

Courtesy of Mr. Nils Hempel - www.spurensuchesh.de

Up in the cockpit, Northrop understood the futility of their plight. He put the nose wheel down to surrender to the Germans, but beneath the smokescreen, they kept firing. Once down, he could not get the wheel back up, and it blocked the exit through the nose wheel hatch. He hit the bail out bell just outside the flak area. With just eighteen combat hours, the crew's wings would be clipped, and they would spend the rest of the war on the ground as prisoners of war of the Third Reich. By the time the mission was concluded, Harold Flaugher would be dead.

## Chapter 15

# A Wing and a Prayer

At the sound of the bail out bell, the crew scrambled from their positions to don parachutes. There was no panic and little conversation. Each man knew what he must do. There was no practice jumping with a parachute from a damaged plane. A man had to get it right the first time. Each was taught to try to land with the wind to his back. Memories strained to remember how to spill the chute, partially collapsing part of the canopy to redirect a chute heading towards a dangerous location. In the haste to depart the plane, each man had to remember what he was taught. A rapid descent from a high altitude would burst eardrums, yet it was best to free fall over enemy territory to prevent being shot by enemy fighters. Bailing out at too high an altitude meant losing consciousness from lack of oxygen. And he must remember to count before pulling the D ring that deployed the chute. In an instant each man had to assess his situation and find a place to bail out that would not result in him being bludgeoned, decapitated or impaled as the plane went out of control dragging plumes of black smoke behind.

Gonzales stood near Flaugher's side, as Jeffers moved from the nose to the bomb bay. Jeffers carried his parachute from the nose and stood near nervous Flaugher as they quickly put on the chest chutes. Jeffers continued toward the camera hatch beyond the bomb bay. Cardenas was anxious as he watched Jeffers and Deimel opening the camera hatch. Flak peppered the ship like popcorn. In the din of battle, Gonzales turned and watched as Jeffers dropped down on one knee, bowed his head and clasped his hands in prayer. Then he arose and stood by the camera hatch preparing to bail out at approximately ten-thousand feet.

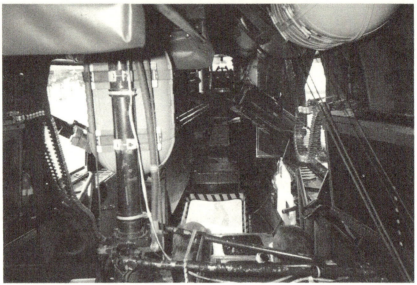

B-24's rear camera hatch where Jeffers, Deimel, Gonzales, Brodek and Clifford jumped

Despite his earlier protestations regarding bailing out, Gonzales was the first man out the rear camera hatch feeling the cold air rush past him. Brodek, Clifford and Jeffers followed him in quick succession as the plane lost altitude. Jeffers pulled the ripcord of his chest chute immediately after exiting the camera hatch as the plane was at such a low altitude. His first emotion was of great relief that it opened as the wind floated him backwards. He had no feeling of descent until he was a few hundred feet above the ground, where the dappled grass and wheat fields lifted gently up to meet him. Safely on the ground and recognizing the predicament he was in, Jeffers' first emotion was anger, not so much against the enemy, but because he knew he would be separated from his wife, family and friends in the squadron back in England. He hoped he would not be shot, and he assumed he would be taken a prisoner of war.

After Jeffers and the others went out, Deimel and Dean went out the bomb bay head first. Northrop remained flying the plane.

Butler, Flaugher and Cardenas balanced on the narrow catwalk of the windy bomb bay. Through the open doors that sunny day, the blue estuary at Kiel disappeared, and the forbidding land of Germany lay in muted colors below.

Flaugher was afraid to jump. He was a tall solid man, and he feared his parachute would not hold him. He had often expressed his fears to the crew. When Northrop told the crew to bail out, Flaugher begged those who remained to push him out, saying he just couldn't jump. The plane was soon to crash.

Butler could see the paralyzing fear on Flaugher's face.

Next out was Cardenas. His tall frame fell through the expanse to the land below.

There was no time left.

"It's time," said Butler.

Butler pushed Flaugher out the bomb bay. It was a relatively safer exit point due to the B-24's huge, vertical stabilizers. Slamming into the stabilizers upon exit, as the beleaguered plane continued on without her crew, was sure death.

Butler waited. When Flaugher had cleared the bomb bay, Butler jumped. He could see Flaugher's open chute far below him.

By then, the plane was over the Danish peninsula.

When all the men were clear of the plane, and it was dropping quickly, Northrop jumped out the bomb bay. Within five minutes all of the men had jumped.

In those crucial frozen seconds over Germany, all ten men of crew #2400, doomed plane #733, plummeted to the farm fields below. What was once a deafening roar of guns and engines melted into a sudden silence. A cacophony of blazing guns, an exploding sea of flak, the urgency of the bail out bell and the deafening roar of the slipstream gave way to a whisper of air through the shroud lines and relative serenity.

The jerked ripcords created a tremendous jolt, as the canopies snapped open. The chutes billowed and floated as the men descended, and the crew watched "Rhapsody" fly on low and undirected without them. Most disheartening was the fact that the rest of the formation had flown on and was returning to England. This crew had reached the end of its journey.

The plane was very low by the time Jeffers fell from the sky towards a sunny green field below. He had been forced to pull the rip cord immediately upon leaving the camera hatch. The G forces, as the chute snapped open, made him feel as if every bone had been broken. The shock of deceleration was so great that his fully-laced boot flew off. A loose parachute strap caused a groin separation when the chute opened forcefully, sharply jolting his groin and back. He could not feel his one leg. His upper leg would be numb for several months, and his back would ache from the jump. He came down in a farm field, and in the distance, he saw a farmer running up to him.

On the ground that day, ten-year-old Gretchen Bartel had a different view. She was standing with her sister outside her thatched-roof home that was built in 1625 in Wagersrott, a small farming community on the edge of even smaller Blick. Many of the people from her village were attending the funeral of a young German soldier, Karl-Hans, that day at that hour. He had been killed in a military training accident. Just after 11 a.m., Gretchen turned to see a huge burning aircraft roar low over her roof. She watched a hatch open, and a man parachuted out into a nearby farm field. Terrified, she watched the plane fly lower, and with a thundering explosion, crash into the nearby woods. The plane had just barely missed the church where so many of the community members attended the funeral.

A young airman stumbled in the farm field and removed his parachute. He had lost one boot and had a gash on his forehead. Local farmer, Nikolaus Clausen, had been cutting his field. Carrying his gun, he ran toward the airman.

"Sweden?" asked the shaken Jeffers.

"Nein" replied the farmer somberly, "Deutschland."

The farmer walked Jeffers across the farm field and down the dirt road near his home. He turned right at the end of the road and took the disheartened airman inside through the front door. He gave Jeffers coffee, and he sat with him for three hours until the German constable came. Local farmers got word he was there, and they came by to gawk at him. Soon, he was picked up, and the German soldiers reproached the farmer for giving the airman coffee. They showed great interest in his parachute and shrouds, fingering the nylon continuously possibly in an attempt at comparison with their own.

1625 German home of Gretchen Bartel where burning "Rhapsody in Junk" flew low over her thatched roof

He was taken at gun point to a pick-up location near a church. A five-year-old girl, dressed in her Sunday clothes for church, stood and stared at him. Seeing her, Jeffers felt for a brief moment that he was home on a typical Sunday morning where little girls arrived for Mass in such dresses. More men with guns came, and they put him in a small shack until the truck came that would deliver him to be reunited with his crewmates.

The plane was even lower by the time Dee Butler had followed Flaugher out. Butler tried to remember to count to ten before pulling the ripcord, but there was little time for that. He could see a farmer plowing below. He could see Germans running in all directions anticipating the landings of the chutes. When his chute opened, he yelled, laughed and cheered despite the fact both of his boots flew off. He swung violently back and forth in his parachute. The ground came up fast, and he landed hard on his feet injuring both of them. His head flew down between his legs, and he was knocked out for a few minutes. By the time he came to and got his parachute harness off, the Germans had encircled him. They were silent and stared at him.

Frank Deimel dislocated his shoulder on the way down, and it snapped back into place when he hit the ground. He lay on the ground dazed and with a cut lip before his capture by the Volksturm, or Home Guard, made up of young boys and old men defending their local towns.

Since Gonzales had been the first man out of the hatch, he could see the rest of the crew coming down around him. Buffeted by the wind, he tumbled for some distance uncontrollably. He tried to direct his parachute away from some blue water he now saw below, but it rocked him violently in the strong wind, and he gave up. The winds took him inland on their own accord. Bullets from ground level flew up at him, as unknown Germans on the ground continued to shoot at the surrendering man. The helpless crew dangled in their parachutes like carnival targets. The best option was to pretend to be dead.

Gonzales soon stabilized, and as he floated down over the green field below, he could see Dean in the distance.

Gonzales hit the ground hard, but he didn't see anyone or hear any sound. He sustained no injuries. Immediately, he buried his parachute as told in the briefings and started walking towards Denmark. At first his steps were slow, deliberate and cautious. Then they became faster and faster until he was running--thinking and hoping he had a good chance of making his destination. He ran for almost an hour. He raced through a berry patch scraping his face on its thorns and then fell to the ground. In the distance, Gonzales heard excited dogs barking. Suddenly, he saw three German Marines in their mid-thirties holding back two snapping, German shepherds on leashes. The German military spoke no English. They motioned to him to get up. Then they motioned to him to raise his hands.

"Hände hoch!"

The men searched him and smiled broadly. They shook hands congratulating each other on his capture.

When Dean jumped, he did not have his own parachute. The parachutes had been repacked the day before. Clifford had unintentionally grabbed Dean's, and the last thing Dean said to Clifford before he left the plane was that if his parachute didn't open he would "whip his ass" when they got on the ground. Prophetically, the chute did not open. Dean frantically and repeatedly beat on his chest to no avail. Finally, the emergency chute opened. After free falling thousands of feet and believing he was going to die, he was relieved to see and feel its canopy open. The force was so great that it blew the bottom of his breast pockets out and yanked off his boots.

Dean slammed into the ground landing half a mile from Gonzales. He had seen the coast line on the way down and hoped he could make it to Denmark or Sweden. He landed in a wheat field, staggered to his feet and struggled out of his harness, leaving his parachute in the field. With heart pounding, he cautiously and breathlessly pushed through a hedgerow. The only sound was his own breathing. In trying to clear himself, he could hear the rip of his felt socks by the wires in them which attached to his leggings. His heart continued to pound, as he tried to clear the brambles. Suddenly, on the other side of the hedgerow, there stood a man brandishing a gun with a fixed bayonet. Other Germans, farmers from the field, threatened Dean with pitchforks. He was surrounded.

Dean saw a man in a beige uniform come toward him.

"Sweden?" Dean asked the man.

The man spoke no English. When he turned, Dean saw a swastika on his armband indicating he was a member of the Home Guard.

All hopes of landing in a neutral country were immediately dashed.

Meanwhile, the Germans marched Gonzales through the field to a railroad track. Dean was taken to the same track. It was almost noon, and there would be no food for a long time. The guards prodded the two along, yelling at them in German. Gonzales, the first of the two captured, walked behind Dean. To make him move faster, the German guard hit Gonzales in the ribs, knocking him down and bruising his ribs with a rifle. He felt his ribs were broken. Dean cursed at the guards, as they pointed their guns at Gonzales after knocking him down. Dean urged Gonzales not to respond.

Further down the track, they found Brodek. In a strange sense of military propriety, the Germans ordered Dean to carry Brodek's parachute, because Brodek was an officer. With the weight of the parachutes, Dean's sore ankles slowed him down. Every time he slowed down, he felt the cold gun barrel at the back of his head. The loose wire still hung from his leg, and the Germans repeatedly stepped on it. With no boots, it was hard to keep his footing. When he tripped, they continued to punch him in the back with a pistol.

In the first village they marched through, one of the German guards cursed at Brodek and called him profane names. A large crowd of hostile people in Schleswig watched them. An older man who was crying broke through the civilians and tried to bash Dean's head with a rock. He was restrained by Dean's armed captors. The horror of the war had touched this formerly peaceful land, and the civilians had suffered greatly with the bombings. The three men were marched past other civilians, and Dean noticed the little girls of the village wearing dresses made of parachute silk.

Dean, Gonzales and Brodek were marched to a large official-looking building they thought might be a court house. Very large high-backed chairs surrounded a fifteen-foot-long shiny table, and Brodek and Dean were instructed to sit on opposite ends of the table. Gonzales was put in a separate room. The Germans ranted at the two in German.

Finally one swung around and looked at normally quiet bookish Brodek.

"Do you understand me!!" he screamed in Brodek's face.

"I understand you, you SOB!" Brodek said.

Gonzales contained his impulse to congratulate Brodek on his response.

The Germans showed them books with pictures of planes urging them to reveal military information far beyond the name rank and serial numbers they gave. Stubbornly, they refused to cooperate.

## Chapter 16

# Death on the Ground

Cardenas free fell from the hatch and tumbled and rolled until he could open his arms and legs to control his body position. When he estimated he was at five-thousand feet, he jerked the ripcord. The white canopy shot upward so high that at first he thought it was not attached to his harness. The air swished past, and he stabilized and felt great joy knowing he was alive. He could see a river below he believed to be the Elbe which ran as far as Hamburg.

But suddenly he heard a popping noise, and he saw bullet holes in the canopy. He remembered his training, and he forced himself to swing side to side to become a more obscure target. Soon, he could see woods below, and he swung to the right until he could clear the trees and land in a farm field. The parachutes were small, only eighteen feet, so his fall was equivalent to that from a two-story window. Once on the ground, he balled up his parachute and buried it under some bushes. He got out his .45 and loaded it and quickly found his compass. He looked at his watch, and it was 11:00 a.m. British time. He had carried his shoes on a wire around his neck, so he took off his flying boots and electric socks and put on his shoes.

Running north through a creek for almost an hour, he saw a farmer in blue coveralls chasing him.

"Halt!" the man cried.

As the farmer closed in to attack Cardenas with a pitchfork, Cardenas's heart beat loudly. He looked around to see if any others were coming. Cardenas took off through the creek bed again and hid under a wooden bridge. Then he heard voices getting closer and dogs barking. His heart was about to explode, and he asked God to make him invisible.

A soldier came under the bridge looking for him, and it was then he saw about fifteen men. He hid his gun and its holster under some dirt and branches and put a rock over it so he would not be found with it. Then they could kill him and say he resisted capture.

"Raus mit Dir!" (Get out!) one of the uniformed men called, poking him with a bayonet.

He was a German Marine.

Cardenas walked up on the bridge with his arms up. He counted seven Marines and three civilians.

"Bist Du Amerikaner oder Englaender?" one man asked trying to identify Cardenas as American or British.

Cardenas identified himself as American.

"Wo ist Ihr Fallschirm?" the man asked inquiring as to the whereabouts of the parachute.

Cardenas pointed to the left away from his buried gun. They nudged him with a bayonet, and the group started walking. A group of men and women approached with shovels, axes and rocks. Behind Cardenas and the Marines, a contingent of blue and gray-suited soldiers arrived. He knew that they belonged to the Luftwaffe, and they were superior to the infantry soldiers. The Luftwaffe men took Cardenas.

"We have to run, or you will be killed by the civilians," called a Luftwaffe lieutenant in English, "Run."

"I'm a good runner," said Cardenas.

The lieutenant shot a round above the civilians' heads, which made them duck to the ground.

Cardenas and the Luftwaffe guards ran all the way to a little town that had cobblestone streets like the ones Cardenas had seen in the southern United States.

The Germans took him to Gudau, near Denmark, where he saw a young woman sweeping the sidewalk.

"Hello, beautiful lady," he said with his customary charm, "how are you today?"

She threw her broom at him. A second young woman threw dirty water at him. He did not care as long as it was not bullets.

At the end of the street, there was a big white building with a black swastika at the entrance. Cardenas was taken to an office with black leather furniture. There was a bed in it, so he laid on it and fell asleep. An officer woke him up with a kick to the stomach. Cardenas could see the swastika on the arm band.

"Get up and stand at attention!" the man yelled in perfect English, "You are going to give me all the information I'm going to ask you."

"I have orders not to provide you with any military information but my name, rank and serial number."

He slapped Cardenas who thought of slapping him back, but reconsidered. Instead, he told him that he was not behaving as an officer would in the United States.

"You are in my hands, and I can do anything I want with you," the man laughed. How many crew members were on your plane?"

"I can't answer that question."

"How many missions have you been involved in?"

"I can't answer that."

Having revealed nothing, Cardenas knew more questioning would follow after they were moved from that area. He was eventually taken to a barn where he met up with Clifford. Few details are known of Clifford's capture.

After two hours, the other officers were all rounded up. Jeffers, Northrop, Butler and Deimel were ordered into a truck. As they climbed in, they noticed a black wooden coffin there. They had no reason to believe that it was for any one of their crew, and they naively assumed the Germans were taking it somewhere in the truck.

After they drove some distance under guard, the truck pulled into a small naval installation, and they were ordered out of the truck by their guards.

Two naval officers appeared for them to follow. They were taken to a long warehouse and entered a room where mines were kept, and on the floor lay a covered body. The guards indicated they spoke no English, and one motioned for someone on the crew to uncover it. All were hesitant. The guard grew impatient, and he ran over to the body and jerked the cover off.

Flaugher!

Jeffers felt a seething anger as he saw the body. The guards motioned quickly for Butler to remove Flaugher's class ring from his cold finger. They stood quietly watching as Butler slid Flaugher's watch from his still wrist and removed his dog tags. He turned and gave them to Northrop, who gave them to a German officer. Then Butler unhooked the parachute harness taking the opportunity to observe Flaugher's physical condition. Butler saw his friend had no broken bones but only a discoloration on his right temple. He noted the chest was crushed, but ironically the clothes were intact with all the buttons buttoned. Seven German military personnel watched as Deimel, Northrop, Jeffers and Butler lifted Flaugher's still body tenderly and placed it in the empty black box. Jeffers noted the sunken chest, and he wondered if a severe blow from some person or persons killed Flaugher.

Deimel looked at the parachute that had been removed from the harness, and it appeared to have opened. Jeffers examined it more closely. None of the lines had been fouled in any way, and no blood was on the chute. Jeffers turned in anger toward the guards with great suspicion.

"Did the chute open?" he demanded to know.

They feigned ignorance of English, but one naval officer shook his head "no."

Jeffers was convinced it had opened, and that led him to believe Germans had harmed their engineer and gunner.

He remembered Flaugher standing at the open bomb bay wearing his helmet telling Butler to push him out. The helmet housing his earphones now lay on the floor near the body. Jeffers picked it up, but there was no blood on it. He examined the ear phones, and the right one had been crushed. The left was still intact. A lot had happened from the time Flaugher fell through the bomb bay. His body had been picked up where he landed, and then it was taken to the naval base, and there was much speculation as to what happened in between. No one on the crew had seen a thing.

They loaded the box in the truck and left for a barn where the Germans picked up Clifford and Cardenas.

A fearful German woman who could speak a little English had been brought to the barn and told the two frightened men that anything could happen to them. German civilians with shotguns kept watch over them. The group argued amongst themselves as to what to do with the men. As the military truck approached, the group realized the military would take charge of their prisoners. The German civilians lined up and spat on the men calling them names and throwing rocks at them as the German military directed the captives to the truck. The civilians tried to hit the crew with their fists and kick them with their feet as the frightened men hurried to the truck. The captives moved forward and looked straight ahead and hoped not to be injured. With the others, the truck took them away.

The truck transporting the rest of the crew pulled up to the building, where Brodek, Dean and Gonzales, held there for a few hours, joined them. In the open-backed truck were two long benches. The wooden box sat between them. Clifford sat on one side and complained of a sprained ankle. With all of the men assembled in the truck, the newcomers noted one was still missing.

The official list of American dead would be received through the American Legation in Bern, Switzerland, for transmittal to the family. The life of the man the crew called a "prince of a man" had come to a tragic end.

"Where's Flaugher?" one of the men asked.

"You're sitting on him," replied Northrop.

## Chapter 17

# Fuer Dich ist der Krieg vorbei

It was a sobering moment for the crew as they peered at the dark wooden box. A favorite member of their close-knit group was gone and taken from them violently it appeared. The crew rode on in stunned silence. Finally, Northrop broke the somber atmosphere.

"Some crew," he said wryly, "not even one got away!"

The crew gave him weak smiles.

Northrop mused about the plane remembering the holes in the fuselage, wings and tail section.

"I wish I could take that plane back to a museum," he said to no one in particular, "so everyone could see what bad shape it was in and kept flying."

Northrop had not had time in England to tell Jeffers that Jeffers was to be made lead bombardier on June 19th. Now, it seemed pointless. Northrop would not tell Jeffers of that fact until nearly fifty years later in an anniversary card he sent.

Along the way, Jeffers told Gonzales that his wife had relatives in neighboring Flensburg. Her mother had a sister and two brothers still living there. That afforded Jeffers no safety now.

The truck wound its way to a German military cemetery. Jeffers and Deimel balanced the back of the wooden coffin, and Dean and Cardenas grasped the front. They set it on the ground outside a small church. A wooden gate led into the rows of graves. Summer birds chirped in the surrounding trees that warm afternoon. Old cement crosses engraved with the German iron cross marked many rows of graves. An old wrinkled German woman about ninety leaned over the wooden box on the ground and placed a bouquet of flowers on the coffin. A wooden cross bearing Flaugher's name would eventually be erected at grave number nineteen at the end of a row in the cemetery in a section blocked off and called the "American Section."

Sadly, the surviving crew re-boarded the truck, and the Germans drove off before the burial. After leaving their friend in the hands of the local Germans, the crew was driven to a naval guard house where they spent their first night.

Clifford and Dean were held in the same room with only one bed. When Dean was taking his turn sleeping, he woke up and heard Clifford saying, "It was a B-24," as his questioners showed him pictures. Clifford pointed to different photos commenting on each. Alarmed, Dean sprung from the bed and told him to shut up and give only name, rank and serial number.

"Fuer Dich ist der Krieg vorbei." (For you the war is over.) were the first words many a captured airman heard. The realization of the truth of this statement was sinking in. It was June 18th, 1944, they were in enemy hands, their families would not know their fate for months, they had no food to eat and they were unarmed---and Deimel noted with some irony, it was Father's Day.

Chapter 18

## *Schloss Gottorf*

"Rhapsody in Junk" burned furiously in the nearby woods. With much excitement, Ernst Hansen, fifteen, ran to the crashed plane from his nearby farm home in Blick. The German military restricted local residents from coming too near the plane for fear of ammunition and bombs exploding, but many took the chance and ran there to find and collect aluminum and Plexiglas from the fuselage and windshield of the plane. The tires had blown out, and broken bits of the plane scattered on the forest floor on impact, and oxygen masks, earphones, navigation charts and shell casings were thrown out in the explosion. Aluminum and Plexiglas were both in short supply in Germany. Plexiglas was often made into jewelry. Soon, the wreckage was completely cordoned off by the German military, and shortly afterward a salvage crew, assisted by Russian prisoners of war, came to cart most of the wreckage away. The Germans set up tents to sleep by the wreckage that night to guard it.

Early evening of the next night, the crew was driven back through Schleswig in close proximity to where they bailed out. The

German truck followed a road that ran beside a large body of water where some of them nearly landed on the way down. Then it turned into an entrance of a fortress. Dark shadows splashed across the walls of the forbidding structure. It was a local military barracks and headquarters for German infantry. Wheels of the German truck slowed, crunching in the gravel, and the truck with the crew passed through two giant black iron gates. The huge structure sat on a small island. Through the mammoth gates was a courtyard.

The big black gates of modern-day Schloss Gottorf, the castle in Schleswig-Holstein, Germany, where the crew was taken for interrogation and where they were held in underground cells

German soldiers scurried around the perimeter. After the hungry men climbed down from the truck, they were taken inside where their personal possessions and identification cards were confiscated. The guards confiscated the escape kits with the silken maps tucked inside. Dean and Jeffers were dismayed to see their money taken. The German guards gave no receipts. The Germans made a list of the men's belongings. According to their records, Clifford carried the most with him, although it was forbidden to carry so much personal identification. The Germans took his Social Security card, Army air base pass, transient crewman pass and a newspaper clipping with a story about Sgt. Cardenas and his relationship to Mexican President Carranza. They took Clifford's quarters assignment card, three identification tags, one Red Cross membership card, one physical fitness test and record, one parachute log record and individual clothing issue record. In addition, they confiscated a leather strap from Jack Gonzales and an identification tag from Alex Cardenas. Watches were also taken. The guards viewed with interest the newspaper article about Cardenas, whose relational status made him even more valuable in their eyes.

During questioning, the interrogator suggested that because the crew had one too many officers, one stating he was a gunner, referring to Brodek, that they were probably all spies and should be hung or shot.

"Were you on a spy mission?" the demanding German kept asking.

The crew gave only name, rank and serial number. They had been taught in briefings that to give more usually meant they would be held longer so that the Germans could extract even more information.

After their interrogation, Gonzales was walked to a winding stairway and then told to go down the stairs to the basement where all the cells were located. The other men soon followed. They were taken to dank ancient underground cells where they remained isolated from one another. They had no idea where they were, but the surroundings were reminiscent of a medieval dungeon.

The brusque guards grabbed Dean's shoes and shoved him in his dark cell. Dean and Gonzales were in adjacent cells, and Gonzales could hear Dean cursing at the guards. The iron cell doors were massive but had a small peephole. Little light filtered into the dismal cells. Upon the door was a paddle to spin to signal that the prisoner wanted to use the bathroom. Graffiti was scrawled on Gonzales's cell wall where someone had been counting long days. All that the men received for nourishment was water.

Most of the crew stayed there one night. Official records show Deimel stayed two nights, but that could be in error. During the night, Gonzales thought he heard many boats passing by, but he did not know which body of water sat adjacent to their cells.

On the second day in Germany, they were given two slices of hard dark German bread. The next morning, they went out into a hallway where they found some British captives also held there. Jointly, they were questioned, and the Germans decided to send them all on for further interrogation and processing. They filled out the necessary papers to transfer all the captured men along with nine envelopes of belongings with the notation, "map material found." Although Dean left without his money, they gave him his watch back.

## Chapter 19

# *Missing in Action*

After 1943, crewmembers knew they faced the possibility of abuse or death at the hands of an hysterical mob on the ground after bail out. Repeated bombings in major German cities set the stage for increased hostility among the citizens. With that thought in mind, the crew boarded the train to Frankfurt. Dean and Gonzales sat side by side on the train facing two German guards who never spoke to them. Gonzales glanced backward and saw Jeffers sitting alone and looking very serious and deep in thought. Several others on the crew sat adjacent to them. The men were hungry.

One of the guards pulled a knife from his pocket and sliced through a piece of blood sausage. He offered it to the prisoners. After seeing the red-tinged fat drip from the sausage, some declined, and some took it but did not eat it.

Back in Norwich, "Rhapsody's" concrete hardstand stood empty.

Upon touching English soil the day before, the surviving sortie crews had thrown their equipment on the ground and put their guns in the trucks. Piles of flak suits crowded the equipment hut swelled with men. The returning men with tired drawn faces, and matted hair had filed into the briefing room in the operations building in sheer exhaustion to be debriefed. Coffee mugs and sandwiches awaited them. Heavy flying boots shuffled into the briefing room. Shoulders were hunched from hours of exhaustive flying and battle, and tired eyes stared at the floor as each man waited his turn for interrogation. In turn, each described what he had seen below, ships in an estuary, bombs that connected to the target or problems on the plane. After some missions, men reflected on the broken Libs (B-24 Liberators) and Forts, (B-17 Flying Fortresses) crippled by a flak barrage that they had seen. Fresh in their minds were broken planes grotesquely twisted into pieces which plummeted to earth through searing flames as formation pilots prayed the pieces would not hit their own planes. After an intense battle in the blue battlefield, a witness might describe planes that erupted into corkscrewing torches or the blossom of counted parachutes, incongruously white against the flak-blackened clouds. The survival of the men seen bailing out of their former refuge was tenuous and often determined by the whim of streaming silk.

The surviving crews chalked up one more mission and returned exhausted to their beds to log sack hours, never knowing if the wake-up call would come only hours later. Like the hardstands, many of the beds no longer were occupied after a mission, and all men knew that the beds assigned to them had only recently been assigned to men who never came back.

Post-mission, reports of June 18$^{th}$ were carefully filed. A returning pilot reported Northrop was last seen under control entering the undercast.

In addition, the report revealed the result of the mission. (Author's notes in parentheses. Following reports copied exactly from old records and reproduced with abbreviations, spellings and time-designation format used by the original writers. Helgoland is the German name for the island notated in the reports.)

> "This information indicates two B-24 groups went to Hamburg. Only one of the 2$^{nd}$ BD (bomb division) Groups went to a TOO (Target of Opportunity).

Stade A/F, (airfield) Bremerhaven, Husum A/F, Heligoland A/F, Wrist M/Y, (marshalling yard) Bremerhaven, Wesermunde and Nordenham were the other targets assigned to the Groups of the 2nd BD that day. A small force of 2nd BD B-24s attacked Noball (V-weapons) targets by GH (Gee) later that day. Over 100 planes that day. Airfield TO (target of opportunity) Heligoland - 8 bombed."

Official 458th mission records for that day revealed the following:

"June 18 was a 2 mission day chalking up sorties 69 and 70. Our 1st missions showed 23 a/c dispatched under the leadership of Major LaRoche and Henson to attack the a/f at Fassberg. G. H. due to 10/10 clouds over the target it was not attacked, but 13 of our a/c attacked Bremershaven on PFF, 8 a/c attacked toos Heligoland a/f visually with poor results . One a/c attacked the m/y at Wrist, G. w hits in the town. Total bombs dropped on these targets, 262x500 GPs. One a/c 733 of the 754th sq. left the formation in vicinity of Hamburg with #1 engine smoking. (see missing in action for names.)"

An attached sheet listed the Northrop crew.

"A further report stated Liberators dove through flak reeling from its hits. At 1021 the formation passed right by Hamburg and at 1031 bombed Wesermunde. The lead navigator's report indicated three parachutes were spotted. The first squadron attacked LR Bremershaven on PFF. Bombs fell just west of M/Y in NE of Bremershaven. The crew passed its IP, and went on to the secondary target. They passed that and went on to their target of last resort. The second squadron bombed Heligoland encountering intense flak from the Heligoland defenses. Their bombs overshot into the sea. There was intense fire from Cuxhaven and from Heligoland defenses."

Some debriefing reports would indicate that #733 left the formation with an engine smoking and was destroyed over or during the raid on Bremerhaven. Lewis Jacobus, Ronald Gulick and Edward Centola in other planes watched the plane leave formation. They filled out reports after they returned to England stating what they saw during this last sighting. Six weeks later, bombardier Centola would once again fly over Hamburg. His plane would take a direct hit, lose both wings and be blown out of the sky killing everyone but the pilot and co-pilot.

Six crews reported Northrop left formation in the vicinity of Neumunster, Germany at approximately 10:20 a.m. at 23,000 feet.

> "He made a one-hundred-eighty-degree turn and headed east. The only visible reason for action," one witness stated, "was smoke from the number one engine."

As the captured men made their way through Germany on the 18th, Air and Sea Rescue was dispatched to find them. It searched again on the 19th. The searchers were told the plane was last seen in Neumunster, but little else. One crew reported hearing an aircraft believed to be #733 calling Air Sea Rescue about 11:00 a.m. over the North Sea. This report was checked and discounted, as it was another aircraft with a similar call sign. When no wreckage was found, the last report was that #733 was believed to have made it to Sweden.

Frostbitten Joe Risko was immediately assigned to another crew and flew two days later still reeling from the loss of his crew and determined to make his thirty-five missions before returning home.

On the day of Flaugher's burial in Germany, on June 21st, three days after his death, the possessions of the rest of the crew were boxed up at Horsham St. Faith to be mailed home. With two crews who were roommates going down just one day apart, strangers to both crews sorted through their belongings hoping to send the right possessions to the right families. Years after the war Jeffers was still trying to find the picture he had kept of my mother and noted he had received a pair of English shoes that did not belong to him.

Sixty years later, Risko's son found a picture of Gonzales and his brother in a group of pictures his father had saved.

Five months after the possessions returned home, the supply officer sent a letter to Brodek's mother.

> "Brodek had more clothing and personal possessions than the other officers whose belongings I have handled. I took care of over fifty officers' personal effects during the time I was supply officer."

Much would happen before Brodek, himself, would see his possessions again. In the meantime, the families back home were following the fighting on radio and in the newspapers.

On June 19$^{th}$ Walter Cronkite wrote of the massive mission of the Second Air Division, and loved ones of the crew following the war read it with interest, not realizing their men were part of it and failed to return.

### "Mighty Yank Air Blow Goes Unchallenged"

### UP War correspondent.

"ALLIED SUPREME HEADQUATETRS, London, June 18, (UP) Blasting the German Army's vital oil supplies without opposition from the Luftwaffe, a powerful fleet of more than 1,300 U.S. Flying Fortresses and Liberators attacked numerous oil refineries in Northwest Germany today, including several at Hamburg.

Three important airdromes in Northwest Germany also were plastered with high explosives and incendiaries as the greatest purely strategic striking force of United States four-engine bombers ever dispatched went out on a non-tactical mission for the first time since D-Day. Eleven Flying Fortresses and Liberators were missing—mostly downed by the intense flak."

"Rhapsody in Junk" was among them.

Chapter 20

# Come In, I Am Your Interrogator

As military intelligence reports were filed in England, the German train car containing the crew sped southwest across Germany bound for Dulag Luft, the designated interrogation center. For crews who were shot down in Italy, Dulag Luft was in the city of Verona, and men were held in the same ancient prison where Christopher Columbus was held. But for crews shot down over the rest of Europe, the interrogation center was near Frankfurt in a town called Oberursel. After more intense questioning there, captives would be sent on to permanent prisoner of war camps. Before arriving in Oberursel the train stopped first at the central train station in Frankfurt where the captured crews were transferred to the tram to Oberursel.

Whenever captured airmen passed through the rail station there, mobs of war-weary Germans tried to get at them to do physical harm, and a few succeeded. Often, it was only the armed German guards who fended off the attackers. As most prisoners were, the crew was paraded through the train station at Frankfurt to await the tram that took them the twenty-minute ride to Oberursel. People stopped and stared at them calling them "Terrorflieger" or "Luftgangsters" and murderers. Some waived their fists and spat at the crew who were grateful to have guards protecting them. The tram ran almost hourly, but prisoners who missed it took the train to Oberursel and walked the one-and-a-half miles from the train station to the entrance of the camp. Seeing advertisements for Coca-Cola along the way was strangely incongruous to the men.

The train station in Oberursel, Germany, where prisoners of war arrived from the Frankfurt train station and where they departed for their permanent camps
Courtesy of Mary Smith and Barbara Freer

For those who walked, there was a water spigot at an Esso station on the corner, but frequently an old woman there would not let prisoners drink. Many a prisoner who stopped to drink was the recipient of a swat from the angry woman who called them murderers.

A new label awaited them at their destination. From that time on they were referred to as Kriegies, short for Kriegsgefangenen (prisoner of war).

Jeffers, Northrop, Butler and Brodek arrived on the same day, June 20th. Records show Deimel arrived on the 21st. Dulag Luft was short for Durchgangslager der Luftwaffe meaning Air Force Transit Camp. It was originally an experimental farm located near Oberursel

Armament Officer 1st Lt. William Brodek's POW I.D. card and pink file card
that the Germans kept on each prisoner
Courtesy of Mrs. Jean Brodek

Pilot, 2nd Lt. Henry Northrop's POW I.D. card
Courtesy of Mrs. Maria Haag

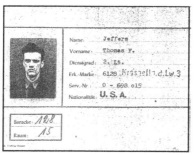

Bombardier, 2nd Lt. Thomas Jeffers' POW I.D. card

Co-pilot, 2nd Lt. Dee Butler's POW I.D. card
Courtesy of Mrs. Kay Gamble

at the foot of the Taunus Mountains. The transit camp proved to be inadequate as the war dragged on, and it was moved to several other locations over the years including outside the town of Wetzlar.

Dulag Luft was composed of three installations; Auswertestelle West, the interrogation and evaluation center at Oberursel, the hospital at Hohe-Mark and the transit camp at Wetzlar.

Auswertestelle West was located three-hundred yards north of the main Frankfurt-Hamburg Road and near the trolley stop. Dulag Luft Wetzlar succeeded Dulag Luft Frankfurt which was formerly situated in the Botanical Gardens of Frankfurt-on-Main and was destroyed in an Allied air raid on Frankfurt.

The beleaguered men of "Rhapsody in Junk" entered a gate and climbed the hill into a fenced area where they were taken into a white wooden building, the Transport Office, for evaluation. Three miles further up the road was a way station, a temporary barracks surrounded with barbed-wire.

The crew disrobed and was searched upon arrival. They were next taken to a room where Red Cross forms were produced, and they were told these forms were expected to be filled out. The Germans wanted far more than name, rank and serial number. The Red Cross form became a tool. How could the Germans possibly notify the downed flier's family if the form was not completely filled out? How, the Germans wanted to know, could they be sure who to contact with the news, without the form?

Although the form initially was quite generic, it quickly progressed to requests for very specific military information. The men were threatened after giving only name, rank and serial number and for failure to complete the forms. They were photographed and fingerprinted and moved to one of three likely locations—the transit camp, the way station or solitary confinement. Most went to solitary where their only companions were fleas.

The cooler, as solitary was known, was an American term borrowed by the Germans. The U-shaped building contained two-hundred-forty, four-by-seven foot solitary confinement cells. Fourteen buildings were scattered about the area surrounded by a security fence on three sides.

U-shaped cooler that housed the solitary confinement cells

One light turned on and off randomly, but it was mostly off. The electricity and heat were controlled from the hall. Temperatures in the cells sometimes became unbearable, and thick cement walls retained the heat. The one window in the room was painted over. The cells had a bed, stool and small table. A tiny iron handle in the cell released a red metal flag to signal a reluctant guard that the prisoner needed to use the latrine down the hall if the guards chose to take him. A washroom and showers were also down the hall, but prisoners were not allowed to meet there. Cooperative prisoners were apt to be taken more often.

A man in civilian dress, who identified himself as a Red Cross representative, entered prisoners' cells the first night and asked the men to fill out lengthy forms which he reiterated were necessary before they could be sent to a permanent prison camp. They refused, and the cat and mouse game continued.

Jeffers spent two days in his cell, and as the others did, banged on the door to use the bathroom when guards were not responsive. While confined, the prisoners were served an ersatz (imitation) tea. It was made from various mixtures of hay, carrots and parched grain. Ersatz coffee, ingredients unknown, was also served. Burnt breadcrumbs and acorns were rumored to be part of its composition. Food was almost non-existent. For breakfast, there might be a slice of black bread, at noon, a cup of sauerkraut soup, and supper was one slice of bread. In discomfort and boredom, the crew consumed the meager offerings and waited to be called.

Small solitary confinement cell, often over-heated, where the crew was held for several days during interrogation

The interrogation methods of Dulag Luft were based upon the premise that if a prisoner was deprived of contact with others, put on a starvation diet, and subjected to other discomforts, he would soon be willing to talk or to unwittingly reveal information that would help the German war effort. Sensory deprivation and isolation were used to "soften the men up" and make them more willing to talk, and the entire crew experienced that and the heated cell. There was nothing to do but sit, lie down, sleep, count the nails in the ceiling boards, pace the floor and to think and wonder about their fates.

The Germans employed there were masters of information, and during the sessions the interrogators told the prisoners more about themselves and their crew than the prisoners could ever have imagined they knew. Much of the information presented to the prisoner was very personal in nature, information that was gleaned from careful perusal of articles in newspapers and from seemingly innocent comments dropped from other prisoners.

Hanns Joachim Scharff, who occupied office number forty-seven, was the master interrogator at Dulag Luft. He was raised in Germany in an upper-middle-class family to be a proper gentleman in the classic sense. A businessman, running a company which imported Adler automobiles into South Africa, Scharff, together with his British wife, Margaret, and his youngest son, Chris, traveled to Germany to reunite with their eldest son, Felix, left in Germany the previous summer. Scharff had plans to visit his mother and grandparents in Greiz and pick up Felix before the war erupted. He was caught there after hostilities broke out and could not return to South Africa. Britain had seized Scharff's property in South Africa as it did the property of all foreign nationals on the side of the Axis powers and interned those foreign nationals still residing in the territory. With his property seized and the threat of being interned, Scharff had no choice but to remain in Germany. He lived with his family in Berlin and found employment in a civilian capacity until he was called up for military training in 1943. He moved his family, which consisted of his pregnant wife, two boys and a newly-born daughter, Della, to the relative safety of Greiz.

In 1943, three days after starting his career as a German soldier, Master Interrogator Hanns Scharff, held his daughter, "Della."
Courtesy of Mr. Ray Toliver

Initially trained as a German Panzer Grenadier, he was destined for the eastern front. Margaret would have none of it. She barged into a German general's office in Berlin and arranged for his transfer. His knowledge of English landed him a place at the interrogation center. As the war progressed, and Allied bombing made it more dangerous to live in Berlin, Margaret took her children to her in-law's villa in Greiz, where she gave birth to another son, Hanns Claudius, and planned to wait out the war.

Although only a private, Hanns Scharff's charming and mannerly demeanor and respect for his opponent, resulted in good rapport with the prisoners. He was a consummate storyteller with a wonderful sense of often self-deprecating humor, and his flair for gentle, yet effective, interrogation did not escape his superiors. His inherent respect of prisoners and low-key interrogation techniques culled far more information from the pilots he was assigned than they ever realized they were giving. Even in the midst of war, he showed compassion for his prisoners many of whom had already experienced brutal treatment during capture. Scharff contacted prisoners' families in emergencies, and he took long walks with selected prisoners up in the beautiful Taunus Mountains. In the heavily-wooded forests, their innocent conversations often revealed valuable information.

The main corridor and Hanns Scharff's Room 47 where prisoners were interrogated
Photographs by Charles Rollings

For those men seriously injured and hospitalized, he made frequent visits to the hospital at Hohe-Mark, sometimes assisting with procedures as he eased the mind of many a frightened patient. His colleague, Dr. Ernest W. Ittershagen, performed countless surgeries repairing broken limbs, bodies and spirits and became an early pioneer in the use of pins to secure broken bones. When the POW x-rays, indicating the use of metal pins fell into allied hands, it was thought at first the prisoners were being tortured by German doctors.

Upon departure, Scharff asked the men he interrogated to sign his "guestbook," and most wrote warm, or tongue-in-cheek, humorous comments on the pages. Years after the war ended, many prisoners whom he had interrogated would reunite with Scharff in friendship.

But Scharff only interrogated fighter pilots. The crew would face any number of other interrogators who worked at Dulag Luft questioning bomber crews.

Periodically, each man was removed from his cell and taken to a room for interrogation. The German interrogators' English was perfect, as many of them had attended school in the United States before the war. With few exceptions, their demeanor was always polite.

"Come in please, I am your interrogator," initiated each session.

"What was your bomb group?"

"What squadron?"

"How many aircraft in your bomb group?"

"What was the target?"

When all questions were once again answered with name, rank and serial number, the prisoner was returned to his cell.

A Captain Hermann was assigned to the crew of "Rhapsody in Junk."

Brodek was the first to be interrogated. He sat across a desk from Hermann. Spread out on the desk was a book containing the whole history of the 458th Bomb Group. The man detailed cogent and up-to-date information on the group and its crews. Brodek was startled at his knowledge.

"Brodek," the man then asked quizzically, "Why are you here?"

The interrogator went on with his questions.

"You are not even on this crew---you are not even a gunner! Why are you flying with this crew?"

While amazed by the information the Germans held, Jeffers was more amused at the way the German berated Brodek for taking such a risk. Brodek told him nothing and was held just two days.

Then Hermann questioned Northrop for a long time. When he was finished, he called for Jeffers.

Jeffers entered the room.

"It is too bad that you had to lose a member of your crew," Hermann said.

Jeffers was convinced the interrogator knew more details than he was letting on. He sized the man up as he would any opponent. The interrogator carried one-hundred-fifty-pounds on his five-foot-ten frame. He wore a blue Luftwaffe uniform, and he combed his straight dark grey hair back over his head. His facial features protruded sharply, and Jeffers judged him to be at least forty-five years old since he mentioned fighting in World War I.

Hermann told him where he, Jeffers, had gone to high school and flight school, places where he had trained, and how many missions he had flown. Jeffers gave only name, rank and serial number for three days of interrogation. By the third day, surviving nights in his over-heated cell, he was just as determined to reveal nothing, and he and his interrogator responded to and greeted each other like old friends.

Cardenas was thoroughly interrogated.

"Look, anything you might tell me I already know and have it here in my records," said the interrogator.

Cardenas smiled thinking that he was lying.

The man took a book out of a drawer.

"You are in the 458th Bomb Group, 754th Squadron of the Eighth Air Force, and this is your third mission."

Cardenas felt a chill run through his body.

"Your commander's name is Colonel Isbell. He was assigned as the second CO of the group in November 1943, and he remained the CO until March 1944 – the longest tenure of one commanding officer in the 2nd Air Division, if not the 8th Air Force… quite a man. Your Squadron Commander is Major Robert H. Hinckley, a bad tempered red-head."

All the information was true.

Often, his interrogator spoke in Spanish.

"You have a German background. Your grandmother is Florencia Strasburger married to General Jesús Carranza and daughter of Jacob Strasburger from Hamburg. I know that you belong to very well-known Mexican families, because Captain Emilio Carranza established the Mexico-to-Washington flying record in 1928. Your uncle, General Gustavo Salinas, was the Chief of the Air Force of Mexico, and both were creators of the Mexican Air Force so as you can see, I know your background."

"How is it possible that he knows all this information?" Cardenas thought.

He remembered that throughout his training they took reports on him at each base, even his background. The Nazis had spies everywhere he had heard. He remembered an old fellow that would bring hamburgers in a little cart and would place himself next to a bridge before the dikes in Corpus Christi, Texas. The FBI caught him hiding cameras and a transmitter in the cart. He had reported every ship departing from the port through the radio, and the ships were sunk in the Gulf of Mexico by German submarines.

The interrogator pressed for information on the Norden bombsight. Cardenas told him nothing. He was returned to his hot solitary cell.

After releasing him once more to the interrogator, he was questioned again.

"Are you ready to tell me the information I requested from you?"

"No sir, I won't tell you anything, even if you kill me."

"That's what I was about to tell you. I'm ordering your execution, because you are considered a spy. You are not American. Here, I have a French credential that says you are a French mechanical engineer named Jean La Ponte."

In England, they had given the crew credentials to help in the case of a crash, so they could identify themselves as French among the Germans.

"You know very well that I am American."

"I, however, am considering it real, so I'm going to execute you," explained the interrogator.

"You then, are acting against the Geneva Convention, where it's established that the prisoners must be respected, fed and protected and should have a bed in which to sleep," Cardenas responded.

The German became very angry and ordered Cardenas out of his office and into a fenced-in area where another two-hundred men had gone through the same questioning. They all greeted each other, and Cardenas thanked God for getting him away from such a horrible fate. He was returned to his cell and left himself in God's hands.

Gonzales was also returned to his cell after many refusals to provide information. The heat was turned up high, and he began to sweat. He sat in his cell trying to determine where the heat was coming from. With the window blacked out and sealed over, it was pitch black, and he had to feel his way around the room, but he could never find a vent or airway, so he gave up the futile challenge. He could only wait and endure.

The crew was released from solitary confinement and sent on to the transitional center for determining which camp they would be sent to. They were led down a long corridor in the morning at the end of which a group of prisoners waited to check out. At the transit camp, the crew had some property returned, but they were relieved of their fleece-lined bomber jackets and boots. In return, they received a Red Cross capture kit consisting of a cardboard suitcase that held underwear, socks, toilet articles, cigarettes, a new khaki shirt and trousers, a wool cap, gloves and an army field jacket. Best of all they had hot showers.

The new prisoners were allowed to send a post card home notifying their loved ones of their capture.

**Kriegsgefangenpost – U.S. censored Mit Luftpost Par Avion**

### June 23, 1944

My Darling Wife,

I am safe and well and am now a prisoner in a German camp. Please wire Mom. I love you very much and will write you as often as I can as soon as I reach my permanent camp. I'll give you my permanent address then so you can write.

Love, Jeff

They were fed more generously, and any wounded were treated in the hospital. The men were given a Red Cross parcel containing corned beef, salmon, pork luncheon meat, cheese, orange concentrate, chocolate, powdered milk, biscuits, oleo, liver paste, seedless raisins, soap, two packs of cigarettes and matches. Suitcases in hand, they set off to the unknown.

## Chapter 21

# Clipped Wings

Hermann Goering, an ex-fighter ace from World War I, had arranged for all officers to be held in the Luftwaffe camps. He respected them as fellow officers and airmen, and it was generally accepted that officers would be treated humanely and would not have to work. Enlisted prisoners were sent to the camps run by the Wehrmacht until after numerous escapes the camps were taken over by Himmler's notorious SS and Gestapo. At that point, the prisoners did not have the benefit of Goering's intervention. "Rhapsody's" officers were assigned to Stalag Luft III in what is now Poland.

The enlisted men, Dean, Gonzales, Clifford and Cardenas were taken to Stalag Luft IV in northeastern Germany which had inferior conditions compared to the Luftwaffe camps. Without the protection of the Luftwaffe, their fates were left in the hands of men of questionable character following the take over of the camps by the Gestapo and SS. Their treatment was far more uncivilized than that of the officers.

The men were sent from the transit camp to permanent camps in groups of fifty to one hundred. Many sent to permanent camps were advised they would travel on a regular train but there was to be no singing or spitting. The railway station was fifteen minutes from Dulag Luft. Some men walked to the railway station down the hill from camp, and some were trucked. There could be as long as a four-hour wait for a train depending on the schedule and the effect of Allied bombings. In addition, there was always the danger of strafing by Allied aircraft. Once again, it was a nervous time for the prisoners as they waited in hostile surroundings.

Eventually, the guards herded the officers into the over-crowded passenger cars. The officers of "Rhapsody" squeezed into a small passenger compartment on the train. Meant to hold only four-to-six passengers, ten men were crowded in. Jeffers watched as one man chose to sleep stretched out up above in a luggage rack of the ancient car which was attached to the end of train.

The shrill whistle signaled departure, and as the cars groaned out of the station headed for Berlin, the reality of life in the enemy's hands sunk in. For hours, the car swayed back and forth in a somnolent rhythm, as its giant wheels sang out picketa-pocketa, picketa-pocketa through bombed out towns across the ravaged war-torn country.

Rolling through the sunny summer countryside brought no consolation. Fear of the unknown, which waited at the train's destination prevented little enjoyment of the sometimes scenic surroundings.

On the journey, the men were given black bread, a chunk of evil-smelling cheese and a piece of blood sausage. It usually took two days from Oberursel to Sagan in the best of conditions when there were no Allied bombings of the tracks or delays due to lack of trains. This trip took four days. Along the route, as Jeffers would say years later,

"We were thrown into a bunch of German jails."

The train rolled into Alexanderplatz Bahnhof (train station) in Berlin which had been bombed with impunity many times. After each fusillade, tinkling glass fell in large masses upon the tracks and platforms from the canopy above leaving stark twisted metal frames. The sight of the blown out windows and structural damage encouraged the worried prisoners as they picked through the remains of the station. Their buddies had done well.

It was a three-hour, approximately one-hundred mile trip from Berlin to Sagan, the home of Stalag Luft III. The area was in the distant realms of Upper Silesia, formerly Prussia. The word Silesia meant sand, and it was that very yellow sand that had made it so difficult for prisoners already confined there to tunnel out of the camp.

It took Brodek five days to reach Stalag Luft III, arriving on the 27th of June. Northrop, Jeffers, and Butler left on June 23rd. Butler and Jeffers arrived on June 27th, but Northrop did not arrive until the 28th. Deimel left Dulag Luft on June 24th, but arrived three days later on the 27th. Gonzales left by himself on a passenger train for Stalag Luft IV, but Clifford, Cardenas and Dean were soon to follow. The officers would not see their enlisted crew until after the war.

When the enlisted men arrived by boxcar at Stettin, a Baltic port town, they had survived an ordeal. On their way to Stalag Luft IV, Allied bombers dropped bombs close to their train, and afterward, fighter planes strafed. During the attacks, the train of prisoners stopped. The earth shook, and sirens wailed. They knew the fighters would fly low to the ground to machine gun anti-aircraft installations, and they especially targeted trains.

Once the men got out of the train, they saw a water hose running. They were desperate for a drink. Cardenas realized then how close to animals they all had become. Instead of organizing themselves so that everyone would have a fair share to drink, the three-hundred men all fought to be first.

It was a three-mile walk from the Kiefheide railroad station to reach Stalag Luft IV. Feeling self-confident about the war, the German guards there boasted to their new captives that they would one day be slaves to the Germans. Dean and Gonzales were put in the same barracks, but at opposite ends. Only months later, newly arriving prisoners were forced to run a gauntlet between sadistic guards brandishing bayonets who set attack dogs against any man falling down in one of the most notorious events in the camps during the war. Hungry and exhausted, prisoners desperately tried to support the men who were so weak they would fall. It was a foreshadowing of what some of the guards there were capable of. At a later date, prisoner retaliation and the War Crimes Trials served up retribution for only some of the guards' misdeeds.

Some prisoners watched the arrival of Cardenas's group. Those prisoners, Cardenas noted, had empty looks in their eyes, and the men were emaciated. The incoming prisoners were put in a big room, and the guards started to go through the list of names. One of the German guards was especially tall and strong, though the incoming prisoners did not yet know his name. They would learn it very soon.

Radio Operator Staff/Sgt. Lawrence Dean's POW I.D card
Courtesy of Mrs. Brenda Morea

Food was scarce, and after a week, the new prisoners drank water to forget their hunger. When a truck full of potatoes was brought in, the prisoners peeled them and returned the peels to the Germans who made paper out of them. Cardenas understood just how serious things had become.

Meanwhile, in Sagan, the officers were learning their fate at Stalag Luft III. The officers' train hissed and slowed to a stop just down from the main train station. The officers peered anxiously out the smudged windows as the train sat on a siding. Slowly, the doors opened. Stiff, hungry and weary, the new arrivals stepped down to the remote platform.

They filed past a tall narrow brick guard house on the left where their papers were checked. Then they trudged up the sandy road for a mile to the camp, their scuffing shoes creating puffs of dry earth with each step. Tall pines, planted in perfect symmetry, lined the road like sentries offering the pleasant fresh smell of pine on the warm summer day. Through a clearing in the pine woods, they got their first look at the camp. The prisoners passed a ten-foot-tall rustic fence made of split pine saplings nailed closely together. Up ahead, they could see the main gate. A huge crimson flag, emblazoned with a black swastika, hung limply from a flagpole. Through the enormous gate on their left, they could see clusters of green-grey weathered barracks, a barbed-wire fence and elevated guard towers. German guards with machine guns at the ready looked down from the ominous wooden towers sullenly observing the new arrivals. Like squat fire plugs, tree stumps sat between the maze of barbed-wire between compounds and the forest. Guards swung open the gate and summarily checked papers. The cluster of men were paraded through and with sinking hearts watched and heard the wooden gate push close with finality behind them.

Now in dirty clothes after their long trip, and most with a thick growth of beard, the men had reached the end of the line. Herded to a forecourt of a stark one-story building, the men were led in one by one for processing. Each was searched, photographed and fingerprinted. He was given a metal identification card with III stamped on it and given a POW number. The men showered and were dusted for fleas and lice.

Bedding, consisting of two thin blankets, one sheet, one mattress cover filled with wood shavings, one pillowcase, one small linen towel and one pillow filled with straw was issued. One two-quart mixing bowl, one cup, knife, fork and spoon were given to each prisoner. There was a German eagle holding a swastika stamped on the utensil handles. If any item was lost or stolen, it would not be replaced.

Afterward, the new prisoners were called to attention. A Luftwaffe officer came out to welcome them accompanied by a Royal Air Force and American Service Officer who led them off for a speech in the theatre. The new men marched from the gate to the theatre with no chance to say hello to old friends as the old prisoners lined up on both sides of the path to search for familiar faces. In the theatre, the new men were given a one-hour briefing by Colonel Delmar Spivey on how the camp was organized, the necessity to be extremely careful to obey regulations, camp activities and who to go to for advice and assistance. Spivey was a pilot shot down in December of 1943 and crash landed on the border of Holland and Germany twenty miles from the Rhine. He was one of the old timers.

The hungry men marched to a mess hall for a free meal put together from donations of Red Cross parcels and German rations. Current prisoners saved items from their own Red Cross parcels to pool to feed the incoming men. Knowing the deprivation they had faced on their own journeys, they felt great compassion for the new arrivals. From the mess hall, the prisoners were taken by a leader and marched to a compound amongst the ten-foot-high double fence and told to find a place to live.

Jeffers and Butler initially chose the same barracks. The room was made for eight men, but it now held ten. Two double-decker bunks were made into triples, and Jeffers took a top bunk. He and Butler quickly discovered that of the eight original bed slats, two had already been donated to the escape committee to shore up the escape tunnels dug into the Silesian sand. They would lose more slats as time and tunnels went on, and soon they were easing into their bunks carefully hoping they did not turn over or move during the night, as they balanced precariously on the two remaining slats.

Fellow prisoners did not immediately accept the new men. They were processed by a prisoners' interrogation society anxious to learn the men's war experiences after being shot down and to be advised of profitable bombing targets they had seen. For security reasons, each new man had to have someone vouch for his identity to confirm he was who he said he was and not a German spy or "stooge." The prisoners were aware that spies could easily be slipped in since so many Germans had lived in the United States and spoke with no German accent. Confirmation of their identity was sought in many ways. If no fellow prisoner could say he knew the new man, questions were asked about sports or other trivia of the United States that any red-blooded American would know. For those who could not find someone who knew them before capture, it could be a lonely existence being given the "silent treatment" by the others until confirmation of identity could be firmly established.

On June 28th, one day after Jeffers arrived in Sagan, my mother was called at work by her sister with whom she had been living back in Ohio. Her sister told her Western Union had been trying to contact her. She left immediately for home. Western Union later delivered the telegram at 6:31 p.m.

> "The Secretary of War desires me to express his deep regret that your husband second lieutenant Thomas F. Jeffers has been reported missing in action since eighteen June over Germany. If further details or other information are received you will be promptly notified. ULIO the Adjutant General."

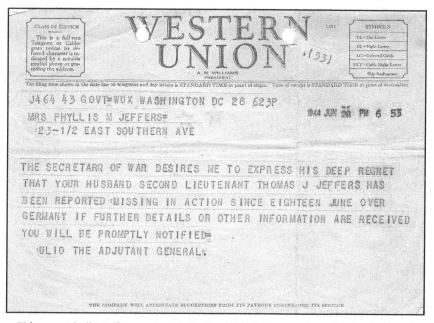

Telegram Phyllis Jeffers received in Springfield, Ohio, ten days after her husband was shot down

One by one, identical telegrams arrived at the homes of the crew causing great worry and anguish. Hank Northrop's mother received her telegram with the sad news on her birthday.

In Tennessee, a taxi-driver delivered the fateful telegram to Dean's parents.

One by one, the families received the stunning news that the boys they sent off to war were missing and may never come home.

Addresses of the crew members were sent to the family members with the advice to communicate with each other and share whatever information was received. Reliance on slow mail service from Germany became the only means to learn of the crew. Often, it would take months to learn anything. Cardenas's mother contacted all of the crew families requesting they maintain contact, pass along any news they heard, and above all pray for the missing men twice a day at the same time together despite the distance of their homes.

## Chapter 22

# Ferrets and Goons

It was unknown how long it would take for the crew's single post cards from Dulag Luft to arrive in the United States. Still worried that their families may not know of their fate, the crew nevertheless fell into the routine of the camps. The prisons were spartan microcosms of their former world. Stalag III ran efficiently for the most part when the men cooperated. It could be abysmal when they didn't. The fate of the men in Stalag Luft IV was determined by the whim of the guards.

Within Stalag Luft III, a small hand-picked group of kriegies ran a super-secret operation, covertly communicating in code with Allied Headquarters and directly back to Washington. Exactly what they communicated and their methods for doing so are still somewhat classified today. Lt. Colonel Albert P. Clark, an early captive, served as "Big S," head of security for the tunnel builders in North Compound. Clark's Spitfire crash landed at Cape Gris Nez, France, in 1942, and he was immediately captured by the Germans. Clark had over six-hundred men working under him in the camp. The Germans grew suspicious of him and moved him and the rest of the American officers to South Compound several months before "Rhapsody's" officers arrived.

Just four months before the officers of "Rhapsody in Junk" arrived at Stalag Luft III, the harrowing "Great Escape" took place as seventy-six men exited late one blustery March night. In the course of two years, the Germans had found ninety-nine tunnels in the camp. Harry was the one hundredth and was dug under Block #104 in North Compound. An iron stove hid its entrance. Only the fact that he had been moved to South Compound kept Clark from going out that night.

Hitler had fifty of the escapees shot as a warning after being convinced that the murder of all of the men, which he demanded, would not be wise. Some men were spared because they were married and had children. Others were not. One named Mueller was spared only because he was arbitrarily pulled back by the dark hand of fate when one of the SS that day was also named Mueller and made note of the matching names and chose to spare him.[5]

When the crew arrived at Stalag Luft III, the shaken prisoners in the camp were still on an emotional roller coaster from the previous escape and tragic outcome. The Northrop crew witnessed the construction of a memorial to "The Fifty" that was built, primarily, by the British and Australians at the edge of the camp where the ashes of the murdered prisoners were interred. The name of each man was engraved in the white stone above the altar-like structure.

In retribution, after "The Great Escape," the Germans called for more time-consuming appells, or roll calls, with guards matching each man's face to his picture i.d. they held in a box on their table. Prisoners played games with them throwing off the count, and it would have to start all over again. One rebellious prisoner, evidently ready for some fun, cut a ping pong ball supplied by the Red Cross in half and put each half over his eyes as he stepped up to the table. The Germans found little humor in the stunt and sent him to the cooler.

Former Camp Commander, Colonel Friedrich Wilhelm von Lindeiner, a distinguished and respected former cavalry officer, had been removed from the camp after the escape, and the new commander, Braune, was not a jovial sort. Reichsfuhrer Heinrich Himmler argued his case with Hitler to have the prisoners taken away from the Luftwaffe and put under SS jurisdiction after the mass escape attempts. Hitler agreed with Himmler, and they agreed to put General Gottlieb Berger in charge of the prisoners. At this late stage in the war Berger had a manpower problem, so he created a subterfuge. He deputized the Luftwaffe camp personnel into the SS. If Hitler asked, he could say the camps were under SS control. This ruse remained in effect until the end of the war.

General Gottlieb Berger, Chief of Central Office SS, General of Waffen SS and Inspector General of Prisoners of War--His fate would later rest in the hands of his former prisoners.
Courtesy of USAFA McDermott Library, Stalag Luft III Collections

The Germans issued notices to the prisoners after "The Great Escape."

TO ALL PRISONERS OF WAR! THE ESCAPE FROM PRISON CAMPS IS NO LONGER A SPORT!

The notice bragged that Germany had kept to the Hague Convention and only punished recaptured prisoners of war with minor disciplinary punishment. The Germans claimed to be protecting their homeland and war industry for the fighting fronts.

> "Therefore, it has become necessary to create strictly forbidden zones, called death zones in which all unauthorized trespassers will be immediately shot on sight."

Dire warnings were posted at the bottom.

> "In plain English: Stay in the camp where you will be safe! Breaking out of it is now a damned dangerous act."

Openly defiant, the prisoners took the fliers and sewed them into coat linings for warmth or used them for toilet paper. At the end of the war, many were brought home for souvenirs.

It was summer in Sagan. Flies buzzed around the crew's barracks. Appells were called several times a day, and in between times, the men walked the circuit on the dirt path. With the heat and dryness came the danger of fire. Large fire pools were positioned in the middle of each compound. In case of a large fire, the water would be wholly inadequate, but the water provided a tank to plunge into. Men mostly sat on the edge of the fire pool talking and occasionally racing hand-crafted wooden boats. During the sultry summer days, some sought relief by swimming in the pools. More than one time in winter or summer a man was thrown into the fire pool by his fellow prisoners.

The wooden huts turned into ovens. Guards sprayed water on roofs with hoses and under floors. In the evening, the kriegies sat outside on the steps or leaned on wooden walls.

The barracks sat up off the ground on posts to discourage the building of tunnels. The Germans had set up a system of specially-trained men to uncover any tunneling activity. These special guards were called ferrets and were familiar with the underside of the barracks having crawled underneath to listen to conversations and spy on prisoners. Jeffers was assigned the task, as were many others, of scratching his head to signal the arrival of a ferret. Watchful men stood in doorways and near windows on full alert. In turn, the word was passed to other men using a vast array of innocent signals to warn the tunnelers of the approach of German guards.

It was not until July 8, 1944, that the battle casualty report from the War Department indicated the crew's status. On July 18th, just before eight in the morning, Western Union printed a telegram.

> "Report just received through the International Red Cross states that your husband second Lieutenant Thomas F. Jeffers is a prisoner of war of the German Government. Letter of information follows from provost marshal general ULIO the Adjutant General"

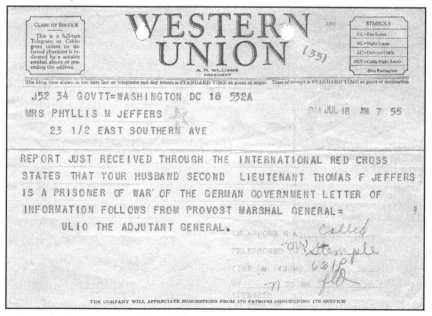

Second telegram received by Phyllis Jeffers

Across the country, families of the other crew members were receiving the same guarded but welcome news. As grateful family members read the words they had been waiting for, the crew continued monotonous walks around the circuit as a regular routine to maintain muscle tone and good health. Jeffers soon found the library, and he was also grateful for the priest that said Mass each Sunday in the camp. Dee Butler found some fellow Mormons and formed a cohesive group. It was a critical time to be in touch with one's God.

The prisoners' world was governed by men they called "goons," the name given to the German guards. Some say it was derived from the cartoon character "Alice the Goon," but no one knows for sure. The guards were suspicious of this label and thought it may be derogatory towards them until a captured officer fabricated the tale that it stood for "German Officer or Non-Com," which gave them some reassurance.

Men designated as tailors in the camp transformed ordinary clothing into "goonskins" for those prisoners who wished to impersonate German guards in their escape effort. Goons oversaw the camp from tall watchtowers, nick-named goon boxes, which were mounted with searchlights and machine guns. In the dark of night, long beams of light swept back and forth across the compounds swathing the enclosures in bright light as the guards searched for escapers. German shepherd sentry dogs, known to the prisoners as wachhunds, were set free at night and ran through the compounds making it dangerous to step outside after lock-up.

The prisoners found goons could be "tamed," and often desired items for escape could be obtained by intimidation, blackmail or exchange of richly desired chocolate, coffee or American cigarettes. In their boredom, the prisoners participated in "goon baiting," annoying the guards and walking a thin line between risking cooler time and pursuing amusement. Some of the RAF men transferred from Stalag I in Barth had been fond of whistling "We're Off to See the Wizard" as the German guards, Glemnitz and Pieber, marched out after each appell. As much as it annoyed the two guards and amused the men of the RAF, the practice maintained the delicate balance of prisoners not over-stepping the behavioral protocol of the camp, while still providing some satisfaction and a hint of defiance. The two guards were transferred to Stalag Luft III no doubt with the tune still ringing in their ears, and it is unknown whether the RAF prisoners there continued the tradition.

Music was one of the few enjoyments that broke the tedium for many a prisoner. The British taught the Americans "I've Got Sixpence," and the Americans taught the British "I've Been Working on the Railroad." In the years that followed, for many of the old timers waiting for the war to end, a whole repertoire of songs could be performed.

Green Death Soup sometimes made with an ox head or weeds was served for meals. German brown bread, hard and unpalatable and filled with sawdust, complemented the soup. Butler ate dandelions as a substitute for vegetables, and he and his fellow prisoners hungrily eyed the stray cats that prowled the camp. The cats were always too fast to be caught. To brighten the dark days the prisoners often saved their rations from Red Cross parcels hoarding British cocoa or American chocolate for months to be added to hoarded sugar for a birthday bash or other special occasion. Dried fruit was fermented into liquor of such intensity that the guards banned its production, but not without an occasional guard passing out from its ingestion.

A tenuous relationship between enemies was maintained as each navigated to find his place on the tightrope that was called wartime living.

Chapter 23

# *From a Lonely Bombardier*

Mail was the most precious commodity to the prisoners. Months could go by without a letter from anyone. It could take months for a letter to go through both American and German censors and finally be delivered, so news was often quite old. Some men never received one letter or parcel. Letters were read and re-read and shared with buddies. My father wrote a handful of letters to my mother. (See Appendix) They were written on a short German form and had to pass through both American and German censors. The German censors were women who were assigned a certain group of men's mail. They came to know the men on paper and from time to time wrote an encouraging comment on a letter that brought bad news. After the war, the women were invited to prisoner of war reunions, and many came.

Jeffers began his limited letters home referring to his unborn child as a boy named "Scrubby." The letters continued advising my mother that he and Butler were together, and the Red Cross was providing help to the prisoners. Like the other prisoners, he frequently requested spices and clothing. He expressed his worry for her and their unborn baby, but he also expressed his hopes for the future when they would all be reunited. The thought of being home for Christmas was always on his mind, and he suggested my mother buy herself a favorite coat she had wanted when he knew he would never make it home for Christmas of 1944. He knew Miriam Butler had had her baby. Months after Butler's daughter was born, Jeffers excitedly ran to the barracks next door where Butler had since moved. He waived a letter from my mother and pulled up a wooden chair to read it to Butler. The letter told of the birth of Julie Anne Butler, which her father had not yet heard. Together, the men celebrated as a sunbeam of hope from a new life in the midst of so much war-time death buoyed their spirits. News in such letters could illuminate the dark mood of the barracks. Jeffers knew his day would also be coming.

The warm days of summer and the tang of fresh cut timber in the camp eased into the coolness of fall. Jeffers had coped with an aching tooth and finally asked a fellow prisoner with little dental experience to pull it out. He never mentioned the primitive dentistry in his letters home.

Within the compounds, fall sports were well underway. Beneath the ground as many as four tunnels were being dug. No matter what else happened in camp, there were always the tunnels. The prisoners' elaborate signaling systems in use to warn of a ferret's approach continued. A simple hand signal set off a chain reaction of gestures that would culminate in the message reaching the desired location. When Teutonic phrases and guttural voices rang out, those men digging were hauled up quickly, and the barracks was returned to some semblance of normalcy before a German guard entered.

The grey autumn days shortened the daylight hours, and the doors were locked. Outside shutters were swung over the windows as darkness fell. By the dim light in the barracks, Jeffers continued to write his letters

By November, he first referred to the death of Flaugher.

### November 6, 1944

My Darling Phil,

Received four more of your letters yesterday and am glad to hear that you and Scrubby are still doing fine. Also happy to know that you are fixed up okay at the Field. I would have had a little trouble signing that application at this time. I was sorry to learn that Mr. Flaugher's son is dead and happy that no one else was injured. I'm sure that they are all okay now. Send me any further news you may get. Please give his parents my sincerest condolences. He was one of the finest men I have ever known.

The last letter written from Sagan was marked November 14th, 1944.

The warm socks in the parcels were taken somewhere in transit along with nuts and other food items that were sent. In the two months that followed, the tide continued to turn against Germany as the Russians moved in from the east. It was rumored that Hitler was adamant that all prisoners of war would either be evacuated or shot.

## Chapter 24

# *I'll Be Home for Christmas*

In November of 1944, Bill Brodek wrote to his sister, Ethel, a secretary for Justice John M. Harlan on the Supreme Court, that it rained the entire month. The monotony and hunger were broken with twice daily appells in the rain for the ten-thousand men. They stumbled from their buildings to line up, often for hours, to be counted by the German guards. If the count was off, they stood longer as the rain poured down, and the ground became mud. Brodek continued to request spices and math books and repeatedly asked for warm clothing. It was the need for the latter that would be prophetic just two months later.

Wet November spilled into the frost of December. The chilled gusts of winter blew into Upper Silesia forcing the men to sleep in their clothes in their unheated barracks. Crude wood-burning stoves offered scant heat. The resourceful prisoners sewed any paper they could find between their thin blankets to protect against the increasingly bitter cold. No matter what they did, they could not get warm.

Back home, that first week of December, my mother was taken

Program from the 1944 Stalag Luft III Holiday Harmonies Christmas program showing the name of Dee Butler
Courtesy of Mrs. Kay Gamble

to Wright Field base and placed in a barracks-style unit where she and other airmen's wives gave birth. Her mother-in-law came from New York, and "Scrubby" arrived in the form of a baby girl, my sister, Diane. Together, my mother and her mother-in-law had Diane baptized.

As the long days of December ran together in an unbroken chain of misery, the harsh blast of the Silesian winter settling upon the camp showed no signs of abating. Condensation from men's collective breath drifted through the cold air around the circuit, now well-worn for those who still made its rounds. Some men never got out of bed. Jeffers' socks had worn very thin from trips around the circuit, and each day he hoped a package would arrive with some new warm ones.

Christmas time in the camp allowed the men to use their stored-up sugar and chocolate to concoct a surprisingly good array of cakes and treats improvised with whatever was on hand. Some men remained morose missing their families, and others made the most of their unfortunate circumstances passing along what little cheer they could offer. Many plays were written and produced much to the enjoyment of a truly captive audience.

The more musical men of the camp produced the Holiday Harmonies Christmas Show at Sagan.

For the festive occasion, the men who attended dressed in their best clothes. Tickets were provided, and even the German guards frequently attended the performances at the two theatres in the camp. In a brief holiday respite, the enemies sat together in the drafty frigid theatre, and they put the war on hold for one day. The homesick men forgot for the moment how miserable they were, as Red Cross supplies had been cut weeks before, compelling ten-thousand men to eat sour bread, sausages of congealed blood, moldy potatoes, thin barley or pea soup and barely palatable cheese. After three weeks of restricted rations, the cherished Red Cross parcels once again arrived.

With the help of a few others, the Mail Officer of Sagan arranged for a special treat for the desolate men after evening appell on that Christmas Eve of 1944. The men waited in orderly formation for dismissal after the count had been taken. Suddenly, the sound of sleigh bells jingled in the distance, and the astonished men caught sight of Santa, an assistant and two kriegies dressed as reindeer, pulling a wagon full of mail. It had been allowed to accumulate over a period of time so that the best present a man could receive that lonely Christmas could be given. Gleefully, the prisoners tore open envelopes and for a few brief moments during the sacred season were a little closer to home.

Rather than locking the prisoners up as soon as it was dark, the Germans made a special concession and let them visit in the various blocks until well after dark. Four inches of snow fell that long-remembered Christmas night. Returned to their barracks and locked in for the night, they paused to hear an American brass ensemble play "Silent Night" in the middle of the quiet compound. It became deathly quiet in the cell blocks as the mellow strains of the original German carol floated on the cold night air, and on that lonely night both German guards and Allied prisoners took comfort in the familiar and nostalgic words. They were all in a place so far from home. Neither side would have chosen to spend Christmas in such a place, and each man had to take small comforts where he could find them.

Religious services were held in the theatre on Christmas day, and the next morning after breakfast North and South Compounds were allowed to visit through the fence. Buoyed by the unexpected mail delivery, the lively men exchanged news of home. On Christmas night, shuttered tightly in their barracks, the prisoners watched as search lights on the goon boxes once more swept back and forth across the shutters with brief periods of faint illumination. The frost-covered dogs patrolled and barked into the wind that drove the swirling snow. Refrains of familiar Christmas tunes faded into the night, and behind closed, and often tearful eyes, each man returned home "if only in his dreams."

## Chapter 25

# The March Is On

For seven months the officers of "Rhapsody in Junk" had languished in their place of imprisonment clandestinely learning of the war's progress through hidden radios. With hopes of eventual release, they became cautiously optimistic but still sent letters home requesting food and warm clothing, for the Silesian winter gathered more fury, and its sting was ever present. They took icy showers to rid themselves of body lice, and they washed their clothing in cold water. Cold never left them.

With rampant rumors of evacuation in the air, the prisoners sensed the need to gain what weight they could and keep themselves in a heightened state of readiness. They were encouraged to get in ten laps a day in subzero temperatures on the one-and-a-quarter-mile track.

Many wondered if the Germans would shoot their prisoners as the Russians drew closer from the east, and the British and Americans closed in far to the west of the camp. Anxious relatives of the men watched the newspapers daily to plot the Russian's progress, knowing their loved one's camp sat directly in that corridor. Some prisoners said they would be evacuated. No one knew for sure, but they all hoped the Russians would cross the Elbe River soon and liberate the camp before any directive came from Berlin.

"Come on, Uncle Joe," they muttered, referring to Joseph Stalin.

But, it was not to be.

On January 12th, 1945, two-hundred-fifty Russian divisions with numerous tanks, covered by an unbroken line of artillery and supported by seven-thousand-five-hundred tactical aircraft, emerged from the eastern bridgeheads and swept across Poland in a little more than two weeks. Altogether, there were two-and-a-half million Russian men. If all went well, the Red Army would soon be in Berlin.

From mid-January, 1945, hundreds of thousand of refugees passed through Berlin. Ten square miles of the city was flattened, and the streets were filled with rubble. What remained of the buildings was miles of decay—jagged broken teeth, smoldering block after smoky block. Bomb craters pockmarked the roads which were jammed with tanks and troops, refugees fleeing from the east, starving children and ragged men and women, all victims of Hitler's mad dream. In the camp, the idea of evacuation once again surfaced.

A uniform thought was repeated throughout the camp, "They'd never move us at night."

Speculating that the evacuation would not take place, the prisoners, however, prepared for the inevitable. They sewed shredded copies of the Allgemeine Zeitung, a readily available German propaganda newspaper, between two of their German-issue blankets for added warmth. The guards, fearful of escapes, limited their food. They warned the men the SS would come in and shoot them as the Russians closed in. The guards kept the prisoners' knapsacks in the block commander's room to be inspected daily rather than confiscate them. Thought was given to how successful the prisoners would be if the guards attacked them rather than see them released.

In the "gen" (information) room, prisoners secretly moved a red string on a map that they had bribed a guard for marking the movements of the troops. Gen could be good or bad, and "duff gen" was unreliable information.

On January 16th, the Russians launched their winter offensive. By January 25th, news arrived that the spearhead had reached three-hundred miles across snowy Poland and paused for a short time at the Oder River at Steinau, forty-eight miles due east of Sagan.

Rumors flew through the camp. Russia had refused to sign the Geneva Convention, so Russian and Polish prisoners did not qualify for treatment under the Geneva Convention Rules. Some had been worked to death in industries or mines. The Allied prisoners had heard stories of some of them used for live target practice by the SS in some areas. For the Russian prisoners, reports of their countrymen approaching gave them a small ray of hope.

On January 27th, at a 4:30 p.m. staff meeting in Berlin, Adolf Hitler's growing concern about the Russian Army, now having crossed the Elbe River, reached its peak. Hitler ordered an immediate evacuation of the camp. The order signaled the start of the twenty-seven-hour march that began in bitter cold and ended with a seventy-two-hour boxcar ride to Bavaria to Stalag VIIA in Moosburg.

Yet, an order was sent from Berlin on the morning of January 27th that the prisoners were not to be moved. But that night the order was countermanded.[7]

The coldest winter in fifty years was lashing the whole of Europe, particularly Upper Silesia. The evacuation was on. Frantic guards rushed from compound to compound.

"Raus mit Euch," they screamed excitedly as they went.

In South Camp, the second act of "You Can't Take It With You" entertained the cold men seated on wooden parcel boxes in the theatre. It was opening night of the play.

At 7:30 p.m., South Compound's Senior American Officer (SAO), Colonel Charles C. ("Rojo") Goodrich, with wiry-red hair and ruddy complexion, clomped down the aisle in his hand-carved wooden shoes. The Southerner was a married bomber pilot from Georgia and a graduate of West Point who had been hospitalized for three weeks before being sent to Friesing, Hohe-Mark Hospital at Dulag Luft and the camp Oflag 21B, before finally arriving at Stalag

Luft III. He had hit the ground hard resulting in a torn shoulder, fractured spine and internal injuries that required surgery. His attempt to bomb the aerodrome at Sidi Hanish, Egypt, necessitated a bail out over Africa causing a broken back, but he was a survivor and duty called.

"The goons have just come in and given us thirty minutes to be at the front gate," he said somberly. Get your stuff together and line up."

He gave the men his oft-heard and recognizable admonition.

"Things will get worse before they get better."

And the snow continued to fall.

## Chapter 26

## *Bash What You Can't Take*

Not only was the situation bad for the officers of Stalag Luft III, but Hitler was emptying the enlisted men's camps further east in Prussia as well, resulting in the so-called "Death March" across Germany that lasted from February 5th to May of 1945. The enlisted men of "Rhapsody" would be unwilling participants in the notorious march also nick-named the "Shoe Leather Express."

At Stalag Luft III, under the bright fence lights, Colonel Spivey, block commander of Center Compound, moved about the camp to notify the block commanders of an imminent departure. The night was cold, but by ten o'clock the snow stopped falling.

With Soviet Marshal Ivan Konev's Southern army within twenty kilometers of the camp, the Stalag Luft III prisoners had little time to plan their journey. Some prisoners built sleds to drag with them, hastily made from Red Cross crates or upended wooden benches. The sleds were so hastily made that many broke after the first hundred yards.

Throughout the camp, there was a mad rush and confusion. Bedrolls were repacked, and men cleaned out cupboards. They destroyed anything that might be of value to the Germans. Bonfires burned piles of old clothes and furniture. Red Cross food parcels were left behind. The men scrambled to their barracks to put on clean warm clothing. Food was bashed that could not be carried. The men, dependent on each other, helped one another into greatcoats and packs. Blankets were tied around shoulders, and the clandestine compound radio was strapped onto a specially-selected prisoner's back. Its earphones were sewn into his cap. In a last ditch effort, some men chipped at the frozen ground to recover buried code books, maps and money. There were plenty of cigarettes, and they would be used to barter with and were easily traded for food and favors. Everything related to escape activities was taken along. Some men were selected to carry the vital escape items: tools, money, maps and travel papers, and these items created an additional burden. The marchers packed the lightest of food, raisins, sugar, cheese, coffee, cocoa powder, prunes and chocolate instead of the heavier cans of Spam and powdered milk.

Ewell McCright, a B-17 bombardier, was a long-held prisoner captured in France where he had sustained a bullet wound to his heel. He ripped the secret panels from the barracks walls to recover ledgers he had kept. After receiving bad news from home shortly after his capture, he fell upon some dark days. Lt. Colonel Clark assigned him the job of chronicling each new admission to the camp, recording personal and military information and details of each capture. Had the Germans found the ledgers begun in October, 1943, they would have been confiscated. In neat and small pencil handwriting, he filled page after page. He would not leave them behind.

For others, much was left behind. Men in solitary were taken "as is" with no chance to pack, eat, or retrieve their precious possessions before being shoved into line. Jeffers and Northrop were in the same block, #128. They quickly gathered their bundles to fall out into the compound. Butler, next door in #129, pulled the collar of his great coat tightly around his neck and met the others in the compound. Deimel was in #126 and Brodek was in #125, all in fairly close proximity, and in quick succession they braced themselves as they stepped out into the snow. South Compound was the first to move out.

In a state of heightened excitement and apprehension, the prisoners prepared for the march..Each block formed its own line facing the gate. With packs well anchored, they stood waiting in the snow. Trembling and stamping their feet in the cold for half an hour, the men nervously checked one another tightening each other's packs. As time passed, it became clear the departure would be delayed, and some of the men returned to their rooms.

Big fires were started in stoves as they burned bed boards and stored up charcoal. Against doctor's orders, many ate big meals continuing to eat what they could not carry, and then they stretched out on their bunks to wait. Soon they were called.

Silesian winters were known for howling winds that could turn snow and ice into stinging missiles. But on this night as South Compound lined up in front of their blocks to be counted, the wind mercifully did not blow. The temperature hovered around twenty degrees, and a bright sliver of moon shone through the dark night. Snow shimmered on the dark pines in the intense glow of the compound lights. Shoes froze stiff, and men puffing blue clouds of breath flapped their arms to stay warm. Heads already ached from the intense cold as about fifty German guards tried to assemble and escort the men. Then the guards, and two or three barking wachhunds pulling fiercely at their leashes, herded the prisoners out of South Compound.

Dressed in mis-matched French and British army issues, the prisoners were reduced to a motley collection of hoboes stumbling forward to be swallowed up by the night. They were off on a journey that would be frozen into their psyches for a lifetime. The initial marchers filed between West and North compounds past the coiled barbed-wire that had separated them for so long. Their fellow kriegies shouted to them wishing them good luck. In columns of four, they stopped to be counted again outside the Vorlager. Eventually the guards flanking them would have to count ten thousand Allied combat officers on the snowy road.

Nervous and freezing guards lined both sides of the road as South Compound exited the camp. At first, there was a lot of shouting from the guards and banter. Men accustomed to formation, the prisoners started out four abreast. After an order was given in German, and the guards slid a cartridge into their rifles, the column moved out towards the west. The first two-thousand men of South Compound moved out at 11:00 p.m. and formed a column a mile long as they cleared the way by tramping down the six inches of snow for the eight thousand that followed behind.

Cold and not knowing where they were going, prisoners of Stalag Luft III are evacuated on Hitler's orders as the Russian Army advances from the east. Courtesy of USAFA McDermott Library, Stalag Luft III Collections

Behind them, the prisoners could see the red glow in the sky, as British prisoners set fire to block #104 in North Compound where "Tunnel Harry" had originated. It was sweet revenge for the "Fifty."

Floating on the edge of the liberating night, deep singing voices of the Australians resounded as they exited the gate and down the road into the darkness. Strong, bass voices sang a spirited version of the old English marching song, "I've Got Sixpence," to keep up morale.

"I've got sixpence, jolly, jolly sixpence,
I've got sixpence, to last me all my life.
I've got sixpence to LEND
And sixpence to SPEND
And sixpence to send home to my wife,
POOR WIFE!"

Decades later, my father would still sing this song. So did the officers at Stalag I at Barth, up on the Baltic, with a spirit of victory and defiance as they marched out of the officers' camp past the Russians in 1945. The prisoners had been confined to the camp by the Russians until their "liberators" were convinced that General Dwight Eisenhower would send all Russian prisoners of war back to Russia. All were forced to return, including the Free Russians who fought on the German side. These were strung up on every telephone pole from Germany to Russia by their Communist compatriots. Only then, were the Barth prisoners allowed to fly to France to be processed home.

The American troops in Stalag Luft III countered "Sixpence" with "Off We Go Into the Wild Blue Yonder." Spirits were high as men marched out and started down the long road.

For many, it had been years that they had been confined, and the openness of the rutted road and the snow-covered forest just beyond their reach for so long was welcome and liberating. It had been a home they hated, but it had been home. They had not known this kind of exhilarating freedom to be outside the fence, and despite the weather, it lifted their spirits. Men struck out into the snowy night with no idea where they were going. Wherever it was, they were just happy to be on their way. Morale was good. The life they had known in this place was one more closed chapter in their book of wartime memories.

Chapter 27

## *Of Historical Significance*

It took eight hours to evacuate the whole camp. South Compound had received no parcels. Six compounds later marched out, each man receiving a parcel, and after the latter compounds raided the Red Cross parcels and took what they could carry, the men threw food to the sixty Russian prisoners in a small area near East Compound. The snow was nearly covered with the coveted food packages. German civilians and the women of the censorship staff ran out to collect what they could. The camp was empty by 4:00 a.m., except for the five-hundred infirm who were later herded into cattle cars by the Germans for a three-day journey to a dirty crowded camp at Stalag XIIID in Nuremberg. The very ill remained and were liberated by the Russians and treated in hospitals or sent home via Odessa in Russia.

The camp took on a ghostly quiet all but for the occasional whistle of the increasing winter night wind swirling about the vacant buildings and penetrating the adjacent pine forest. The occasional bang of a flapping wooden-window shutter, left unlatched during the hasty evacuation, echoed forlornly through the still night. What had been the chaos of evacuation was supplanted by the silence of reflection. So many lives had intersected here.

The camp had known the genius of "Big X," Roger Bushell, mastermind of "The Great Escape," and murdered by the Gestapo. He was only a memory now to the prisoners held the longest who had known him well. As they left without him that frigid night, many could still envision his face, and more than one man regretted he was not with them. His daring accomplishments at the camp would transcend time. The tunnel, Harry, left behind would be his lasting tribute.

Former resident Douglas Bader, a double amputee and famous legless British fighter pilot, became a legend for his escape attempts, and through his autobiography, "Reach for the Sky," the hero of many a young British boy after the war. Despite losing his legs in an aircraft accident before the war, the brash fighter pilot served with great honor. With the call sign, "Dogsbody," Bader seemed invincible causing his men to believe he was "bomb-proof, bullet-proof and fire-proof." He often smoked a pipe on his way back across the English Channel after vicious battles in the sky, defiantly pushing back the cockpit cover and unclipping his oxygen mask. He held the stick between his good knee and the tin one and struck a match to light his pipe. Then he flew up next to his comrades and puffed wisps of smoke into the slip stream. As a prisoner, he did his best to create havoc in Germany to the point German guards threatened to, or actually took his artificial legs away to thwart his escape attempts. When Bader bailed out, he lost one of his artificial legs and damaged the other. While hospitalized, he asked the Germans to return to the wreckage to locate the missing leg. This they did and promptly repaired it. Now, with one-and-a-half working legs, he planned an escape at the same time Reichsmarshal Hermann Goering was granting special permission that allowed the RAF to drop a replacement leg packed in a wooden crate. It was dropped over St. Omer, France, where Bader was held. But the day before the wooden crate from England arrived, Bader went out of a hospital window on a rope of tied sheets. He was returned the next day and found the new leg waiting for him. From then on, he was closely supervised.

Later, when he was moved to Stalag Luft III, Commandant von Lindeiner strongly suggested Bader serve his time at the Lamsdorf Medical Compound. When feisty Bader defiantly refused, Oberfeldwebel Glemnitz stood at the head of a contingent of guards to have Bader forcibly removed from the camp. But it was not before Bader threatened to remove his legs and jump in the fire pool, so that befuddled guards would have to flail about trying to fish the legless man out. When he finally agreed to leave, ten heavily-armed guards escorted him out. He marched through the center as if he was inspecting the troops.

Lt. Col. Albert P. Clark, a West Point graduate and fighter pilot from San Antonio, Texas, was one of the youngest lieutenant colonels in the camp. One week after Bader was sent from the camp, Clark was given his bunk. He was the first USAAF fighter pilot taken prisoner of war in Germany. Head of security during the planning of "The Great Escape," he would prove to be a rock to his men throughout their ordeals and a role model for young men who were tested to their limits. Loyal to his men, he would stay with them through each emotional trial and even sacrifice his own early return after liberation to "close the gate" at Stalag VIIA in Moosburg, Germany, after being assured each of his men was safely headed home.

Clark's friend, Lt. Colonel Robert M. "Moose" Stillman, had arrived at Stalag Luft III after Clark had been told he was killed over Holland. Coming in over the coast of Holland, the B-26 pilot had the tail of his plane shot off, and the plane crashed upside down in a fireball with Moose still in it, leading his squadron mates to conclude that he had been killed. Two weeks after the crash, he was delivered to Stalag Luft III from a German hospital, and he arrived with two black eyes and a broken little finger. As they sat out the war, Clark and Stillman were roommates.

The camp had been home to Jerry Sage, larger than life, from Spokane, Washington, who became the camp's Houdini and made escape an art form. One of his greatest feats was convincing the Germans he was a downed airman when in reality he was working for the OSS (Office of Strategic Services) as a spy behind enemy lines in Africa. Major Sage had evaded the enemy before being captured and flown to Sicily and on to Germany. It was an amalgam of Lt. Colonel Sage, who years later, was the model for Steve McQueen in the movie "The Great Escape." Sage had hidden a compass during his stay in Stalag Luft III. He requested that a fellow kriegie kick and break his ribs in order to be taken to the local German hospital to facilitate an escape effort. While there, he arranged for a "donnybrook" to be staged by fellow bandaged and injured prisoners while he stole a German alarm clock, tucked it into his coat and walked out. Later, he scraped luminous paint off the clock hands to place on the tip of the compass needle to aid him in further escapes.

When Sage was captured in Tunis, he joined Richard "Wings" Kimball, an American fighter pilot, and RAAF (Royal Australian Air Force) pilot, Lt. Southard, at a temporary holding camp in Sfax, Tunisia. They fixed Sage up with insignia indicating he was a fighter pilot to cover his OSS involvement. The Germans flew the three to Sicily on a JU-52 stopping over there before flying on to Naples. At the airport in Sicily, the captured men saw a great commotion. Prisoners who had been aboard a German ME-223 transport flown out of Africa after capture, had landed just before the JU-52 and were being harangued by their German guards who were threatening to shoot them when they arrived in Naples. As they deplaned, one paratrooper who had smuggled aboard a timed-delayed thermite fire cartridge hidden in the arm sling of a captured doctor dropped it down a hole in the plane's floor. As he and the doctor were driven away from the German airport, the ignited plane burst into flames and burned to the ground. The unlikely saboteur was legendary paratrooper and Scottish military chaplain, Murdo MacDonald who was with British parachute forces captured in North Africa.

After MacDonald was driven off, Sage was separated from his two companions for special interrogation. He would not see them again until he eventually arrived at Stalag Luft III. "Padre Mac," as MacDonald was later called, served as chaplain for the American prisoners in the camp and sustained many a forlorn man through the ordeal of imprisonment. Sage had been removed from the camp before the current evacuation, but his boundless energy and spirit had become contagious to many men whose own spirits had wavered in the dismal surroundings.

For so long, the dank camp was home to Wing Commander Harry Melville Arbuthnot "Wings" Day, an Englishman renowned for his own amazing escapes, and who served as a role model for many a man at the camp. Bushell and Day met in 1941 at Dulag Luft and had at that time both been considered "permanent party" at Dulag Luft assisting others who were to pass through later. Day had asked for a kitten at Oberursel and was instead given a cat he named Ersatz, (artificial) most fitting as everything given in Germany seemed to be a substitute or imitation. The stories of his escape attempts were legendary.

Through that massive gate had stormed Lt. Colonel James Rhea Luper, a West Point graduate and B-17 pilot, whose plane exploded in the sky over the bay in Stettin, Germany, when he was bombing an oil refinery. All that was left of the plane was the right wing panel. Luper bailed out just before it exploded. He was picked up by the Germans in a small boat and treated for cuts and a leg injury. Luper was renowned for his many gigs (demerits) at West Point. It is said that he racked up more than any cadet since Ulysses S. Grant. He married the Commandant's daughter. Stern and granite-jawed, with piercing intimidating eyes, the ex-captain of West Point's boxing team was marched into the camp in 1944. Many of the prisoners that saw him come in groaned as they had suffered under him at the Army Air Corps training camp, and shouts of "Hey, they got Luper!" rang out in astonishment as he had come through the gate.

Among those who studied law at the camp was future United States Attorney General, Nicholas Katzenbach. Many law students had completed more than one year of law classes within the shabby confines which was recognized as legitimate credit after the men's release.

Great feats of bravery and courage, and cunning escape attempts had taken place in this camp. The personalities were unique and memorable. Now the mass of men, both known and unknown, marched out into the night.

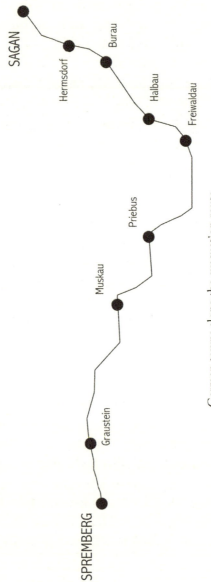

German towns along the evacuation route
Courtesy of Mr. Nils Hempel - www.spurensuchesh.de

## Chapter 28

# *Winter's Bitter Lash*

The first column, South Compound, marched south and then west. The first village south of Sagan was Hermsdorf nestled just before the tiny village of Burau. The narrow winding road then snaked through Halbau, Friewaldau, and turned west to the only town of any size, Priebus. The bass voices sang for the first few hours of the march, and the column stopped briefly every thirty minutes to adjust packs and blanket rolls. The order to march had been by blocks with the SAO and staff initially taking positions at the tail of the column, so that they could assist stragglers. German Lt. Wiggenhaus, was the officer in charge of South Camp, and his confusion about the route made the march all the harder.

For some men of South Compound, the first long stop after five hours was at the top of an autobahn overpass. A stiff rising wind whipped across the overpass where the frigid men stood in the open. It sculpted the fallen snow into two-foot high snow drifts at the edges of the road. Gazing up the road swirls of iridescent snow straightened to horizontal gusts providing little chance of relief. Men built crackling fires from logbooks and watched as ashes of long-cherished letters drifted upward effortlessly into the blackness of the night sky. Straining horses gasping vapored breaths into the cold night air could not move wagon loads of food and German equipment, so the men were issued bread and margarine to lighten the load.

After forty-five minutes, the march continued in silence. Echoes of lively songs had faded long ago and were lost to the night. The joyful singing was replaced with a collective groan as straps of packs dug into weary shoulders, and exhausted men pushed themselves forward by necessity. Their common enemy, the vicious cold, was as deadly as Fockewulfs or ME 109s splitting their formation and ripping through their collective resolve. The mantle of frost was their constant companion, and snow drove hard into their faces which were lowered and angled to brace against the fury of its force.

The disheartened troops soon deteriorated into a stumbling mass. The men pulled their newspaper-reinforced German-issue wool blankets tightly around their hunched shoulders and marched in two feet of snow drifts. Ice formed on eyelids and moustaches. Exposed flesh was often futilely covered as they were pushed to their limits against the elements and struggled to force one foot ahead of another. Men dropped at the side of the road from fatigue and cold. Every two hours the column stopped while men huddled together on the road, legs outspread toboggan style, each leaning on the man behind. Many were too weary to speak. The crunch of boots and exhaustive groans of the beleaguered were often the only sounds that permeated the stillness of the night.

An old German guard marched in the deep snowdrifts at the side of the road.

"Muede, muede!" he cried out.

The prisoners thought he was crying out for his mother, but soon learned the German word for tired was "muede."[8]

Extra shoes, clothing and souvenirs that had been jealously hoarded for so long were dumped indiscriminately on the side of the road. Packs were rearranged upon aching shoulders, and men who fell were encouraged to get up and come along or get in the wagon that followed the column.

When the guards called for them to halt for ten minutes of rest, the exhausted men flung themselves on the ground. But breaks brought more intense cold as immobile bodies covered in sweat cooled down immediately. So bitter was the night that their trousers froze to the surface of the road. Some men remained standing for that reason, and others chose to stand and smoke rather than eat. The long line of men once again dug through packs and discarded more items too heavy to carry leaving a scattered trail in their path. Cans of margarine were the first to go. The men had coated their faces and lips with margarine early in the march, but could no longer carry the only soothing and protective balm they had. In the midst of the blowing snow and darkness, German civilians, mostly old men and women and children under twelve, crunched through the snow moving in ghostly shadows collecting what they could gather in their frozen arms.

When brief rest periods were over, the guards, as tired as the prisoners, pushed themselves to move out.

"Raus!" echoed repeatedly from the German guards with guttural voices trailing off down the line triggering each new order like falling dominos. Weary stiff men arose from the hard cold ground for as far as the eye could see, struggling to their feet under the weight of their packs.

"Fertig machen!" (Prepare to move!) called the guards.

German convoys moving west also occasionally overtook the men forcing them to jump to the left to let the convoys pass.

"Raus! Raus mit Euch!" and "Was ist los?" (What's the matter?) rang out as hunkering German guards tried to count, corral or urge their reluctant charges onward.

They marched the rest of the night, and South Compound was still marching at daybreak. Many men could no longer feel their arms or legs. Men fell asleep as they marched yet, like robots, they were driven on under a power they could never have thought was their own.

According to records held at the Muzeum Martryologii in Zagan, Poland, some of the men of South Compound detoured at Priebus to a town called Grosselten five kilometers off the march route arriving at noon. Today it is called Przewóz and is forty-five kilometers from Sagan (now Zagan). By the Polish account, some of the group slept four hours in barns there and returned to Priebus in the morning. An account in *Clipped Wings* indicates the same route. Those at the head of the line marched eighteen miles and found shelter in buildings of a labor camp in Freiwaldau. Those following ripped planks from the buildings to build fires, despite the risk of being shot by Germans.

Accounts vary on the topic of shelter, time and location of stops along the way for South Compound, with some men indicating stops and some claiming never to have slept anywhere until Muskau. Some weary men in the column stopped only for periodic rest.[9-14]

Jeffers and Butler found shelter when the column finally staggered to a stop at about noon in Grosselten. Surprisingly, the German farmer provided the men with hot water for coffee or oatmeal from their Red Cross parcels. The exhausted men fell into three large barns and sank down in the hay. Clark and Stillman huddled together on the first level among a mass of men. They pulled the hay over top of them to try and keep warm. Others went up in the lofts of the giant barns. Those taking off shoes to rub numb feet found their shoes frozen and were not able to put them back on. The farmer kept a small stove going where they were able to de-ice their shoes and re-grease them with more margarine if anyone had kept enough. It was too cold to sleep.

When the march resumed at 6:00 p.m., the SAO and staff changed positions to the front of the line where they had to contend with Lt. Wiggenhaus's poor conduct of the march and with his various excuses and broken promises regarding rest and food.

Barns along the march route
Courtesy of Mrs. Valerie Burgess

The interior of one of the barns in Grosselten where the prisoners stayed.
Courtesy of Mrs. Valerie Burgess

"It is desirable to reach the destination before the other compounds," was the only explanation offered by Lt. Wiggenhaus when pressed why the men received so little relief.

The men leaving Freiwaldau/Grosselten continued to walk west in the snow for thirty-three hours covering thirty miles before the first night's rest. In spite of their attempts to protect themselves, the biting wind stung the marching scarecrows as they marched on exposed stretches of open road. The bread, by now frozen, was impossible to eat. Boots and clothes coated with snow froze solid. With heads down and eyes on the feet of the man in front, they marched on.

The fear of the Russians emptied a mass of bereft humanity onto the same road. The desperate and panicked refugees fled from their homes hoping to escape retribution from the invading Russians. The refugees were mostly old men, women and young children who plodded along or rode on broken-down carts pulled by half-starved horses and mules, barely strong enough to walk. The refugees had nowhere to go, and the prisoners pitied them. Some of the hungry men offered the children bits of chocolate they had saved from Red Cross parcels, and one weary prisoner gave his worn woolen gloves to a crying German toddler to warm her bare frostbitten hands. So many times, the basic tenets of humanity superseded the cruelty of war.

The horse-drawn wagons with frozen wheels, barely turning, clattered down the crowded narrow road. Walking German troops, some wounded, were also on the road begging cigarettes from the prisoners as the German troops made their way to engage the Russians. Periodically, fresh German troops in white snow gear took up positions along the way and took scant notice of the prisoners.

Spent German guards continued to march through the deepest snow at the edges of the roads beside the column, and the oldest men, hardly fit for the trek, threw away heavy packs they could no longer carry. Down the line, an elderly German guard who had been kind to the kriegies was practically carried by two Americans, while a third prisoner toted his rifle.

"We were all in the same boat," my father told me decades later, "we were just trying to survive."

Frostbite became a fact of life, making fingers and toes tingle and turn white until the progressive numbness eliminated any feeling at all. As he tramped along, Jeffers pulled a frozen loaf of German brown bread from his overcoat pocket and took a bite of bread followed by a bite of frozen margarine. He ran out of bread long before the margarine. Men dropped with frostbite and twisted ankles, and soon order disappeared, but they regrouped, and survival instinct made them drive on.

Lt. Colonel Clark was reluctant to abandon his two huge scrapbooks that he had assembled during the long years of his confinement. He offered a case of Scotch to anyone who would get them home. Lt. Colonel Willie Lanford took him seriously and dragged them over the snow on a makeshift sled. Lanford was a Squadron Commander who bailed out of a burning B-17 and landed very near Belgrade, Yugoslavia, incurring flak wounds to his side. At the invitation of Lanford, Col. Goodrich and four others added their packs on the sled and took their turns at pulling.

The cover of Lt. General A.P. Clark's scrapbooks now on display at the Air Force Academy's McDermott Library. The scrapbooks he kept in Stalag Luft III survived the winter evacuation march and also his confinement in Stalag Luft VIIA. The Germans confiscated many of the pages when he arrived at the latter camp. After the war, the scrapbooks arrived in Texas, beating him home.

Courtesy of USAFA McDermott Library, Stalag Luft III Collections

A creaking wagon followed the column, and exhausted men were loaded into the wagons until they were strong enough to march again. Despite the cold, their clothes were drenched with sweat. Some men stayed behind with exhausted comrades rubbing the men's wrists to keep them warm until the relief wagon arrived.

Even though Article Seven of the Geneva Convention specifies that prisoners of war are not to be marched more than twelve-and-a-half miles a day, South Compound covered thirty-four-and-a-half miles in twenty-seven hours with one four-hour stop in barns and stables before arriving in Muskau. A few men passed out or were delirious. Food or water was seldom available or was denied them. They ate whatever they carried. Some bartered and exchanged cigarettes, the long-held prisoner of war currency, or sometimes traded soap with the German civilians for an onion, egg, bread, a potato or hot water. People they met were generally kind and considerate, but isolated groups of SS men who crossed their paths berated the locals for associating with the Luftgangsters.

There is no question that the men in South Compound suffered the most on the march traveling long distances with only brief rest stops, so succeeding groups would have room on the roads. Theirs was the longest march of the group as the Germans tried to find faster routes for those who followed behind. The prisoners blamed Wiggenhaus, and some thought he may have intentionally abused the men, but it is also possible that higher authorities were pressing him to keep South Compound moving as Russian guns boomed in the distance. Regardless of the cause, the beleaguered men of South Compound were continually prodded along, forced to violate the marching rule of the Geneva Convention as the column wound its way through winter's ice and snow and the death throes of the Third Reich.

Miles into the march men had called for Murdo MacDonald.

"Padre Mac, you're wanted at the back," became a common call as the padre fell back to stay with a fallen man. Then he would return to the front. The padre, both paratrooper and religious counsel, remained a constant comfort for those who needed him.

*Rhapsody in Junk* ✷ 173

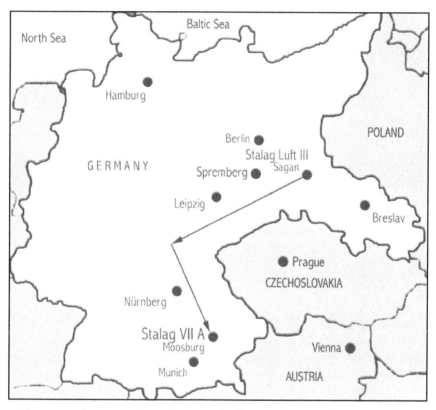

The evacuation route from Sagan took the marchers to Spremberg where they boarded boxcars and continued on southward to Moosburg, Germany, and Stalag Luft VIIA.

Courtesy of Mr. Nils Hempel - www.spurensuchesh.de

## Chapter 29

# Merciful Muskau

The route was confusing, and the Germans back-tracked the men of South Compound more than once. In such moments, authority occasionally broke down, and tempers flared as men so tired of being out in the cold were pushed to their limits.

Butler had matched himself with Hal Gunn on the march, as the block commanders recommended partners to look out for each other. They took turns carrying a loaf of German bread, and Butler carried raisins in his pocket. Blinded by the onslaught of snow, Butler could feel Gunn's hand slide into his pocket for a taste of raisins and was thankful his friend was still with him. Beside them, was their roommate, Woodie.

Gunn, who was dressed in an old blue British RAF long coat, was a B-17 pilot who had sustained flak fragments to his face after the flak destroyed his controls over Hull, Germany, where he was bombing a rubber plant.

Woodie was a Tuskegee Airman, piloting a P-40 that crash-landed in Italy when his engine caught fire after an intense flak barrage. When his reception in a block of Southern fliers was not cordial, Butler and Gunn arranged for him to be transferred to their block where a close friendship was cultivated.

Each step the trio took was a desperate effort to move one inch closer to what was ahead. Visibility was limited as the bluish cold and fatigued men ahead drifted into clouds of condensed breath. The men continued on until halting for a brief stop when Butler and Gunn noticed Woodie was no longer with them. They asked if anyone had seen him. None of the men in the plodding line that could still answer had seen him--except one. Someone said he went off into the forest saying he needed sleep. Butler and Gunn backtracked for half an hour to find him. Finally, they found him with his back against a tree. He was stiff and cold and losing consciousness. For half an hour they worked with him.

"Come on, Woodie," urged Butler, "We may need your help. We've all got a better chance to survive, if you join us—the three of us will all look out for each other."

The wind chill was below ten degrees, and a man could easily succumb quietly and slip away into death's cold hands.

"Get up, Woodie," said Gunn, "you can't stay here!"

Butler wrapped Woodie's arm around his shoulder, and Gunn supported his other arm. With his friends' help Woodie was half-carried, half-dragged, along until he could once more function on his own.

Further up the line, Ewell McCright struggled with the secret ledgers he had hidden in an old pair of pants and tied around his shoulders. After so many years of keeping the ledgers, he was determined they would eventually make it home with him.

Fatigue and frustration showed at rest breaks. Men prodded by German guards refused to move on until they repacked parcels. Another group, which had stopped in the woods by the roadside, was accosted by a guard leading two barking wachhunds. Impatient, the guard felt the prisoners were not moving fast enough, so he turned the dogs loose on them. Uncharacteristically, the hungry dogs raced forward and licked the men's hands and ate the remaining meal they found there. The contented dogs trotted back to their master wagging their tails.

The long column turned northwest towards Muskau. The weather changed between snow, rain and hail as the line staggered up a hilly road. A twelve-mile march through the night brought the line across an icy bridge on the outskirts of Muskau's industrial area at 2:20 a.m. It was the 29th of January. They would rest for thirty hours.

Entering Muskau, which was a pottery town and once a pretty summer resort, the men could see two tall chimneys of a glass factory looming ahead in the village. Thankfully, civilians came out with hot water. Upon arrival at Muskau, approximately fifteen per cent of the marchers were incapable of marching unassisted, and a larger number were on the verge of physical and nervous exhaustion.[15] Colonel Goodrich informed the Germans that further marching without rest would be flatly refused [16]

The glass factory as it looked in 2004 with a locked fence surrounding it since it had been abandoned for a new facility many years before

After standing two more hours in the cold, the men now totally exhausted had realized their worst distress. The wait in the cold was remembered by many as their darkest hour. The first night had its difficulties, but the march into Muskau in the early morning hours, only to be left standing for hours in the cold with no respite in sight, was far worse. Finally, the men were directed to accommodations in the factory with the large smokestacks. Stories about extermination surfaced in the murmurs of the crowd. Reports from newer prisoners, and information from their clandestine radios, provided the horrific news of the Jews fate in extermination factories. The smokestacks looked ominous.

But instantaneously, Muskau was turned into a make-shift transit camp with local citizens coming forth to aid the prisoners.

The first men inside the glass factory could barely move, and many huddled near a large furnace leaving those behind them stranded in the bitter cold. A voice cracked like a whip.

"You men move back!" cried Colonel Davy Jones, an ex-Doolittle Raider, taking charge and pushing through the impasse.

He advised the men to back-off and find a better place to sleep.

Frigid, and barely able to take one more step, the mass of men expended its last ounce of energy and lurched inward to allow more men to enter.

By 4:00 a.m., with great commotion, townspeople joined the men and offered their comfortable homes to some of the prisoners.

Lt. Colonel Clark chose to stay with the men.

The factory with its dirt floor was warm, and there was a kitchen upstairs to prepare the first hot food that many men had since they left Stalag Luft III. There was also running water.

A spiral staircase led to the factory's furnaces which were white hot, and the prisoners reveled in the warmth. Jeffers slept on the concrete floor near a big furnace surrounded by machinery. He fell down exhausted by the warmth of the fire, and the butter he carried melted in his pocket. His feet and hands were frostbitten, and his shoes were stiff with ice.

When senior officers insisted the men needed more rest, the Germans acquiesced, and the prisoners spent an extra day there and slept one more night before starting west again after their respite. Some men slept for twenty hours and could barely be awakened.

## Chapter 30

# Rolling Cells

The next morning, the men left Muskau. Thankfully, it had stopped snowing. There were fifteen miles left to go to culminate the march to the railway junction at Spremberg.

Before they left the glass factory, the kriegies said prayers. Then they headed out. Just ahead, the street angled to the right, and they faced a bulky gray stone building of four stories. They marched past the large archway door of the Town Hall as they moved out and turned west toward Graustein. Their long column, now five-men abreast, twisted over the hills and along the banks of frozen streams past white-shrouded country estates. Along the road, they saw one-man fox holes freshly dug. Roadblocks and tank emplacements impeded their progress. In the last futile months of the war, the aged men in the Volksturm had been called up to defend the German homeland and were seen training in each town the column passed through, often using the most primitive of weapons, some marching with broomsticks on their shoulders.

Dysentery, thought to be started by Spam and corned beef that had frozen in the cold and was eaten before it defrosted, added to their misery. Hundreds of men squatted along the road.

The side roads cut through forests and small towns where they bartered with the inhabitants swapping cigarettes and soap for apples or eggs.

The men left the back roads for the broad autobahn choked with refugee traffic. They shared the highway with a parade of wagons drawn by oxen and piled high with furniture, bedding, mirrors, clocks, hay and crates of fowl. They arrived in Graustein at 6 p.m. and slept in barns, some occupying the burgermeister's (mayor's) barn. Clark and many others found shelter crammed into chicken coops. Roused from the hay, early the next morning, they marched downhill towards Spremberg.

The weather had eased some. Blisters, stiffened backs and legs and the pain of frostbitten feet and hands still plagued the men. With a slight thaw, the cobblestones were uncovered, and sleds had to be pulled over the wet roads. Visibility was much better, and the biting winds disappeared. After a rest and change of weather, some measure of good spirits was restored. Each man that was able helped the man next to him. Perseverance had brought them this far. Each footstep forward was a small victory.

Finally, their march was nearing its end.

Just outside Spremberg, Russian prisoners pulled 88 mm anti-aircraft guns into position. By noon, South Compound arrived in Spremberg.

They were met by Major Simoleit, the Sagan Executive Officer, who told them no food would be forthcoming unless certain leather belting, allegedly pilfered at Muskau and used to pull sleds, was returned. Col. Goodrich called his block commanders forward for questioning. The block commanders gave him a sharp military salute as some German officers in the area grimaced. Since the assassination attempt on Hitler, the Fuhrer forbid the use of the traditional military salute in Germany. The Heil Hitler, straight-armed salute, was expected in its stead. The special meaning of the traditional military hand salute given by the block commanders in such troubled times was not lost on the German prisoners who witnessed it. After the small drama played out, the belts were located and returned to the Germans.[17]

The men were then led up to a large square building, a German training facility, and were marched out onto the grounds behind the building in narrowing circles until the entire column of two-thousand men was standing on the field. The rising temperature created traces of snow and slush. For two hours the men were counted.

At this beautiful military post, the Stalag Luft III prisoners were allowed a hot meal. At a field kitchen, the Germans ladled out hot barley soup from a large steaming vat as the men filed past. It tasted like ambrosia to the hungry and cold men, who collected it in empty cans from food or drink.

Spremberg was a Wehrmacht (German Army) training station and school for mechanics. It was also a tank-training facility. German Tiger Tanks with muzzled eighty-eight guns sat atop flat rail cars pointed east. The young fearful German Panzer drivers who trained there looked barely old enough to shave. The fate that awaited the prisoners in Spremberg when they were packed into filthy boxcars and sent away on a horrendous odyssey towards Bavaria was described by some of them in later years as worse than the march.

From the training center to the rail yard was two miles through the town. They did not spend time at the railway station in Spremberg but were loaded onto boxcars in a more isolated area. After the men were marched there, they were packed sixty-to-seventy men into waiting French 40 and 8 (forty men or eight horses) box cars. It was late afternoon. The men took up residence where pigs had recently departed with no benefit of cleaning. There were no windows, and the only light and ventilation came through cracks in the wooden sides. The cars were pulled by an old hissing engine leaking steam and hot water. Knowing the Allies often strafed rail cars was a cause for concern. Guards hurriedly ordered the reluctant and protesting men aboard. Many more prisoners to accommodate were on the way.

Original French 40 and 8 box car used by the Germans to transport animals and prisoners
    Courtesy of the Wright-Patterson Air Force Museum, Dayton, Ohio

Long line of French 40 and 8 box cars waiting for the prisoners down from the main railroad station in Spremberg, Germany, in 1944
    Courtesy of USAFA McDermott Library, Stalag Luft III Collections

## Chapter 31

## *Center Compound*

South Camp had been gone for several days from the glass factory at Muskau when Colonel Spivey and General Arthur W. Vanaman, both senior officers from Center Compound, arrived in Spremberg. General Vanaman was the only American general captured by the Germans. He had knowledge of the Ultra Codes, super-secret information that deciphered German codes, so he had been prohibited from flying for fear of capture and interrogation. Much to Allied Command's horror, he flew what he thought would be a "milk run" and was captured after his bail out over Germany in 1944.

By four in the afternoon, it got dark in Germany during the winter, and in that late afternoon darkness Center Compound, following in South Compound's footsteps, marched into Halbau. They approached a quaint church which was a beautiful and peaceful sight, surrounded by glittering mounds of pristine snow, soon to be trampled upon by heavy boots. The soft snow stretched out invitingly from the church door as the dark shadows of night descended on the property.

The church was opened by the mayor, and cold miserable prisoners jammed every corner inside.

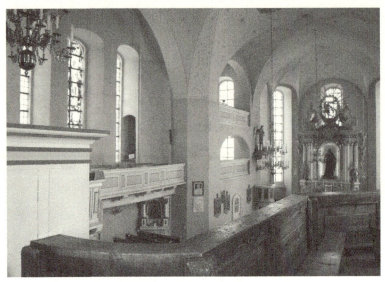

Interior of the church in Halbau
Courtesy of Mrs. Valerie Burgess

Church in Halbau where Center Compound slept
Courtesy of Mrs. Valerie Burgess

No one was allowed to lie down, since he would occupy too much space. The pews were crowded as tightly as possible with men sitting or standing. The balconies and steps were covered with exhausted men. Another thirteen-hundred men milled about outside until they were directed to the morgue and all the crypts that could be forced open. Some men built rough shelters on the lee side of the building, and a couple of hundred more could find no place to get under cover, so they were sent to the school.

By 8:00 p.m., the men bedded down. General Vanaman slept on the altar. Fights broke out in the church as men pushed beyond their limits tried to cope with the crowded conditions. Colonel Spivey spoke from the altar in harsh terms telling the men things could be a lot worse for them during the war and warned them that the next man fighting would be thrown outside. A blanket of silence fell upon the men, and they settled down and fell asleep. Spivey joked later that General Vanaman, stretched out where the lectern had been on the altar, looked like a living sacrifice about to be offered up for who knew what.

A surprise awaited the two SAOs (Senior American Officers) in Spremberg. Spivey and Vanaman were singled out by the Germans and told they would not be boarding the trains. Instead, they, with three other officers, were taken to Berlin to meet with German generals and civilians without the knowledge of Hitler. It was hoped that the meeting would convince the men to entreat their superiors to join the Germans in an allied fight against whom they considered to be everyone's enemy, the Russians. The Germans plied the two with fine food and wine, and General Gottlieb Berger, founder of the SS and Commander of all the prisoners of war in Germany, attended the meetings. It was he who had previously deputized the Luftwaffe camp personnel, trying to comply with Hitler's wishes that the camps all be under SS control. He was responsible for the brutal treatment of Russian prisoners, a million of whom died, but his treatment of the American and British prisoners was more humane. The men of Center Compound went onto the trains without the two officers.

General Berger eventually sent General Vanaman and Colonel Spivey from Berlin to Switzerland with messages for General Eisenhower and Prime Minister Churchill, which were ignored. At Vanaman's insistence, Berger also arranged for the Red Cross to reinstate the delivery of Red Cross parcels and in particular to deliver emergency food rations to the starving prisoners who had for so long been on the roads of Germany heading for Bavaria. This reinstatement was carried out by the so-called "Great White Fleet" of Swiss trucks driven by Canadian prisoners of war.

## Chapter 32

# *Train of Misery*

The rail trip to Moosburg required two days and two nights with an additional one night in the cars after arrival at Moosburg. The over-crowded train filled with the men of South Compound had left for Moosburg at 7 p.m. and traveled twenty-four hours to Chemnitz where the main station was bombed out. The journey was like no other any of the men had experienced. It was claustrophobic, it was stifling, and in Jeffers' case, it was his twenty-fourth birthday.

The men in some cars got bread and margarine and cans of meat. Many got nothing. When the rolling prison stopped at a station, black coal was shoveled into the firebox. There were frequent stops but often the doors didn't open. What sounded like a hailstorm lashing the train turned out to be machine gun bullets from American fighter planes.

Not all men could sit or stand at the same time. The fearful crowded men tried to organize rotations in cars changing position every hour moving men away from cold outside walls. A full colonel riding in Jeffers' car insisted on lying down as many men stood. One old guard was assigned per car, and often as he slept, a kriegie held his rifle. Such was the insanity of war. When the wooden doors were infrequently rolled back, guards faced the train holding their automatic rifles at the ready across their chests. They were as tired as the prisoners.

The filth and stench were unbearable on the journey. For sixty hours the moving cells lumbered through occasional rain beside the frozen countryside and bombed out cities. The claustrophobic wooden cars traveled through Dresden, Chemnitz and Zwickau. The men wondered how much longer they could endure the stifling confinement.

Ten days after the train passed through Dresden, a center of German cultural history, Allied bombers destroyed the entire city, which was also full of thousands upon thousands of refugees fleeing from the east. No one knows for sure how many were killed those fateful days, February 13th and 14th, 1945, but estimates indicate between seventy to one-hundred-thirty thousand lost.

Before arriving at Moosburg, the train stopped only twice to let the men out for breaks. Once had been in Chemnitz. At 2:00 p.m., the cars stopped on the curved track of an isolated siding in Regensburg.

"Aussteigen!" (Climb out!) the guards called to the sick and tired men.

Despite Clark's warnings, some of the men drank out of the contaminated big tubs of holding water for the locomotives, such was their thirst.

Smoke from a recent air raid was still visible there. Regensburg was a prime target due to the presence of a fighter aircraft assembly plant there.

The men were let out to relieve themselves, and civilians in the area stared at the incredible sight of an endless line of two-thousand bare bottoms squatting in the snow. By now, many of the men were vomiting and had diarrhea.

Shortly afterward, the men were loaded back into the horrid boxcars at gunpoint.

Sixty years later, Clark told me of the stop in Regensburg.

"While we were in the station, a German armored division which had been going the other way, stopped on the next track. The men were traveling on the flat bed cars with their tanks. We figured they were on their way from the Italian front to the war in the West. These soldiers looked tough, and when they realized we were Luftgangsters, they swung their weapons on their tanks around and aimed them at us. Air raid sirens started to wail, resulting in a quick departure for both trains in opposite directions."

Only one-hundred-forty miles from Switzerland, Clark went down the line of cars during the stop at Regensburg giving the word that anyone wishing to escape was free to do so. Money maps and compasses were distributed.

Some in Jeffers' car leapt down and took off running. Jeffers chose to stay. Thirty-two jumped off the train under cover of darkness but within two weeks were picked up and returned. Despite their capture, with each step south they knew they were seeing the end of the war and the crumbling of the Nazi regime.

Four-hundred kilometers after leaving Spremberg, the torturous transport pulled into Stalag VIIA at Moosburg, thirty-miles northeast of Munich, in the early morning hours. It was still dark, and the train sat on a siding with the men locked in its fetid cars until daylight. They pounded on the rattling doors all night for water and asked that the sick men be taken off the cars, but the guards only threatened them with rifles.

In the still of night they could hear dogs yapping outside the cars and could only imagine what awaited them on the outside. A cool misty rain covered the cars and showed no sign of stopping.

Gate at the entrance in Moosburg. The large sign at right designates it as Prisoner of War Camp VIIA.

Courtesy of Moosburg Online

Modern-day picture of the front gate area in Moosburg, Germany

## Chapter 33

# Moosburg

Stalag VIIA had been originally constructed to accommodate ten-thousand men, but now it held eighty-thousand. The German staff was Wehrmacht, not Luftwaffe. The commandant was pro-British and anti-American, and Col. Goodrich found him to be unreasonable and arbitrary in his decision making. The commandant was thoroughly despised by both the prisoners and the Germans. The prisoners were predominantly French with thirty-eight thousand there. The camp held fourteen-thousand Russians, and another fourteen-thousand prisoners were combined British and Americans, but all other allied nations were represented. The Germans were running out of places to keep so many prisoners. Stalag VIIA would hold one-hundred-and-thirty thousand by the end of the war.

When the massive wooden boxcar doors finally opened at 8:00 a.m., February 3rd, the filthy men, gaunt and unshaven, many with sunken eyes circled in black, peered out. They blinked against the sudden light as the boxcar doors were pushed back. With their last ounce of strength, they stumbled down stiffly from the cars, helping down the weak and sickly. Slowly, they made their way down the muddy road between the train track and long barbed-wire fence to the rows of green-shuttered beige stucco buildings on the other side. They marched through the single gate, bore to the left past a tall wooden tower and in a grey mist delivered themselves into the hands of the Wehrmacht—no longer somewhat protected Luftwaffe prisoners.

Upon arrival in dimly-lit Moosburg, many men trudged another half mile through another gate to an area that looked like and smelled like a stockyard. Horse stalls and barns and a sixty-foot slit trench for a toilet greeted them. It was in constant use due to the deteriorating condition of the men. Soup was handed out that was hardly more than a puddle of grease and weeds, and bread was in short supply for everyone.

The men were shown to a desolate barbed-wire enclosure with two long empty sheds where there was only floor space. For four days they stayed in what they called "The Snake Pit" trying to tolerate overcrowding, cold and mud. The shack provided no beds, fuel or food. Most men were sick, cold and damp, and everyone was covered with fleas and lice. From the second to the sixth of February, the men settled where they could before going into the camp proper. For the third time, there was not enough room to have everyone lie down at once, so many did not sleep.

In the Nordlager (North Camp), small groups were taken to be deloused and sent to the main camp. They eyed the showers again with the same trepidation they felt in Muskau, but to their relief the men had the luxury of their first warm-water showers with soap. The showers were brief but an unbelievable luxury.

The transferred prisoners were finally moved to the main camp. There was no coal in the camp. The men burned bed boards for heat, and many stayed under blankets in bed all day to keep warm.

Bunks in the stucco buildings had filthy vermin-infested burlap palliasses on the beds. By filtered light coming through the cracks, the men could see bedbugs, lice and fleas crawling everywhere. Men's bodies were livid with welts from insect bites, and many men hung their meager blankets out all day in hopes of ridding the fabric of the biting beasts.

An aisle six-feet wide ran the full length between rows of three-high, twelve-man bunks. Four-hundred instead of two-hundred crowded into each barracks. Tents supplemented the crowded buildings, and some men opted to sleep in air raid trenches rather than stay inside.

The four hundred in each barracks obtained water from one faucet and one hand pump. Sanitation measures were totally inadequate. There was no hot water, and the men were left to wallow in the filth of living in severely over-crowded and totally inadequate conditions.

The German food ration consisted of one-half cup of warm water for breakfast, one cup of thin watery soup for lunch and a little black bread for supper with an occasional extra issue of cheese, margarine and blood sausage. On Wednesday, February 7$^{th}$, they got their first Red Cross parcels.

For four to six weeks, the men kept on their same filthy clothes without benefit of any washing facilities. There was no sanitation system in place, no cooking facilities and increasingly, straw was spread over the floors of the barracks to be used as bedding.

Dysentery was the norm as the men wallowed in the filthy make-shift accommodations. Some of the men, who had been the strongest on the march, now began to lose hope. Disease ran rampant, and medical treatment was practically non-existent. By the end of February, partially due to the bombing of the railroads, supplies of the Red Cross parcels were cut off in Moosburg. Now, the men had to rely on what little German food they were given and were reintroduced to Green Death soup. For nearly three months, their meals were extremely meager. There was constant trading amongst the prisoners, with some prisoners assisting others who had lesser trading skills, and prized possessions were bartered away in the interest of filling an empty stomach.

The "Great White Fleet" of emergency provisions arrived at Moosburg one day, much to the jubilation of the hungry men. One third of a parcel per man was all that was allowed, but even a fraction of a parcel was better than none. Intestinal ailments became a reality that evening for men who ate too much after being on reduced rations for so long. With the arrival of the Red Cross parcels, the Germans further reduced each man's German rations.

## Chapter 34

# *Stalag Luft IV*

The enlisted men from "Rhapsody in Junk" began an even longer march south through Germany in early February as their camps were evacuated. From day one, they had endured the sadistic treatment of *Feldwebel* (sergeant) Hans Schmidt, better known as "Big Stoop." At six-foot-seven, he was an oafish heavy man with unusually large hands. The giant from Stalag Luft IV at Gross Tychow, where Clifford, Gonzales, Cardenas and Dean were held, had burst men's eardrums with one slap and had shamelessly stolen prisoners' provisions. There were many there who wanted to get even with him, and probably no man was loathed more. He marched out into the snow with the prisoners and accompanied them all the way to Moosburg.

While barely existing in their camps, the enlisted men had also learned the value of a Red Cross parcel. Camp leaders in Stalag Luft IV never were put in a position to check on the arrival and distribution of parcels as camp leaders had been in other camps. War crimes testimony after the war indicated the theft of Red Cross parcels by the Germans in Stalag Luft IV. While there, the gunners of "Rhapsody in Junk" and their fellow prisoners shared one parcel divided among eight men. It contained one can of Spam, two packages of Old Gold cigarettes, one can of pate and a can of KLIM to make milk. The Germans doled out one-half cup of soup every day at 2:30 p.m. and no more food until 2:30 the next day. It was supplemented with brown bread, margarine, dehydrated sauerkraut, rutabaga, kohlrabi and horse meat. Once a week they each got one potato. On the one day a month they received the parcel, they each received four cigarettes and were so happy many sang until midnight. There was never enough food. The average weight loss was fifteen to twenty pounds.

Now, as they marched out, each man was handed a Red Cross parcel that had been stored in the German warehouse. Piled up for an undetermined length of time, these were the boxes they should have been receiving all along. The thin men had been barely sustained on barley soup and occasional horse meat and sauerkraut, so the accumulation of parcels was quite a surprise to them.

Their camp had no bathing facilities, and they washed in pans of water. They burned lice-infested burlap mattresses filled with shredded paper in their pot belly stoves for warmth, as the barracks, like Stalag Luft III, were also unheated.

Not knowing what the future would hold, the prisoners marched out of the barbed-wire enclosure. For some, the march would last almost four months until May 8th. Most of the men would end up in boxcars traveling to Nuremberg.

The enlisted men from "Rhapsody's" crew made the three-mile hike from Stalag Luft IV to the railroad yard in Kiefheide and were locked in boxcars for two days before the train started moving.

For the most part, the trains were marked with the white letters POW on the top as dictated by the Geneva Convention, but the Allies often thought this was a ruse, so sometimes the trains were strafed. When the train arrived in Berlin, the 8th Air Force was bombing the city. The men had nowhere to go, so they remained in the cars trapped and terrified until it was over.

When the train arrived in Nuremberg on February 8th, the men were held at Stalag VIII. From that vantage point they excitedly watched bombing raids and fighter plane dog fights. One night, they watched with delight as the RAF hit an underground ammunition storage facility, and explosions were heard for many days and nights.

With the Allies closing in, the prisoners of Stalag VIII were evacuated again on April 8th. Dean, Gonzales and Clifford marched from Nuremberg to join the officers at Moosburg.

When the large column split, Cardenas marched in a different direction. Guards drove the men hard to keep up. On February 18th, Cardenas felt his body was giving up, and he slumped down on the ground. In his delirium, he heard a guard coming toward him with a bayonet.

"Lord, please save me," Cardenas pleaded under his breath.

Suddenly, he felt fire on his backside, so he stood up, and the sharp bayonet went through his index finger. With great anger, Cardenas studied the guard's face for future retaliation. Then he wearily and reluctantly rejoined the column.

Soon, the men walked alongside a property, and when they were about fifty meters from a house, Cardenas saw an old lady staring at them from inside. He waved at her until she saw him.

"Frau, haben Sie Brot und Eier?" (Lady, do you have any bread and eggs?) he asked.

She waved telling him to come to her.

"Wish me luck. I'm going to see the old lady!" he said to his friend, Felipe.

Cardenas ran and jumped over the window sill where he saw the frightened old lady. He showed her his ring that she liked, so she offered three loaves of black bread and eight eggs in exchange for it. He put them in his hat.

When he was ready to return, the guards had their backs to him, and he waved to Felipe indicating that he should distract the guards. Felipe and another friend, Blacky, started a mock fight. When the guards tried to separate them, Cardenas ran back to the group with the bread tucked under his jacket and the eggs still in his hat. He gave a loaf to each of his friends and kept one for myself.

After much walking, Cardenas saw a cow eating a beet. He broke away and went over and took it from her. He cleaned the slobber off and ate it. Later, he saw a kitten drinking milk, and he reached down and took the soured milk and drank that too.

The weary men kept marching until they reached the Elbe River. While there, they saw four P-51 Mustangs, and with much delight, they waved enthusiastically to the pilots. The pilots saw them, turned around and started shooting. Cardenas ran behind a tree, but since there were twenty men doing the same thing, he ran and jumped in a small fenced pig pen. The pigs scattered, and bullets hit the fence and house. After ten minutes, everything was over, and when Cardenas stood up, he saw a man's body that was killed in the attack.

There were many dead bodies along the way, but the prisoners kept walking. The next day, British Hurricane fighters flew over, and the prisoners were paralyzed with fear and froze in their tracks. But the British knew about the friendly fire by the Americans the day before, and they did not fire but waved back instead. From that day on they had air protection, both from the British and Americans.

The march from Stettin in Poland, to Luxembourg took eighty-seven days. The Germans knew liberation was at hand, so they permitted the men to light fires to heat some potatoes. It was May 2$^{nd}$, 1945, when they saw British tanks. Cardenas ran excitedly in a zigzag pattern towards a tank to avoid any possible shooting.

The top of the tank opened.

"Are you Yanks ex-POWs?" the driver asked.

When Cardenas said they were, the man opened a big jar of peaches in syrup and handed it to him, and he gratefully took two. Soon, all the prisoners got their own.

When the Brits freed the prisoners, Cardenas found the guard who had sliced his finger. He took custody of the German guard's gun and bayonet. The guard begged not to be killed.

"I do not kill unarmed men," Cardenas firmly told the scared German. "I have honor."

The guard was then taken as a prisoner.

The camp of the British tank group was some distance away, and the men were told to head that way.

Sgt. Alexander Cardenas wearing British clothing given to him upon his liberation
Courtesy of Mr. Scott Walton

When Cardenas saw a farm ahead, he asked the farmer for a couple of horses. Only one had reins. Cardenas got on one, and with much help from the farmer, Blacky got onto the other one. He fell twice and decided he'd rather walk.

Cardenas rode west and found a river. He grabbed tight to the horse's mane and crossed the river finally reaching the camp. A guard pointed his rifle and stopped him. He asked if Cardenas was a Yankee prisoner, and when he responded affirmatively, he was allowed on base.

Once on the base, Cardenas was given bread to eat and washed it down with Carnation milk. The British welcomed the prisoners that filtered in happily, and after feeding the starving men, they took all of their clothes and sprayed the men with insecticide. The thin prisoners could see the lice, nits and ticks falling dead from their bodies.

"Let's see who makes a bigger pile out of those," Cardenas said to Felipe.

Then the men bathed. They could not get the soap to lather, and Cardenas told the Brits their soap was useless. The Brits told him to keep scrubbing as the layer of dirt was too thick for the soap to penetrate. Soon, Cardenas felt his skin burning as layer on layer of dirt gradually ran down the drain.

Afterward, the men shaved and got haircuts. Cardenas's hair by then was shoulder length. The British gave the men clean clothing, and Cardenas stuffed rags in his shoes that were too wide.

The British, according to regulations, took the German guard's gun from Cardenas, but he came home with the bayonet.

## Chapter 35

# *Dean and Gonzales*

The column of men Dean and Gonzales marched in was not in a hurry on their sixty-mile march. As winter turned to spring, they were enjoying the fresh air and their freedom, having been locked up every night prior to the march. Along the way, German women ran out to offer the thirsty men water. But the men's terror was not over.

On the third day of the march, they too, experienced the terror of allied fighters flying above them and opening fire. Men and guards scattered into the woods, and Gonzales hid behind a tree. German vehicles had traveled on the same road with the prisoners, and when the Allied pilots saw them along with a column of three-thousand men, they mistook the entire group for the enemy. Several men were wounded or killed during the attack.

Gonzales was determined to escape.

After a tiring day of marching, it began to rain. The Germans knew they could not make the next village by nightfall. They bedded the men down in a rain-soaked open field where they huddled under thin blankets. In the morning, the guards prodded the weary men to march on. Gonzales and his friend, Russell, stayed hidden under their blankets as the group began to move. Just as they were about to escape, three Wehrmacht guards came back to check the area and found the two of them. They told Gonzales and Russell that had they been SS guards instead of Wehrmacht, no doubt the two prisoners would have been shot. The guards reasoned the war would soon be over, and the men would be going home. They encouraged Gonzales and Russell to join the others. But the two prisoners were not convinced.

In the village where they had stopped for the night, Gonzales and Russell crawled low to the ground between guards to sneak out of a farmhouse barn. They knocked on the door of a farm house, and the German occupants fearful the two visitors were Russians, shook with terror. The duo explained they were Americans and just wanted food. With some relief the farmer's wife handed them cake, bread and ham. Gonzales put the treasured items into a bag and thanked the couple, but before departing, Russell tore a picture of Adolf Hitler off the wall and told the couple he was a bad man. With extra rations in hand, the escapees waited until dark to sneak back to the barn. They moved stealthily but found the guards had changed position. At just the right moment, the two waited to crawl between them. With their food in hand, they safely made it inside the barn and shared what they had with the others.

The next morning, April 16th, they started the final leg into Moosburg. As they approached, they could hear cannon fire in the distance so they knew the Allies were close.

Thirteen days later, the fighting would all be over.

Chapter 36

# The First Taste of Freedom

In late March, air raids, mostly flown by the 15th Air Force out of Italy, intensified over southern Germany. Prisoners were ordered to stay inside during raids but now defiantly watched the exciting action. Exploding bombs were heard, and the strong vibrations were felt under the men's feet. The planes were so close that if bombers went down, the kriegies saw the chutes. The sight was bittersweet, for not all the crews survived. General George Patton's Third Army was still one-hundred miles from Moosburg.

The early thaw that warm spring turned the ground to mud, and the men were ankle deep in it since the camp had been built on a swamp fostering a constant supply of mosquitoes. Slats and other wood were burned for campfires. Clouds of black smoke rose from hundreds of small cookers, and fires burned in the open air choking out any chance of breathing clean air, but warding off to some degree the onslaught of the flying pests.

A long trench was the common open-air latrine. The latrines gave off a terrible stench. Filled to overflowing, an epidemic seemed inevitable. The SAOs called a strike. They and their men refused to report for twice daily appells to be counted. Discipline had broken down, and the Germans had no clue how many men were there. The angry guards threatened to use force, but kriegies returned back inside their barracks. Dogs were brought in, and pistols were drawn. Eventually the commandant backed down, and the "honey wagon" rolled in that night and pumped out the latrines.

The first week in April, the Luftwaffe took over as administrators of the airmen when conditions in the camp further deteriorated. On April 9th, South Compound was moved across the road into big tents with Center Compound prisoners, as more enlisted men, including Gonzales, Clifford and Dean arrived at the camp on April 16th. Five large tents were erected, but the shelter was not sufficient, and prisoners slept outside all over the compound. Lean-tos made of blankets appeared, and beds were laid on the bottom of slit trenches.[18]

During the whole month of April, the prisoners could hear P-47 and P-51 fighter aircraft strafing targets in and around Moosburg. On the 9th, the men looked upward to witness five-hundred B-17s from the Third Air Division of the Eighth Air Force, escorted by three-hundred-and-forty P-51s, pass overhead just west of Moosburg en route to bomb Munich. Their spirits were raised immensely. The prisoners eagerly plotted the advance of the allied front on their hidden maps.

The guards soon began escorting prisoners outside the camp to barter for food.

Jeffers and his friend, Charles Church, collected what cigarettes and candy they had and followed the guards outside the gate and across the bridge on the Isar River. They hoped to trade for bread or sugar. With the lax security and futile attempts to control prisoners, as many as seventeen prisoners spread out and agreed to meet their guard at a designated point at a certain time.

Jeffers and Church approached a farmhouse just past the bridge and banged on the door. A frightened German woman called down from the window.

"Ve haff nussing, ve haff nussing!" the frightened German woman shrieked from her upstairs window.

The men explained they were Americans and only there to trade for food.

Relieved they were not Russians, she came downstairs and let them in and traded with them. Then the two went up the road to another home. Having traded for a few carrots and eggs, they sat at the kitchen table conversing with the pleasant couple who lived there with their beautiful daughter. Another knock came on the door. This time the woman was met by several German soldiers. Like Jeffers and Church, they too, had cigarettes they wished to trade for food. The woman invited them in, and the motley group of traders sat at the table talking to each other.

The woman showed Jeffers and Church the wedding picture of her daughter who was married to a handsome German soldier who had been captured by the Russians. Jeffers noted what a handsome couple they made. A later photo of him, once dashing in his uniform, showed an emaciated man whose collar barely fit around his neck. He was still held as a prisoner and would probably never come home.

Jeffers and Church returned to the home several times each time graciously greeted by the woman. Upon one visit, two prisoners from India were there trading. The woman told all the men they could return later for baths in the deep luxurious tub there. She told the men the Americans could have baths first and then the Indians. Church and Jeffers told her they would return the next day to enjoy the long-awaited treat.

When they returned the following day, the couple was distraught. The two Indians had come and taken their daughter. They dragged her to St. Kastulus Catholic church at the edge of the camp and raped her there. Jeffers and Church tried to console the anguished parents, but there was little they could say, and they commiserated with their German friends as the cruelty and brutality of war continued to go on unabated around all of them.

Now, parts of the camp were unsafe to enter, and a desperate "every man for himself" air was apparent. Long lines were everywhere and between the unsanitary conditions, lack of adequate nourishment, despair as the war continued on and the overcrowding, it was hard to be optimistic.

On April 13th, 1945, it was Jeffers' wife's twenty-third birthday, and he missed her greatly. Next, came the news that President Franklin D. Roosevelt had died the previous day. Men, already desolate, wept openly. Men still on the march from northern camps passed the word of the death, and one kriegie with a trumpet played "Taps" as a column stopped on the open road to remember F.D.R. In Stalag VIIA, on April 15th, a memorial service was held, and a sole trumpeter played "Taps." Other nations' prisoners stood at attention and saluted.

The air raids continued, and men sat outside and watched. At no time, day or night, was the air free of planes. Discipline in the camp broke down further, and daring prisoners broke down fences inside to move about more freely. There was no retribution.

Modern-day twin steeples of St. Kastulus Catholic Church which could be seen by the prisoners from inside Stalag VIIA in Moosburg, Germany

The twin steeples of St. Kastulus can be seen in the distance. Before the 1945 liberation, the men of South Compound were moved to the tents due to overcrowding in the camp.
Courtesy of USAFA McDermott Library, Stalag Luft III Collections

## Chapter 37

## *Bavarian Redoubt*

As the Russians closed in on Berlin, Hitler devised new plans. In one plan, he proposed the kriegies be taken to Berlin to be put in cages in the middle of the main street, Unter den Linden, where they would be bombed by their own planes. The alternate plan, which he became adamant about, was to move thirty-five-thousand Allied prisoners further south in Bavaria to hold as hostages in the hopes of achieving better truce terms. The so called "Prominente," prisoners he felt held the most value, had already been identified, and many were held in various secure castles. These were men who were related to senior Allied figures and were, therefore, held as bargaining chips to be used at the appropriate time. Hitler spoke of establishing an Alpine Redoubt near Berchtesgaden where his Eagle's Nest sat high up in the mountains. General Berger was instructed to take the prisoners to the mountains south of Munich and hold them. If the Germans were unsuccessful defending themselves, the prisoners were to be executed. This came about because Hitler's mistress, Eva Braun, learned that Berger opposed the execution of prisoners. Accordingly, she had intervened and told Hitler, who was unaware of Berger's opposition, to give the signed order to Berger. In her mind, any other officer who received the order would have carried it out.

Day by day, the Germans turned to more desperate solutions.

> "The great Bolshevik offensive has now crossed the frontiers of Germany," announced the Germans.

Urgent pleas went out to the Allied prisoners printed on fliers.

> "The men in the Moscow Kremlin believe the way is open for the conquest of the Western world. This will certainly be the decisive battle for us. But it will also be the decisive battle for England, for the United States and for the maintenance of Western civilization......Please inform the convoy-officers of your decision, and you will receive the privileges of our own men for we expect you to share their duty. This is something which surpasses all national boundaries. The world today is confronted by the fight of the east against the west. We ask you to think it over. ARE YOU FOR THE CULTURE OF WEST OR THE BARBARIC ASIATIC EAST?"

The brutal reputation of the Russians followed them. Stalin viewed Russian prisoners of war as traitors. His own son, Yakov, a Russian artillery lieutenant taken prisoner early in the war was held with some Allied prisoners at Sachsenhausen Concentration Camp. Upon learning of his father's brutality in the massacre of fifteen-thousand Polish soldiers at Katyn, Yakov threw himself into an electric fence at the camp and committed suicide as the American and British prisoners testified later.

Despite the plea from the Germans, the kriegies were not convinced of the German wisdom to join their side. Instead, the prisoners were told by the Germans on April 18th to prepare for another march south that would take place in three days. But within the dismal confines of the camp, Lt. Colonel Clark and his men were operating their clandestine radio monitoring the BBC and Radio Luxembourg. They heard of a new Allied agreement broadcast on

Radio Luxembourg. The agreement had been reached through the Swiss Protecting Power between the Allies and Germany. It forbid the transfer of Allied prisoners to Bavaria to Hitler's Alpine Redoubt and also prevented the Allies from moving German prisoners out of Europe. On April 22$^{nd}$, the new Allied agreement was accepted, but the German administration in the camp had not been told.

On April 23$^{rd}$, the Germans told the prisoners to line up at the gate.

"You'd better check," Clark said defiantly, "There's been a new deal, and we ain't going."

The Germans did check, and no prisoners were moved.

## Chapter 38

## *Tanks!*

On April 27th, some kriegies reported seeing tanks at the crest of the hill a mile north of Moosburg.

On the 28th, it rained all day. American fighters flew over Moosburg and waggled their wings in recognition of the prisoners below. One came so low and fast it sent everyone running for cover. As fighting got even closer, the men were ordered by their alarmed guards to stay in the barracks. Closed inside, eager eyes peeped out of holes and saw Allied soldiers in the fields around the camp.

Clark heard the guns and knew the end of his thirty-three months of captivity was at hand.

"Soon," said a despondent German guard to him, "our roles will be reversed."

Jeffers and Butler envisioned returning to the new babies born in their absence.

Sick men, including Col. "Rojo" Goodrich, whose stalwart presence had for so long been a source of encouragement and security for the men, was now confined to his bunk having given up hope. But the reverberation of the guns signaled that now help was on the way.

Dee Butler huddled in the cramped kitchen quarters of his barracks. Men there ate what they thought would be their last kriegie meal behind barbed-wire, as they listened to the bullets zing through the compound, and explosions from a distance showered them with ceiling plaster and shatterings of plaster from the walls.

On the evening of April 28th, the prisoners spotted armored vehicles pulling into town. They turned out to be an SS contingent.

The liberation had begun when the highest-ranking prisoner of war, U.S. Army Colonel Paul "Pop" Goode, captured at Normandy, and British RAF Group Captain Kellett, left the camp before midnight and strode into Headquarters of Combat Command A, 47th Tank Battalion, with a message from a German commander requesting a creation of a neutral zone surrounding Moosburg. The Germans had been negotiating with the attacking army attempting to arrange a peaceful surrender of the camp in exchange for securing several Isar River bridges that led back to more secure lines. The proposal was rejected outright, and the Germans were given until 9:00 a.m. the next day to submit an unconditional surrender or be attacked at that hour.

As artillery shells flew over the camp during negotiations, the German guards initially gave every indication they would fight, but very quietly, they left in trucks during the night of the 28th. The majority of the guard force was pulling out, leaving only a skeleton force behind. One kriegie climbed a watch tower in the morning to verify it was abandoned.

On April 29th, at 6:00 a.m. the men could hear the booms of heavy cannons and guns in the distance. Shortly after daybreak, a group of American kriegies near the main gate watched two German staff cars with red crosses painted on their sides drive up. Goode and Kellett climbed out and strode into the camp.

"You guys better find a hole," Goode warned, "The war is about to start."

A few remaining German guards deserted their posts and turned their weapons over to their former prisoners.

Upon his return, Goode brought a piece of white bread back into the camp after his breakfast of bacon and eggs on the outside.

He shared it with Clark and others who had not seen white bread for three years. To the grateful men it was like cake. As they enjoyed it, they heard the Germans blow up the two local bridges over the Isar.

Within the jagged barbed-wire enclosures prisoners were preparing for a church service to be held at ten o'clock. By 9:45 a.m., many men had gathered on the open plaza and waited for the service to begin. The start of the church service was halted as planes flew over, and the kriegies began to hear rifle fire. The battle was on.

At 10:00 a.m., two American P-51s roared in low shooting up the camp. Men in one of the guard towers began to shoot at the planes. The Allied plane turned and came down with its powerful guns spitting bullets and ripped the tower into kindling. Within a minute or two, mortar shells landed in the town, and stray bullets whistled into the camp. Men dove into slit trenches and fox holes as fighters flew low on strafing runs. The German guards advised the men to stay inside and close their shutters. Some men dove under barracks. Butler jumped into a slit trench as fast as he could to escape the flying bullets.

The Germans fired from the church steeple of St. Kastulus, and SS troops on the outside of the compound yelled for the remaining camp guards to join them in the fight. They entered the camp demanding loyalty. Most refused, because the Swiss Red Cross told them that if they stayed and guarded the Allied prisoners, preventing them from breaking out and getting killed by their own forces, the guards would receive special treatment. The SS threw grenades into the guards' barracks and killed some of them for their refusal.

Butler watched two of the helpless guards taken behind a bush and shot through the forehead by the SS. At the same time, more SS troops climbed to the top of the cheese factory adjacent to the camp and began firing.

The cheese factory adjacent to Stalag VIIA still exists today.

In the beginning, when the shooting started, there was only the sporadic rattling of small arms fire coming from somewhere in the woods just outside the fence. SS troops dug in downriver and along a railway embankment a mile away as they desperately fought to defend the town of Moosburg. Within minutes, the noise from the incessant firing of hundreds of small arms and heavy automatic weapons was deafening. A fierce, but brief, battle raged. In the bell tower of St. Kastulus, Germans fired on Americans as they fought within the town. By 10:30 a.m., the resisting SS troops, the last hold outs for the Third Reich, were dead on the road and in the fields.

In the midst of the firing, men hit the ground and took cover. Clark braced himself as the ground shook with one collective and memorable thud resulting from thousands of men all hitting the ground at the same time. Jeffers turned to see a fellow kriegie put a thin cooking pot on his head offering meager, yet, comical protection. Kriegies erupted everywhere, scrambling for cover or attempting to burrow into the hard ground. The more adventurous were climbing on top of the buildings and guard towers to watch the excitement. Bullets ricocheted over the compound, and several kriegies were hit, but none seriously. The shooting stopped. Then--deathly quiet.

Camouflaged Sherman tanks of General George Patton's Third Army rolled over the hills to the northwest about 11:00 a.m. The unmistakable rumble and clanking of heavy armor approaching the camp from somewhere outside the perimeter fences signaled the nearing end of the battle. American forces were coming directly toward the camp and moving fast. Puffs of smoke rose above the tanks. A tank shell blew a hole in the mail building, and small arms fire hit the roofs. The American 14th Armored Infantry Division of the U.S. Third Army, nicknamed "The Liberators," had arrived.

One of its Sherman tanks pushed down the barbed-wire to be greeted by thousands of jubilant men. So many of them jumped on the tank, that not one inch of it could be seen. High atop the tank sat jubilant Al Clark, "Moose" Stillman and friend, Dick Schrupp one of two photographers Clark asked to record the historic event.

Defeated and unresisting, German guards waited at the gate. An American officer approached, and a German officer outstretched his hand, but the American refused it. He only saluted.

Two P-51s with loud engines followed doing victory rolls over the barracks and tents. Fifteen minutes later, the fighter planes made passes again but this time rocking their wings or tumbling in acrobatics. An enormous cheer went up as hopeful kriegies ran out and cheered and waved.

The Germans were taken away in trucks. Only then, were the covert flags of many countries brought from their hiding places in the battered barracks and openly displayed with great pride.

The first liberating tank comes down the main street of Stalag Luft VIIA on liberation day. The top of the cheese factory can be seen in the background at the left.
       Courtesy of USAFA McDermott Library, Stalag Luft III Collections

The American tank pushes down the barbed wire amidst the jubilation of the confined prisoners.
       Courtesy of USAFA McDermott Library, Stalag Luft III Collections

Men standing on rooftops watch their fellow prisoners of war surround and climb atop the first Sherman tank through the barbed wire at Stalag Luft VIIA. Men kissed, patted, tried to hug and spilled tears of joy over the tank.

Courtesy of USAFA McDermott Library, Stalag Luft III Collections

## Chapter 39

## *Unrestrained Joy*

Jeeps rolled into the camp first, and men weeping joyfully reached out to touch the drivers. Feelings not expressed for long months and years were finally being freely released as men rushed to welcome their liberators. Some liberators found their scrawny and dirty brothers, and at least one liberator that day found his son.

Tank commanders responsible for pushing down the ten-foot-high wire gates were kissed shamelessly by jubilant screaming men with tears streaming down their cheeks. The mood was one of total and unrestrained joy.

"How long have you been on this drive?" a jubilant and breathless Butler called to an approaching tank driver.

"Twenty-four hours," came the reply.

"How did you withstand the pace?" Butler yelled up to the driver.

"If the old man can, we can," he laughed.

Some men ran to pat and kiss the tanks. Jack Gonzales offered a prayer of thanks to God for their freedom. Amid the shouting and cheering of the newly-freed prisoners, Lt. Harold Gunn made one final entry in his diary.

"This account was begun by POW # 1613 but is being finished by Lt. Harold W. Gunn, USAAF."

POW #6128, Thomas Jeffers, whose prayers were answered, was also free.

K rations and C rations were passed around from the tank drivers, and moist-eyed liberators on olive-green trucks and in the tanks were overcome with emotion.

As tanks rolled on the cobblestones of the ancient city of Moosburg, all eyes turned to the two tall steeples of St. Kastulus Catholic Church. Machine gun bullets splattered against the steeples ripping a crimson and black Nazi flag from its base. There was another period of quiet. The Nazi flag was pulled down, and at 12:30 p.m., before the eyes of thousands of men, the American flag was raised on the steeple. Eight-thousand American kriegies faced the church, came to attention and saluted. Years of pent-up emotions trickled down their cheeks.

Afterward, the American flag went up in the town. To the dismay of the ecstatic prisoners, it was quickly taken down. Within minutes, the flag once more flew brightly in the town. It had been run up upside down.

Eight of the ten men of "Rhapsody in Junk" sent to Moosburg celebrated in great joy along with thousands of other brave men who were coming home after a sacrifice that defeated a tyrant and allowed freedom for the generations that followed.

Sobs and laughter were the only anthem needed when the Nazi flag came down and the Stars & Stripes was hoisted up in its place on the camp flagpole that day. Martin Allain, a B-26 pilot who had crash landed in Tunisia in 1943, after bombing rail yards in Sousse, had smuggled a flag into Stalag Luft III to be displayed for identification if the Allied planes appeared one day. He sewed it between two blankets and took the flag hidden within the blankets on the long winter evacuation march. Before thousands of cheering kriegies, the dirty malnourished man scurried up the flagpole and ripped down the detested Nazi flag.[19]

Doors of St. Kastulus Catholic Church where Jeffers visited after his liberation from Stalag VIIA in Moosburg, Germany

Two soldiers unrelated and both named McCracken were prisoners in the camp, and by chance, both of their brothers came that day to rescue them. The camp had held four sons of American generals, General Patton's son-in-law and humble men who had only known prison life for the past five years.

A correspondent from WLW radio in Cincinnati, Ohio, struggled to find his way through the throngs of celebrating men. He found and interviewed Jeffers at the camp. Jeffers sent his love home to his family via the reporter who sent a letter about the interview to my mother. She had not had a radio on to hear it.

The sight of Old Glory waving atop the flagpole at Stalag Luft VIIA on liberation day brought tears and sobs from thousands of newly-freed prisoners.

Courtesy of USAFA McDermott Library, Stalag Luft III Collections

1st Lt. Martin Allain scrambled to the top of the flagpole at Stalag VIIA to attach an American flag.

Courtesy of Lt. Col. Renita Foster, United States Army

## Chapter 40

# *Biding Our Time*

In a few hours, loudspeakers were mounted on poles. Army chow was served to the starving prisoners, and soon music was hooked up. Much to their amusement, the now free men listened to the popular "Don't Fence Me In." The haunting strains of "At Last" entertained and touched each man. The upbeat "Pennsylvania 6-5000" was played over and over.

The liberated kriegies walked in and out of camp exploring their newfound freedom. Trucks came in with food, water and doughnuts. The prisoners tore holes in the wires around the camp and walked out into the fields to look around. Inside the wire, some men played games while waiting for their departure. There were two more days of hunger until more trucks came in with food. White bread, chicken, turkey, ham, beef stew, salmon, pasta and meatloaf were delicacies most men found too good to be true. Most men started throwing up what they ate as their stomachs had gone so long with so little food.

Latrines clogged, and rubbish piled up as the men tried to be patient. Food was still in short supply, so men were determined to forage on their own. The mood turned sullen as they were free but not quite free, and men were turned back at the gate by American guards. The area was still not safe, and gangs of unpredictable Russian and Polish prisoners caroused in the streets of Moosburg causing their own deaths and the deaths of others. Russian prisoners went on a rampage in the town looting, seeking revenge, committing rapes and stealing food. Some in their euphoric state drank benzene they found thinking that it was alcohol and died. The people of Moosburg feared for their lives.

For one, in particular, revenge was brutal. One prisoner witnessed two prisoners of war whooping with excitement, as they carried a guard's head in a bushel basket. They claimed it was "Big Stoop." Another prisoner recalled seeing "Big Stoop's" body spread-eagled across a road with a pickaxe in his head.

A group of Russian generals held in the camp posed happily for a picture. Upon their return home, Stalin would have them all shot as traitors.

General Dwight D. Eisenhower repeatedly ordered that former prisoners stay put. Many could not restrain themselves and hitchhiked to Paris or elsewhere. He had made an agreement with French General Charles DeGaulle that French prisoners would be released first. It took ten days until the American prisoners left.

Two days after liberation, Gonzales stood in the crowd that greeted General George Patton as he arrived in his command car. It was brightly shined and suitably decorated with sirens and spotlights and a four-star flag. He was immaculately dressed in whipcord trousers, boots, battle jacket, two ivory-handled pistols and a helmet polished to a high sheen. The prisoners crowded around but kept a respectful three or four-feet away, and no one touched the command car. Patton was an imposing figure with his harsh face, and he stood rigidly at attention, a man more than six-feet tall, weighing one-hundred-and-ninety pounds. He spoke through a microphone attached to the loudspeakers on his car and addressed the crowd in an uncharacteristic high-pitched almost falsetto voice thanking the men for their sacrifices. Then after a brief inspection of the camp, he was gone.

The day after liberation, April 30th, Hitler and his mistress, Eva Braun, committed suicide in his bunker in Berlin. Ironically, the concentration camp at Dachau, near Munich, was liberated the same day. With the war going badly, General Berger was more conciliatory than he had been in earlier days and no doubt was currying favor with the Allies, for he knew what was coming. His treatment of Russian prisoners had been, and continued to be, subhuman. He knew his days were numbered.

Chapter 41

# A Reversal of Roles

In Greiz, Germany, interrogator Hanns Scharff's wife, Margaret, gathered up her three sons and daughter. The rural area there had been mostly untouched by the war, but that was about to change. At the end of the war, the American armed forces penetrated into the "Russian" zone of Germany and requisitioned the family villa as their regional headquarters. They allowed the family to stay in the basement of the magnificent villa, while they occupied the upper floors. During this time, the Americans became close with Margaret and her children. When the American forces were obliged to withdraw thirty-five kilometers to the west so the Russians could move in, they took Margaret and the children with them, against regulations. Their familiarity with the now-desperate family convinced them to make an exception and try to get the family to safety. Margaret and her children, hidden by blankets, rode in the back of an Army truck and were dropped off in a town called Hof in the western sector.

Meanwhile, ebullient and masterful Dulag interrogator, Hanns Scharff, fled the interrogation complex in Oberursel with several others carrying files, typewriters, and his log book and guest book, along with general records. He had been ordered to Weimer to set up an intelligence operation there. He had been the prisoner's friend, and true to his form, he carried a suitcase filled with items that had belonged to downed airmen killed in action, so that the individual items could be returned to their devastated families. Each crash site had been searched, and all of the dead fliers' belongings were tagged and catalogued for return to their next of kin.

When the location at Weimar proved to be untenable, the relocation was switched to Altenburg, and twenty-nine prisoners, twenty-eight of whom were American, had to be moved from the cooler at nearby Nohra Air Base. But Patton's tanks were closing in fast coming along the autobahn. With twenty-nine unguarded Allied prisoners on a flatbed wagon behind a borrowed new red Mercedes fire engine, Scharff slipped behind the wheel and raced to Bad Sulza at top speed. He dropped off the prisoners in Bad Sulza before proceeding to the rail station at Leipzig.

In Bad Sulza, Hanns loaded up the Germans. One major, one captain, three sergeants, one corporal, two female secretaries and an enlisted man hopped aboard the fire engine already laden with all the files and typewriters. At sundown, they caught the train and arrived in Leipzig on track one at midnight. Leipzig was the largest railway station in the world at that time. Scharff's group had less than thirty-minutes to board if they were going to make it to Altenburg, and that train left from track thirty-six. Racing through the bombed out train station on a commandeered heavily-loaded baggage vehicle, he had only three-minutes to spare. He crossed a weakened spot on the platform, and the vehicle and all it carried fell twenty-feet into a bomb crater swallowing up the files and records as Hanns barely leapt clear. Only the suitcase and some personal items remained. Seconds before the train pulled away, Scharff boarded with the seven others and fled Leipzig, suitcase still in tow.

With dawn breaking, the German contingent climbed from the train at Altenburg. In the distance, Hanns could hear Russian artillery. The Luftwaffe at Altenburg was getting nervous about the safety of the two secretaries, and Scharff suggested driving them to Gera, where a director of his grandfather's textile mill lived. He commandeered yet another car, and as he dropped them off, sirens were wailing as Patton's troops neared. When he arrived back at the base at Altenburg, it was deserted. He and four men replenished their supplies there, donning new uniforms and set out on foot to escape the enemy.

Hunger overcame them, and they stopped at a farmhouse where they saw milk cans.

"Sir, we are very hungry soldiers and would it be all right if we took a drink of milk from one of those milk cans?" Hanns asked.

"Of course! Help yourself. Be my guest."

"Thank you so much, my friend. It's nice of you to be so kind to four hungry German soldiers."

"What? German soldiers! I thought you were American officers! Be off with you. Get off this property immediately!"

Hanns now clearly understood what the future held for him.[19]

Approaching a small village two hours later, Hanns saw it was occupied by American troops. Before surrendering he thought it was best to change into civilian clothing and leave the other three men so he could make his way alone to the villa at Greiz to find his family. He crossed the autobahn through an underpass, but an American squad captured him and took him to a post where several other Germans were being held. The Americans did not know he could understand English when one of them advised his fellow soldier to check the men over closely.

"The ones in uniform are no trouble, but the guy in "civvies" has a military passport and may be a spy," he said.

They had orders to execute spies!

With great alarm, Scharff took off running at full speed for the forest as bullets tore through the trees. He found the spot where he had buried his Luftwaffe uniform and put it back on. Then he ran back through the underpass and caught up with his three German sergeant friends just as they surrendered. He turned over the suitcase to the authorities, who turned it over to the Red Cross. He was loaded into a truck for a long ride, and as he rode, he anticipated the bleak future of prison life.

Scharff was trucked to "The Hell Hole of Bad Kreuznach" prisoner of war camp, a field that sat within acres of German vineyards. The camp was overseen by American armed forces. Without the greatcoats, rucksacks or blankets that were taken and thrown in a pile as prisoners entered the field the prisoners were ill-prepared for the weather.

Scharff squeezed his way into the crowd taking his place among the tightly-packed German prisoners. There were no facilities, no barracks, no toilets, nothing--just bare hillside, which turned into mud the moment it rained. It was an open-air camp that already held ten-thousand prisoners, and the numbers kept growing after the German surrender. The field was so crowded that no one could lie down on the muddy ground. Traditionally, the twelfth through the fourteenth of May was the time of "Eisheiligen," or time of the "Ice Saints" in Germany. It was a common cold snap when spring rain turned to sleet. With the bitter winter of 1944-45, the three saints, Pankratius, Servatius and Bonafatius, were out in force spreading sleet and a cold chill across the land.

With no food, shelter or warm clothing, the tired and dirty German prisoners of war started to sing at midnight and sway back and forth in unison in the sleet for warmth and to bolster their morale. Scharff hunkered down against the cold. Guards fired rifles indiscriminately into the darkness to quiet the men. By morning many were dead, victims of disease and exposure to the elements. Daylight revealed the man next to Scharff had been shot dead.

The United States was ill-equipped to house the influx of thousands of prisoners. Because he was a translator/interpreter, Hanns was taken on daily rounds to mark an X on the foreheads of the men who died during the night, which averaged about one-hundred.

One day, he found his cousin, Oskar, and the men embraced. Oskar saw the slightly preferential treatment Hanns had been afforded because of his English skills. Hanns offered to make Oskar an interpreter also to better his dismal condition, but Oskar's English was almost non-existent. He practiced the one English joke he knew about a large and small elephant and recited it flawlessly for the American lieutenant and was approved.

A compassionate officer took Scharff to the supply shed, where he received warm clothing but no greatcoat. They found Cossack-style fur hats, and Scharff convinced the lieutenant to give him one for Oskar. Strangely attired, the two translators made their way through the camp that held over one-hundred-thousand German soldiers.

As Hanns struggled in the camp, his future daughter-in-law's father, a German soldier, was declared missing in action in France. It was believed he was killed by French partisans while his unit was retreating towards Germany. However, his body was never found. After the war, German Chancellor Conrad Adenauer negotiated the return of German prisoners held by the Russians. Not all came home, and many were executed or kept as laborers for the Soviet Union, only to eventually die in a foreign land. Monika Scharff who years later married one of Hanns's sons was too young to understand the difference between the Western front and the Eastern front. In the fifties, as she watched news clips of jubilant German POWs from Russia reuniting with their families, she was hoping against hope that her father would be among them and come home too. It made no sense, but she was too little to understand. She remained a little girl watching and waiting for a young father who would never come home from the war. Just like the Allies, so many German children would never know or see their fathers.

Margaret and the children made their way to a refugee camp in Belgium, while Hanns sat in the wretched camp. Her English relatives soon arranged for the family to fly from Brussels to London on a DC-3. Once in England, they stayed with relatives until Margaret decided it would be more beneficial to be declared "Displaced Persons." Being DPs entitled the family to a government grant which enabled them to travel back to their home in South Africa. After months of staying in the safe haven of family, Margaret and the small children checked into a DP camp set up just outside Glasgow, Scotland. After some time living there, they were allowed to board the Caernarvon Castle steamship for the first civilian trip made to South Africa following the war.

Conditions in Bad Kreuznach where Hanns was still held were so appalling that the overwhelmed Allies knew they had to do something. They decided to release all of the Germans who had previously lived in what was now the Russian sector to let the Russians deal with them. Finally, Hanns would go home to his family at the textile mill in Greiz, where he had spent his boyhood years and where he knew they waited.

The German prisoners were loaded on railroad freight and flatbed cars, and they headed east. Hanns was then trucked to within thirty kilometers of the textile mill and villa in Greiz and walked the rest of the way. It was late one evening when hungry, exhausted and suffering intense pain from a gallstone attack, Hanns pushed open the villa gate where the family valet met him and fed him. He asked for his family, but he was told they were no longer there. Only his mother remained determined to stay and protect the villa and her belongings.

The valet warned him he must not stay as the Russians would arrive at any time, since the Americans left the Russian-designated sector. But Hanns was too tired and saddened to move. He fell into bed and into a deep sleep.

Just as the sun came up, he was awakened.

"Hanns! Wake up! Listen!"

It was his brother Eberhard who was left to run the mill during the war.

"During the night, the last Americans left Greiz, and some Russian forces are already in the outskirts of town. They'll be here at the villa later this morning!"

Eberhard feared they would both be arrested as Nazi collaborators. The Russians would confiscate the villa and mill, justifiably they reasoned, from collaborators of the Nazi regime. Eberhard had sent his family west when local industrialists started being arrested in the Soviet sector. The brothers would be tried by a Soviet military court immediately if they did not flee.

An American officer friend of the family showed up at the villa and told Hanns he had fifteen minutes before the Russians came. The officer agreed to take Hanns and his brother to Hof in his jeep, but they had to leave in ten minutes. Hanns was speechless and dazed, and he had few places to turn. He knew he was losing his boyhood home, and he reached for what he could find to remember it by. Standing in his father's study, he picked up a little bronze figurine of three Prussian soldiers linked together in lock step which stood on his father's desk, missing the Prussian sergeant who commanded them. He put the little bronze soldiers in his pocket and walked out of the villa into the waiting jeep never knowing if he would ever see the villa again. The brothers were joined in Hof by Oskar who thought it a good idea to offer their services as translators to the American Counter Intelligence Corps (CIC) stationed in Hof. Hanns was immediately hired by Harry B. Toombs, an agent of the CIC, as his personal translator.

Bronze Prussian soldiers taken by Hanns Scharff at the end of the war from his father's desk at his boyhood home in Greiz, Germany
Courtesy of Mr. Hanns Claudius Scharff

Immediately, the Russians arrived and moved into the villa. They took Hanns' mother as a housemaid and cook for the Russian commandant who brazenly occupied the villa keeping his vodka cooling in the toilet. Early in the fifties, they moved out and turned the villa into a youth hostel.

After the CIC operations were closed down, Scharff returned to the familiar hills of the Taunus Mountains just above the former Dulag Luft base to live without his family. In need of many supplies in post-war Germany, his mother sent him a package. It was plundered during transit, and when it arrived only an empty box filled with packing paper remained. Slowly, he tipped the empty carton, and he heard a dull thud. Amongst the paper scraps on the floor stood the little Prussian sergeant which the thieves had overlooked and who was reunited with his marching Prussian troops ready to take command.

## Chapter 42

## I'll Be Seeing You

On May 3$^{rd}$, the first contingent of ex-prisoners of war left Moosburg. The next day, my mother received a letter from radio station WLW notifying her of the war correspondent's interview with my father on the 29$^{th}$.

> "When we received the news about the liberation of your husband, we tried to call you, but were not able to reach you. Our WLW correspondent interviewed your husband who says he is well and sends his love."

The item had been carried on the Sohio newscast of May 2$^{nd}$ at 12:30 p.m., just three days after the interview.

Most men were taken by truck the twenty miles northeast from Moosburg to Landshut, a former Luftwaffe base used by C-47s to fly the men out to France. Men often waited for hours or days for the planes. Jeffers chose another path.

Up at 4 a.m. on May 8$^{th}$, Jeffers, Church and another friend made their way to the recently captured Brukmuhl Airport at Straubing, Germany, where C-47s were bringing supplies to the camp. Straubing sat at the confluence of the Danube and Isar Rivers. After unloading,

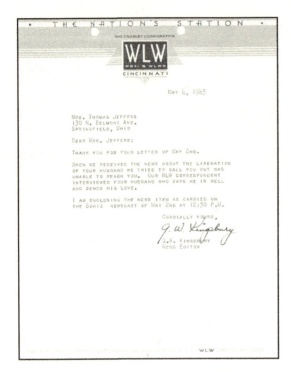

Letter sent by radio station WLW in Cincinnati, Ohio, to Phyllis Jeffers. It later hung in her grandson, John T. Walton's, office at WLW.

the empty planes were flown back to Namur, Belgium. Jeffers and his two friends and another small group of enterprising prisoners asked if they could fly back to Namur. They climbed aboard and took their places on the aluminum benches and prepared to leave Germany. While in the air, on their four-and-a-half-hour flight, they learned Germany had surrendered. As they flew onward, Allies around the world turned out to celebrate in the streets on long-awaited VE Day.

Arriving in Namur, they found a plane to fly them to Liege, Belgium, and then went on to Camp Lucky Strike, near Rouen, France. It was situated at St. Valery, between Dieppe and Fecamp on the Channel Coast of northern France. The area had been part of Hitler's impregnable Atlantic Wall, and now the vast arena of tents was one of a number of huge tent installations named after cigarette brands and set up to process the troops coming in on trucks and buses. The reception center slowly started processing the surge of soldiers waiting to return home. Long lines of men filled the camp. Ex-prisoners of war were to get top priority. Long

The vast tent city at Camp Lucky Strike
Courtesy of USAFA McDermott Library, Stalag Luft III Collections

Continual new arrivals added to the long lines at Camp Lucky Strike.
Courtesy of USAFA McDermott Library, Stalag Luft III Collections

designated as kriegies, the men now became RAMPs, Returned Allied Military Personnel. But in their minds, the kriegie label would never disappear. The RAMPs were to be automatically promoted, but many were not through a paperwork mix up. Jeffers and some of the other crew never were. Each RAMP got three-hundred dollars in back pay. Jeffers bought a small gold cross to present to his baby daughter when he returned to the States.

Upon arrival at Camp Lucky Strike, the men shed their worn clothes and were deloused. They showered and were issued new uniforms and identification cards.

Bedding was issued, and they were assigned a tent where they slept in their clothes, as it was still cold in May.

The next day, the men received a physical exam. Gonzales stepped on the scales and found his former one-hundred-seventy pound weight had dropped to one-hundred-twenty-eight. Much to their dismay, the ex-prisoners in the camp were given a canteen of eggnog for energy every four hours for the first two days before full meals could be taken. Afterward, they were fed five small meals a day. German prisoners of war prepared huge pots of creamed chicken and were able to eat very well themselves.

The RAMPs were debriefed by intelligence officers and began the waiting game. Most of the crew filed reports on Flaugher's death. Movies were shown in larger tents, and the RAMPs could not miss the irony of watching, "The Thin Man Returns Home." For my father, the 29th was always a unique day. He was called up for the service on the 29th, left for Europe on the 29th and was liberated on the 29th. In years to come, the prisoner of war reunions would always be held on the 29th to remember liberation day.

Patience ran thin, and at times no one seemed to be in charge. Before many men had been processed, General Eisenhower showed up to plead once more for patience.

On May 29th, Phyllis Jeffers received the telegram she had been waiting for.

> "The Secretary of War desires me to inform you that your husband 2/Lt Jeffers, Thomas F. returned to military control 29 April 45. Ulio the Adjutant General."

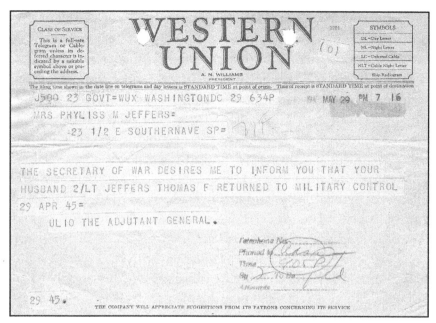

The final telegram Phyllis Jeffers awaited

The day finally came, and trucks moved the men to the harbor at LeHavre, France, to be loaded onto troop ships. Jeffers gazed at the hulking ship, The Marine Dragon, that would take him home. It left late in the evening, and the next morning it had crossed the English Channel. The men took one last look at the White Cliffs of Dover.

There were a few stormy days at sea, and it was too rough to go up on deck. Waves crashed into the bow and washed completely over it. Bracing themselves as best they could, the men looked to the back of the ship where the waves were so high the men were looking straight up at them. In the next moment, they were looking far down into the waves as the rocking ship plunged down against them. With each next wave, they again viewed the sky.

Much to his surprise, Jeffers spotted Clifford and Dean on board. He had not seen them since interrogation in Oberursel over ten months before. Food ran short on the voyage, and Jeffers asked Dean if they had any extra food in the enlisted men's mess hall. The two went down below, and everything was gone until the next morning. Dean offered Jeffers an orange left from dinner but with his new appreciation of food and realizing how precious the orange was, Jeffers declined, not wanting to deprive Dean of it. Their paths crossed in passing one more time on the ship before it docked.

When the weather permitted, the men watched movies on deck. Dean reveled in the fact he could eat in the open air and not be bothered by gnats or any type of bugs as he had in Stalag Luft IV.

Although the war in Europe was over, the liberty ships went in convoys sailing erratically, due to the possibility of some German U-boats which may still have been in the open sea. The diversions lengthened the trip. The Marine Dragon zigzagged across the Atlantic dodging icebergs and finally made its way into Boston. The ship pulled into Boston Harbor June 11th at the dock of the old Boston fishing pier. Crowds cheered, and as Jeffers left the ship, he looked upward to a window where men with their arms around young American women cheered enthusiastically. It was only when he looked closer that he saw that the men were Italian prisoners of war.

## Chapter 43

## *Into Waiting Arms*

After arriving in Boston, Jeffers spent the night at Camp Miles Standish. From there, he boarded a train to Camp Atterbury, Indiana, where he saw Dean aboard the train and then lost him for the next sixty years. After further processing, he caught a Greyhound bus for Springfield, Ohio. He rode for hours on the bus until it slowed down and ground to a stop in my mother's hometown. She and her sister and brother-in-law greeted him as he stepped gingerly off the bus. He was twenty-one pounds lighter than when he left. With great joy, he met my sister, Diane—"Scrubby." She was nearly six-months-old. My father was back in the arms of his family. He had enlisted when he was twenty-one years, seven months, and he had aged considerably in the years since he had signed the enlistment papers.

A week later, Lt. Colonel Clark having "closed the gate" behind him at Moosburg, made his way to Landshut and on to Camp Lucky Strike, but not before he noticed the Russians had rolled up every bit of barbed-wire at Moosburg to take home with them leaving little behind that was usable. Frustrated with delays at Camp

Thomas Jeffers finally meets "Scrubby," his daughter, Diane.

Lucky Strike, Clark was sent to Rouen, France, and later arrived in Paris. Solemnly, and with much respect, he went to Mass at Notre Dame and dropped down on his knees in the silent cathedral in thanksgiving for his safety through his thirty-three month ordeal. In a very short time, he would be home in Texas.

Dean returned to Tennessee and called his father to say he was coming in on a bus from Knoxville. Dean's father had no car, so he called a taxi. When Dean got off the bus from Knoxville, the taxi driver drove father and son home. Upon their arrival home, Dean's father tried to pay the driver, but the driver would take no money.

"No sir, it is my pleasure," the tearful man said, "because you see, I am the one who brought you the sad news almost a year ago. So, it is my treat."

Butler boarded a former Gem luxury liner. He was bedfast with swollen feet and ankles, so his buddies brought him food. Soon, he was well enough to go topside and witness the arrival into New York Harbor. He, along with many others, wept tears of joy at the graceful sight of the Statue of Liberty who stood tall to welcome her fighting men home. Butler boarded a train and passed through small towns where strangers gave the returning soldiers ice cream and milk to thank them in small part for service to their country.

Soon, he arrived at the Hotel Utah in Salt Lake City, a town that represented his religious heritage and held strong memories of his training days with Flaugher and the crew. Up on a balcony, stood Miriam, who had arrived with her father. She stood on the balcony

Dee Butler greets his new daughter, Julie Anne.

watching for him and not coming down until she could see what he looked like after his many privations. After a lunch, where he drank as much milk as he could hold, he saw his daughter Julie for the first time and was once more filled with great joy. And something else made him very happy--the taste of peanut butter that he had missed so much.

Gonzales's Navy victory ship left from Southampton, England, shortly after Jeffers, Dean and Clifford departed. On his flight from LeHavre to Southampton, Gonzales got his final view of the chalky White Cliffs of Dover before he boarded his ship. In the past, he had test-fired his guns out past the Channel. Now he sat as a passenger in the new era of peace, a young man yearning to go home. Ten days later, he would be home in California. The ship pulled into Boston May 29th. Gonzales left Boston for Marysville, California, on a brand new train covered with "POW" and "Welcome Home" banners. It was filled with soldiers and newspaper reporters who interviewed the soldiers all the way to California. At every train station where they stopped, people met the train, cheering the soldiers and bringing food and gifts for them.

Arriving in Marysville, he boarded a bus for Camp Beale where he stayed for about a week and then took another bus to Los Angeles.

He stepped off the bus into the arms of his mother, father and family. His mother hugged him, shocked to see her athletic son's skinny frame. Parties of celebration ran continuously. After two weeks at home and celebrating his twenty-second birthday, he reported to a convalescent hospital in Santa Monica, where he was nursed back to health for four months. His three brothers still served overseas.

Gonzales craved hamburgers, milkshakes and candy bars, although he could not eat them at first. When he could finally tolerate the missed foods, he smiled broadly remembering how good they were.

The British had flown Cardenas from Luxembourg to Brussels, Belgium, where he stayed in a three-story building enjoying the normal beds. He left Brussels for Normandy, France, where he was once more in American hands. He and nineteen others went to Paris after getting a three-day pass and one-hundred-dollars for expenses. They took the train and visited in Paris all day and went to the Lido at night.

He returned to Normandy and took a ship back to Portsmouth, England, where they took on injured soldiers. After a few days at sea, a storm arose.

Cardenas asked the captain for permission to go to the front of the ship to prevent seasickness. Two sailors walked him with harnesses attached to a side cable all the way to the front of the ship. The ship dipped down, and waves of ten meters came up and over the ship. Cardenas grabbed the cables hard, as the sailors did, and the ship tilted up so much that the water ran off the ship's deck.

It stormed for two days, and on the fifth day of the journey, the weather calmed down. Two days later, Cardenas cried with happiness when he saw the Statue of Liberty on the horizon. As he came down the gangplank to the docks, there were women everywhere trying to kiss him.

All the military personnel heading south were put on a train towards San Antonio, Texas. All along the route pretty women in every city stopped to greet them. Cardenas asked for a pass to go see his parents and brothers. He was given thirty days and took the train home.

When he saw his father, who was at the station to meet him, they fell crying into each other's arms where they stayed for a long time. Father and son finally left the platform. Up ahead, Cardenas could see his house. He cried tears of joy as he knocked on the front door. Once inside, everybody hugged and kissed him. Cardenas's mother tearfully embraced him. She ran her hands over his entire body to make sure he was "complete." A bayonet scar was etched into his little finger. She had fixed him the one thing he had missed so much—enchiladas. Many Mexican meals would follow to fill out his thin frame.

After months of deprivation and confinement, the crew of "Rhapsody in Junk" was home surrounded by the welcoming arms and love they had missed.

In Bloomdale, Ohio, the Flaugher family would have no celebration.

## Chapter 44

## R&R

Returning prisoners of war were ordered to report to one of a half-dozen centers by a certain date. My parents boarded a Pullman train with their new baby on August 15, 1945. They had just boarded the train when they learned Japan had surrendered. VJ day for them was celebrated on the train, and by the time they got to Florida, the celebrations were over.

They were quartered at the Ocean Grande Hotel right on the beach. All meals were provided and served and prepared by German prisoners of war in a mess-hall type setting.

Dean was home for sixty days and then went to Miami also for "Rest and Relaxation." Walking down Collins Avenue, Dean and Jeffers met again. They discussed what may have happened to Flaugher, and they speculated he may have actually been killed by the Germans after parachuting out. Jeffers said he had reported all of this to the authorities. Gonzales had done the same. They saw Cardenas in Miami as the two strolled along Collins Avenue in the blazing sun and were thrilled to be reunited with him.

Dean and his wife, Frances, stayed at the Monroe Towers on Collins Avenue. He was there two to three months. During a physical, the dentist detected a dark spot up in his gum above his front tooth requiring dental surgery, so he needed to stay longer to recuperate. He went back to his barracks to recover, and Frances returned home alone on the train. Dean was due to get his Tech/Sergeant's stripe the morning she left. Instead of getting his promotion stripe, Dean accompanied her to the train station. He never received his stripe and returned to Tennessee several months later.

With rest and relaxation behind them, all the men of the crew went their separate ways to start new lives. Some returned to advance their schooling, and some married and started families.

Some of the crew exchanged Christmas cards, but other than that, most contact was eventually lost. They bought homes and changed addresses, and soon they lost track of each other--some for over sixty years.

In 1946 Jeffers attended the first Stalag Luft III POW Reunion. Left to right are highlighted Lt. Col. A.P. Clark, Thomas Jeffers and his friend Charlie Church in the foreground with whom he visited German homes in Moosburg trading for food.

Courtesy of USAFA McDermott Library, Stalag Luft III Collections

## Chapter 45

# Fading Away

Decades passed, and the war stories told so proudly diminished as more current matters took precedence. Our family moved numerous times as Jeffers made the Air Force his career, and we traveled a great deal as my father pointed out the wonders of the world to us. There was no place he would not go, and few things he would not try. His time in captivity taught him to appreciate all that the world had to offer.

The stories of my father's war experiences were silenced and forgotten when in his later years he had several small strokes. His imprisonment, his plane and his crew vanished from his mind, and he would never speak of them again. Over eighty-years old, he gradually lost most of his memories, and he suffered from dementia. He and my mother were forced to give up their home, and they moved to a nursing home closer to my home. The family packed up everything my parents owned and had collected after nearly sixty-two years of marriage. On the shelves were my father's favorite books. I looked them over and in my curiosity pulled out a book entitled, *The Interrogator*, 'the story of Dulag Luft Master Interrogator, Hanns

From six decades past, the faces of Lt. Colonel Albert Clark, Lt. Colonel "Moose" Stillman and Lt. Dick Schrupp, jubilant atop a Sherman tank at Stalag Luft VIIA in Moosburg, Germany, on the day of their liberation, April 29th, 1945
Courtesy of USAFA McDermott Library, Stalag Luft III Collections

Scharff. The subject of the book had autographed it to my father at a kriegie convention no doubt, even writing my father's prisoner of war number in it. I had remembered seeing the book on the shelf for years, but I never asked him much about it or who Hanns Scharff was. Had this been the man who interrogated him? I knew nothing of this man.

I brushed the dust off of his books stacked neatly on his bookshelf. There was Clipped Wings, which chronicled his days at Stalag Luft III. I gently turned the pages. Many of the pictures were taken with secret cameras made by the prisoners and hidden from the Germans. In one picture, I looked into the face of Albert P. Clark, who grinned from the top of an American tank with his roommate, "Moose Stillman," on liberation day. I had met Clark, since promoted to Lt. General, at the memorial dedication of the 458th Bomb Group at Wright-Patterson Air Force Base decades later and at a prisoner of war reunion I attended with my father. I remembered we had our picture taken together.

Jeffers' grandson ex-Marine, Tom Reiling, saluting the grave of Sgt. Harold Flaugher in the American Cemetery in Belgium. This picture hung on Jeffers' wall until the day he died.

Courtesy of Mr. Tom Reiling

I gathered all my father's files in boxes. There were letters to a Jeremy Baulesch who "godfathered" Harold Flaugher's grave in Belgium. It was not uncommon for Belgians to godmother or godfather the graves of Americans killed in action in gratitude for the Belgians' freedom. My father had written to Jeremy expressing his thanks. He spoke of Harold's dedication to his job of keeping the aircraft in the best possible condition before combat missions. He wanted Jeremy to know just who this man was he was caring for. Over the years, Jeremy sent pictures of himself standing at the grave, and years later my nephew, Tom, an ex-Marine, visited and had his picture taken saluting Flaugher's grave. "For Harold" Tom had written on the picture as he presented it to my father, who sobbed when he saw the emotional image. I took the treasured picture to hang on the wall of his room at the nursing home.

In the bedside table drawer, I found a most curious item. It was a small, black notebook, and on each page was the name of a state and under that a restaurant. He had listings for forty-eight states, and sometimes there were comments about the specialty the restaurant served and the occasional comment about the bar there. I had absolutely no idea what this was, as I knew he could not have visited all these places, but the notebook was old and for some reason he kept it.

His shadowbox of medals hung proudly by his desk, and his WWII uniform jacket and hat were carefully placed in a garment bag beside the jacket my mother wore for their wedding.

The shelves and his files were rich with personal history of which he could no longer speak. There was a file holding the crew pictures of the Morley and Northrop crews, young vibrant men kneeling and standing with their newly-formed crews so many years ago in Topeka, Kansas—all innocent faces unexposed to the horrors of war. There was a file with a single obituary in it—that of his roommate in England, Bennie Hill, which told of his passing away after the war. My father had felt it was very important to keep it.

# Chapter 46

# Still Standing Tall

We sold my parent's home in one day, and John and I went back to represent them the day of the closing. We entered the home one last time. The house was a shell now, hollow and cold with memories of conversations in every room. My father's records and tape player had blared out his favorite 1940s tunes so many times. "Underneath the lamp post, by the garden gate…my own Lili Marlene," and the lilting melody of "Moonlight Cocktail," which was "their song," still lingered.

"Marielaina, you're the answer to a prayer," he would sing out loudly, and the humorous "Fuehrer's Face," my father had sung with gusto much to our amusement. I had recently taught it to my two small grandchildren.

"Now, that's what I call real music," he would say after he'd finished singing or listening to the war-era music.

Dancing to "In the Mood" and playing high-spirited games of Parcheesi in the dining room faded like elusive wisps of smoke never to return.

The seven grandsons and his only granddaughter, Robin, who had passed through the rooms, were mostly grown now. We had celebrated my parent's birthdays and their 50th wedding anniversary there, and the resonance of their laughter and voices like distant echoes were not as easily removed. The last thing we did was take down the musical door chime that played "Off We Go Into the Wild Blue Yonder" each time someone rang the bell. My parent's presence was still so much there in the empty rooms and stayed behind as we softly closed the front door one last time.

The nursing facility was twenty minutes from my home, and the staff considered the Jeffers like family. The pretty building had a front porch that faced the street, and a line of tall white wooden rockers ran its length. On windy days, I was amused that the unoccupied rockers swayed back and forth by themselves as if pushed by some invisible hand.

While there, I took my parents to a large state park nearby where there was a deer pen, and we walked over to feed and pet the deer there frequently. Due to injury or weakness, the captured animals were confined within the metal fence missing the freedom they had once experienced. They longed to leap and run along the lake and through the dense tall green trees, but their condition would not permit it. My father, in particular, liked to see them, and it seemed to give him great peace and comfort to watch their beautiful faces and soft innocent eyes. Helpless to care for themselves, their fate was up to their captors, and they relied on others to be fed and sheltered. My father held small bits of broken carrots in his hand which was brown-specked with age, to feed the small deer held behind the wire. They were mostly young does, typical of the deer we often see running loose on the streets and highways of our county, which is heavily over-populated with deer. Larger ones must have stayed hidden, for I never saw a large deer in our area.

Not long after my parents settled in, Max Flaugher, brother to Harold, came to visit. He drove down four hours with a box of Harold's mementoes. His purple heart, his letters home from England and his high school memorabilia--the small collection of a short life, all sat within the box. Max brought an old movie from

The American flag is raised at Moosburg on liberation day. Shadows of war-weary but joyful prisoners saluting the flag are visible on the wooden fence.
Courtesy of USAFA McDermott Library, Stalag Luft III Collections

Harold's high school days. Now, I could put an animated face with the name I had heard for so many years. I watched Harold's antics during his class trip to Washington D.C. Eternally young, it seemed like it was just yesterday in his youth that he frolicked with his classmates. Max and I spoke of his brother that evening at dinner after we had left my parents.

"You know," he said, "Your father has had flowers put on Harold's grave for the past sixty years."

I had never heard that, but it did not surprise me. My father's loyalty ran very deep.

I made a request of our local State Representative that my father be given his Prisoner of War Medal. Before too long it arrived, and a formal presentation was planned at the nursing home. All the residents and staff gathered for the presentation and reception. No one stood taller and prouder than my father as the colors were paraded in. As a former prisoner of war and veteran, he could not re-tell the story of the American flag being raised in the Moosburg camp on liberation day without choking up no matter how many times he told it.

His patriotism and love of country was unwavering. It was not only for himself that he stood tall, but it was for Harold, and the crew and the men who gave their lives in the tragic war from which he was lucky enough to return.

 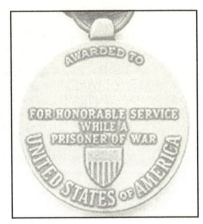

Prisoner of War Medal
Courtesy of Mary Smith and Barbara Freer

Thin and becoming frail, he stood at attention as his medal was presented. His grandson, Tim, in Army green saluted his grandfather sharply, and a strong salute was returned. Then he donned his WWII jacket and crush cap. My mother, weak and pale, stood by his side to recapture the picture of them taken so many years before as she pinned his bombardier wings to his uniform jacket in Texas. A newspaper photographer snapped their picture as they replicated their original pose. The original picture sat on a table in front of them. That picture, and the new one, appeared on the front page of the local newspaper the next morning. A reception with punch and cake followed accompanied by piped in 1940s music.

Three weeks after the ceremony, my mother's health continued to fail. The transition from her home to a nursing home had been hard for her. Despite her own physical problems, she still tried to take care of my father for nine months. She was in a room in the same building, but it had become increasingly hard for her to walk to his room to care for him. In her confusion, she collapsed by his hallway in the early hours one morning, when she normally should have been asleep, and I think she sensed her own end was near as she tried to see him. She was put in Hospice care and remained there only one week. He sat with her in Hospice brushing her hair until the end, and she died at 10:35 p.m., November 22, 2003, after he had gone to bed. Diane, who had come from Michigan, and I were with her, and we faced the sorrowful task of telling our father of her death the next morning. He had been married to my mother for so long, and her death left him alone for the first time. I found it hard to use the term widower for him. And suddenly, long before I was ready, I was motherless.

The family gathered in his room, and we helped him dress. He slid into his warmest coat with the button at the neck, and I once more stretched the over-stretched elastic loop over the top button. We took him to her funeral Mass, and on a cool November day she was laid to rest in Springfield. Bundled against the cold wind, he stood desolate at her grave. Head down and hands in his pockets, we held his arms and steadied him as he heard the priest's final prayers at her gravesite. So many of life's experiences they had known together on their long journey.

After everyone returned home, my father was in my complete care. It was a blessing in disguise that he could not always remember that my mother had died, and he often spoke of her as if she were still living. It blunted the pain for me to some degree not to watch him mourn. But on a deeper level, I always sensed he knew, and for him, his own death would be welcomed.

## Chapter 47

## Now Alone

Michael Fox, a County Commissioner, who had come to witness my father's medal ceremony, decided after seeing it that all World War II veterans in our county should be recognized. He arranged for a lavish luncheon for them at a local hotel, naming the project Operation Heroes.

Just three weeks after my mother's death, I dressed my father in his sport's coat and tie, and John and I took him to the luncheon. We sat with two-hundred-and-seventy elderly warriors who had gathered to accept the salute for their World War II accomplishments.

Music of the era played, and each man received a certificate of appreciation. Only one-hundred-fifty or less were expected, but hundreds more came forth, and another luncheon was arranged. Before it was over, nearly six-hundred-fifty World War II vets were recognized. Commissioner Fox pulled me aside at the luncheon where I took my father to receive his certificate.

"You know your father started all this."

How pleased he would have been to realize that, but in his humility would have flatly denied it.

I watched the unsteady gait of so many who fought the valiant battles. The hands that flew the planes and launched the torpedoes and cradled the guns were spotted with age. The sharp eyes that peered through gunsites and bombsights of the past strained a little harder. The lines of time that defined these wonderful faces told the story of battles fought and good lives lived. Dignified business suits substituted for Army and Marine uniforms and helmets, Navy life vests and Army Air Corps bomber jackets, but underneath nothing had changed. As I sat feeling privileged to be amongst these heroes, including my own, there was a hush in the room. Then the announcement came.

"We got him!"

At first a low murmur—then wild cheers of the aging men erupted in the jam-packed room as the capture of Saddam Huessein that day was announced. The clapping was deafening and long-sustained. Their youth and enthusiasm returned. Those to whom they had passed the torch were lavished with their praise. To be cheered by these veterans was the ultimate cross-generational salute. The old boys still had a lot of patriotism and fight left in them, and my father was right there enthusiastically clapping with them.

Diane came from her home, which was four hours away to help, but on a day-to-day basis my father depended upon me. There was so much I wanted to ask him during our visits, and so much I wanted to know. I was lucky that he had related many of his experiences over the years, but there were still gaping holes. For so many years, he tried to find out exactly what caused the death of his friend and crewmate, Flaugher. Now with his memories gone, I felt the torch had been passed to me to continue the quest.

Grandchildren came to visit, and his brother came up from Florida to see him. We went on outings with the staff and residents, and we went to sing-a-longs. We held the puppies people brought in to show the residents and made craft projects together. Yet, his life was empty. This vibrant man who had always been so accomplished and sharp was fading from me, and at some low-level understanding he was no longer fulfilling a need and was feeling useless. He had always been an active and social man, and now all he did was sort through his clothes and lie on his bed. He spoke of missions and parachutes, and day after day, he repeated the donning of many pairs of socks and a warm hat. When I arrived to pick him up, I would find him in a warm coat even on a summer day. He wore his heavy gloves and had more gloves in his pockets. He adamantly insisted on keeping them there.

When I took my father outside, he always came over to make sure my coat was fully buttoned, and I stretched the worn elastic loop over his top button of the favorite old winter coat at his request to make sure it was secure to keep his neck warm. It came to be our ritual. I can only guess what was going through his mind as he relived an indelible experience that was seared into the deepest recesses of his mind. Now, in the twilight of his years, the memories surfaced in their own jumbled way.

I took my father on errands with me, and the one thing that would always catch his eye were contrails in the sky as we drove. Mid-sentence, he interrupted me to point out the sweeping white vapor trails in the sky. He seemed mesmerized by the ethereal plumes as they streamed across the blue sky and evaporated before our eyes. He never failed to point them out.

We went grocery shopping as we had done with my mother. It was odd that now there were only the two of us. I handed him each item, and he methodically placed it into my basket in a precise order. We were a common sight at Meijer Department Store, him in his layers of clothes pushing my basket, and me handing him everything for inspection. On days when he could not walk well, I suggested that I push him on one of their long carts with a short wooden bench just behind the basket. At first he was hesitant, but I told him it was his B-24, and he jumped aboard. I ran with him as fast as I could through the parking lot for take-off, and he held on tightly. He motioned with a sweeping swing of his arm as the wind riffled through his hair and mine.

"When you get up there," he said with great authority, "Peel off!"

How many times he must have heard that term after dropping his bombs when Northrop would return to the safe shores of England to land.

I had given him a stuffed penguin, years before, and it made the trip with him to hospital rooms and nursing facilities. A flightless bird had seemed fitting. Now, it sat on his bed, and when grandchildren came, or when there was nothing else he wanted to do, we threw it quickly to one another. He could still fool us by looking at one of us and throwing to someone else. At one point, he took it to another resident's room and left it, and the hunt was on until I found it and returned it to its proper place on his bed.

Often, we would look through books. I showed him pictures of Stalag Luft III and Stalag VIIA, and for a few moments he would remember faces from so long ago. I showed him something I had found about actor Donald Pleasance, a former prisoner held at the officer's camp Stalag Luft I at Barth. My father had enjoyed his performance in the movie, "The Great Escape." I read aloud how Pleasance had been a conscientious objector but later joined the RAF. Post war, he was the only actor to have appeared in both "The Great Escape" and its television sequel, "The Great Escape II: The Untold Story," playing one of the would-be escapees in the first film and one of the German executioners in the second. Strangely, when he acted in "The Eagle Has Landed," he even played the role of SS and Gestapo chief, Reichsführer Heinrich Himmler, who had ordered the murder of "The Fifty" Stalag Luft III escapees, thus completing the full circle of roles from German murder conspirator, executioner and victim, an odd coincidence so long after his prisoner of war days. It was as though the fog had lifted, and for a moment, my father seemed to understand it all, but the moments were short-lived and soon he just stared at me.

## Chapter 48

# In Search of the Crew

I called ninety-one-year-old General Clark one day, and we talked about the war and the prisoner-of-war experience. He was Superintendent of the Air Force Academy from 1970-1974 and retired after thirty-eight years of service. He was still living in Colorado Springs, and soon we became pen pals. I looked forward to his letters, and he also sent me his memoirs that were about to be published. No matter what I asked him, he was ready with an answer. The general had definite opinions on matters, and he spoke them to me without hesitation. He invited me to the Academy with a promise to show me through the library's special Clark Collection, dedicated to Stalag Luft III. I told him I would try to visit there.

My father had told me some years back that he had tried to find his crewmates. I decided one day to pick up where he had left off. It would be wonderful to meet them and listen to their stories of the crew days. He had received a Second Air Division Journal for years with stories of the 458th Bomb Group, and I looked at the list of names that were responsible for the newsletter. I called Emmett Cook in Texas, a bombardier shot down in Sicily in 1943. He had bailed out of a spinning B-17, and the aircraft blew up burning his hands as he sought to bomb the shipping and docks at Palermo. He said he had no water for three days. Emmett was in touch with a film company making a film on Stalag Luft III and told me all about it. He was as enthusiastic as a young school boy talking to me about the war. He told me others to call. I called Christine Armes in England who was planning a monument dedication to the 458th, and I called other board members who would know about the next prisoner of war reunion to which I hoped to take my father.

Another letter written to the Journal also took my eye. Darin Scorza, son of a 458th navigator, Sam Scorza, wrote to request information on men of the 458th since he was starting a website to honor them. I emailed him immediately and asked him to include my father on his website. In our initial communications, we found that Darin's father, whom he lost in 1987, had been injured in a plane called "Rhapsody in Junk" causing him to miss several missions with his crew. Darin quoted from his father's journal:

> "It had the old type super chargers. A few minutes after take-off, the terrific pressure from the outside air forced the top hatch open. It hit me on the head and stunned me for a few minutes. It hurt plenty all through the mission, but it's okay."

I had to tell him my father was shot down in that plane! Darin told me there were sixty-three boxes of 458th materials at the National Archives in Maryland, and each box held one-thousand pages. German records had been brought over after the war as well as old mission and personnel records. It was a place we both wanted to visit. Darin told me how to obtain my father's Missing Air Crew Report (MACR) from the Air Force, and he gave me the crew's correct MACR number to ask for. I sent him two crew pictures I had, that of the Morley and Northrop crews, for his website, and I monitored his guestbook for letters pertaining to the men I was looking for.

Unbeknownst to me, others were seeking the same information. I posted a message on the Mighty 8th Message Boards stating I was looking for the crew of "Rhapsody in Junk." Local and European military researchers responded immediately. One was Ed Reniere in Belgium who monitored the site. He had grown up in occupied Belgium, and years later paid back the men who liberated his country by helping veterans and their families trace crews and planes. He gave me all the men's serial numbers and further information on each. Coincidentally, Lawrence Dean posted an inquiry trying to find his crewmates shortly thereafter. Ed responded to both of us in a joint email. Jack Gonzales's brother-in-law, Jack Whetstone, posted a letter in Darin's guestbook inquiring about the men of the crew not long after that.

After finding each other, the Dean, Jeffers and Gonzales families emailed back and forth between Ohio, Tennessee and California. Dean's daughter, Brenda, and I emailed frequently exchanging copies of old documents, letters and pictures. Soon, Gonzales's brother-in-law put me in touch with Gonzales's daughter, Linda. That led to phone calls to their home, and happily, I spoke with Jack and Lawrence themselves. I had a million questions for them. Better than that, the two men initiated calls to each other and heard each other's familiar voice after sixty years much to their daughters' delight. They wanted to speak to their old bombardier, but it was too late, as he was now more confused and incapable of meaningful conversations. How he would have loved to have spoken with them.

I located navigator, Deimel, and called him in Texas. With Ed Reniere's help from Belgium, I traced three more on the crew and sadly found Butler, Northrop and Brodek had passed away. He told me also that Clifford had died, and I looked further for an obituary, but I could not find one. I turned to an independent researcher in California for help hoping I could locate any family he had.

> "I did not find an obit for Charles Clifford. He died 29 Aug 1985. If he had no relatives and died alone, the county may have done an autopsy on him to determine the cause of death, and then it would not be in the paper for some time, and if no relatives claimed him, no obit."

Although I was disappointed that no leads materialized, it was sadder yet to think that he had died, and no one had claimed him.

I eagerly called Northrop's son, Michael, one night, and spoke to his wife, Sherry.

Then he sent an interesting email.

> "Wanna hear something wild? Just a few days ago, before you spoke with Sherry I had a dream: I was in a car being driven into the desert by a man whose face I could not see. The car stopped and I got out. In front of me was a rusty old airplane, half buried in the sand with only the top of its wings and upper half of the fuselage visible. The rusted hulk was huge and full of holes. It was a B-24. Eager to explore, I walked around it until I could find a place to enter. I entered the plane from the wing gunner's port. When I began to look around inside I was amazed at how well it and its contents had been preserved. I began to notice little details like maps and gadgets strewn about and that the plane's four engines were now running and there were people shuffling about. I walked to the front of the plane and into the cabin where I saw the copilot who turned and gave a thumb's up and then smiled at me. I then looked toward the pilot's seat where I saw a yellow post-it note stuck to the steering wheel. It read "Hank." I sat in the chair. I was my dad.
>
> A few days later you called."

Michael led me to his sister, and I had to smile when I heard her name—Marielaina. She spoke of losing both her parents and was still grieving for them. They also had another brother. Marie, as she was called, worked with a young man named Alejandro Cardenas who had a great grandfather in World War II, and we thought we might have found a connection to the missing Cardenas, but that turned out to be another false lead.

But there were other bright spots. Ed helped me locate many of my father's roommates from Stalag Luft III in Block 128, Reardon, Downing, Kauffmann, Branch, McDarby, Beatty, Koch, Roberts, Kaplin, and Tribbett. These were names I had never heard him mention, but were written on a scrap of paper in his files. I called Tribbett, whose son had moved in to take care of him in California, and the ex-POW and I had several conversations, but too many years had passed, and he could not place my dad.

Ed, in Belgium, had sent me two websites related to a Robert Beatty, pilot of "Heavenly Daze," a B-17 that had crashed in Holland. After dialing several likely phone numbers in Pennsylvania, I hit the jackpot. Eighty-seven-year old Robert and I had a lengthy conversation. He remembered my father's name, but that was about all. I told him I was going to send him two websites sent to me from Belgium that Ed had accidentally come across that discussed his crew and his mission that fateful day. Not only that, the Dutchman who had set up one of the websites was desperately trying to find any of the men on the Beatty crew, because he had just found pieces of the plane and a tail section. The small town wanted to pay honor to the men of the crew. I immediately emailed the Dutchman and Robert to connect them.

Two weeks later, I took the mail from my mailbox, and I saw the return address of Beatty. After I had called him, his memories came back more clearly, and he remembered a story about my father. On one grim overcast day when the men had nothing to do but stay inside on their bunks, he told me my father read to them out of a novel. The story contained a lot of French phrases, and as he got to each one, he purposely mispronounced it to make them laugh. He grew up with a mother who spoke perfect French, so he knew all the correct pronunciations.

"He sure brought us up out of the depths of despair that day," Beatty said, "Nothing ever seemed to bother him. I can still see him lying up there on the top bunk."

I continued in my quest to find Cardenas. My father had found him years ago in Mexico, but then lost track of him for decades. I wrote to the last address he had, and received no reply. I called

Cardenas families everywhere, and I found it is as common a name as Smith in Mexico. I ran into continual dead ends. One day I found there was a man by that name at Wright-Patterson Air Force Base not far from me that I guessed could have been his son, and I called his office to find he was on vacation. He worked in the very area my father had worked at one time. I waited until the day he returned and anxiously called only to find that he was not the one I was looking for. I called the Veteran's Administration to see if they had someone by that name in Mexico who might still be receiving a retirement check. They said they did. They requested that I send a letter to him via their agency, and they would forward it. I did as they asked, and waited for months with no reply.

I found Brodek's wife and his son, and when she sent pictures, letters and documents, I got to see what he looked like for the first time.

I found Bennie Hill's son, Blaine, who kindly sent me information on his father, who had been the lone survivor on the Morley crew. He had come across a letter my father had written to his, and he sent it along to me. The lucid words conveyed concern for his former roommate and anguish over the loss of Bennie's crew. I found and talked to the sons of the two men who watched "Rhapsody" go down as they flew in the same bomber stream, but their fathers had also passed away.

After I found several members of the crew, I went to the nursing home to tell my father the news. I pointed to each face in his crew picture showing those I had found. He studied their faces and said nothing, but he gave me a big smile.

## Chapter 49

# *Worldwide Research*

During this time, I drove almost daily to see my father. One day when I did not go, I received word that his older sister, Lorraine, had died in New York. He had been close to his sister, but they did not see each other much considering the geographic distance between them. I did manage to put him on the phone to her several months before. I called the nurses that night and told them I would be in the next day to tell him his sister had died, so they might prepare him.

"What was her name?" the nurse asked.

"Lorraine," I replied.

There was a long silence.

"He has been asking for a Lorraine all day long and all night long," she told me.

We were both stunned by his instinctive knowledge that something had happened.

I visited the next morning, and the picture of him with his sister and brother that had been on his dresser was moved. I put it back in its place. I told him she had passed away, but he was not as nearly as upset as I. Perhaps, he did not really fathom what I was saying to him. But when he saw my tears, he held me in his arms with my head on his chest as I had done as a small child, and he patted my back. For a few moments we absorbed the depth of the loss on our own levels, and he told me not to cry. He had experienced so many losses.

The next day I returned to researching.

Having gotten my hands on archive records, and having found some of the crew, I began to research their war experiences more deeply, often taking documents to read in his room while he slept. I had received the MACR from the Department of the Air Force and found it fascinating to read through.

I pored over the pages that combined both American and German records. Words the crew had written in reports just after the war leapt off the pages--words that had not been read in over sixty years. They gave the order of bail outs, and Butler, Clifford and Cardenas pondered what had happened to Flaugher. German KU (Kampf Flugzeuge USA) (Battle Planes USA) report #2245 stated Sgt. Flaugher was found dead on the 18th of June at Kappeln near Schleswig. That was at 10:00 a.m. Also at ten, the Germans picked up Dean at Kappeln near Schleswig The captain and commander of the local naval air base also stated Brodek, Cardenas, Northrop, Butler, Jeffers, Clifford, Deimel and Gonzales were all picked up at ten. I assumed these were rough estimates, and I also knew there were time changes in the summer, especially between England and Germany, and that is why some of the times in reports I read did not always reconcile. Ed tried to clear it up for me:

> British Summer Time (one hour ahead of Greenwich Mean Time) was in use in Britain and by the US Army Air Forces based there on 6 March 1944. This coincided with the Middle European Time in use in Germany and in the Luftwaffe." According to info found at www.srcf.ucam.org/~jsm28/british-time British Summer Time (BST) was indeed Greenwich Mean Time + 1, but the "Double British Summer Time" (DBST) also known as "British Double Summer Time" (BDST,) in use during the

war was in fact "GMT + 2." From 1942 on, BDST/DBST started after the first Saturday of April [see the 1942 Regulation] and what is mentioned above, for a mission in March, means USAAF and German times should be the same in their respective reports at the time (March.) But at the time of your Dad's last mission (June 1944) DBST/BDST was in force, so the "10:20" mentioned as the time the ship left formation could be "9:20" in British Summer Time (BST) - only one hour ahead of GMT - which was in use in Germany, according to the text in italic above. So the German "10:00" is in BST and not DBST/BDST in my opinion. Hope I'm right and this clears things up.

Ed

I could tell it was not going to be easy interpreting the reports.

Having tackled that one, I returned to the MACR. It went on to state that Harold Flaugher was buried on the twenty-first of June, 1944, at a Schleswig military cemetery. Upon the MACR page was a faded address.

There was an interview done after the war in which co-pilot, Dee Butler, reported that Sgt. Flaugher's body was placed in a coffin by officers of the crew and taken to a cemetery.

> "Sgt. Flaugher's chute opened when he left the plane. His chest was crushed, but no other bones were broken. He had a large discoloration on right temple, and it is my theory that he was struck with a blunt instrument such as a butt of a rifle. None of his clothes were torn, and it seems as though they would have ripped if he had struck some object in his descent to the ground. His body was stiff. I would estimate the time I last saw Sgt. Flaugher from bailing out to the time we were shown his body in a warehouse to be approximately 3 hours. Yes, everyone, without exception cleared the plane."

Sgt. Clifford stated in a written report that Sgt. Flaugher did not want to jump and asked to be pushed from the plane. Dee Butler agreed to help him and gave him a push out of the hatch. He speculated Flaugher's parachute didn't open, but that was later denied by the others. Clifford stated that Lts. Northrop and Deimel after capture were taken to pick up and carry Flaugher's body to a point where they put it in a casket. Northrop was given the engineer's watch, ring and money belt, all later taken by the Germans. Clifford stated he saw the casket and the personal effects. He also stated that they were held at a local police station and then taken to Kiel Naval station guard house before leaving for Dulag Luft near Frankfurt for interrogation.

Personal accounts by Butler and Cardenas gave the order and location where the men jumped from the plane, either camera hatch or bomb bay. At one time all the men probably filled out reports, but this was all that was sent.

A report was included regarding the wreckage. The German KU report stated at 10:25 a.m. at Brau-Holz, 10 km west of Kappeln the Germans found what was probably a B-17, 100% loss and that nine of ten prisoners were transported from Schleswig to Oberursel. They noted that Sgt. Flaugher had died. The plane was salvaged by "salvage battalion 3, 11 III one B/l Schleswig" according to the report.

Being one of the "B-24 Boys," my father would have been justifiably outraged that the Germans thought his plane was a B-17.

There was one last page I found tucked in the MACR. It had the name of a bombardier, Morris Epps, who was shot down the same day but not in the same place. A clerical error had placed the errant page in my father's crew report. When I saw it, I noticed the error and put the page in the wastebasket by my desk. From time to time I saw it there, and soon I found myself taking it back out. I went online to see if I could find anyone by that name. After several phone calls, I located Epps's wife and his daughter, Becky Lawson, who had been trying to find out information about her father for years. He had died some years ago. I told her how to find his MACR, and I sent her the page I had received.

I copied my father's MACR and put it in a binder to give it to him. So many times when I visited him, he was carrying it with him, and he loved to read it, often making notes on it. I read many books on the war and did much research, and I could not shake the idea from my mind of going back to Germany to find the crash site of his plane. I had read of several people who had done it, and I posted an inquiry on the Mighty 8th website.

I got an immediate response from pilot, Kevin Pearson, a B-17 aficionado and military researcher in Alaska. He had personally dug out a crash site in Germany, and he had been to Kiel. He was excited about the proposed trip and was instrumental in tracking down mission and military history and explaining the intricacies and mechanical aspects of flying to me. He even recommended a great hotel where he had stayed when he visited the submarine pens in Kiel. Kevin became a constant source of information when I needed it.

Likewise, Darin Scorza was invaluable providing me with 458th history and interpreting archive military charts and mission records. During the war, the pilots and crews had great affection for their planes, and Darin knew the men and the planes. It was clear that back then there were "B-24 Boys" and "B-17 Boys," advocates of the Liberators and Flying Fortresses, or Libs and Forts as they were called. Darin and I were "B-24 Boys," just as our fathers had been. Researcher, Kevin, was clearly a "B-17 Boy," and we took turns good-naturedly singing the praises of our respective favorite planes. I found there was also a rivalry between the 8th and 15th Air Forces during the war. The men of the Fifteenth Air Force sarcastically composed a ditty, sung to the tune of "As Time Goes By."

> *"It's still the same old story, the Eighth gets all the glory, while we go out to die. The fundamental things apply, as flak goes by."*

Ed continued to answer any question I threw his way. Within what seemed like an instant, he fired back prisoner of war numbers, planes' serial numbers, phone numbers, German archives and newspapers, addresses and anything else that would help me in my quest, including translations. He also kept me informed of what the weather was doing in Belgium.

Almost daily, new leads arrived in my inbox, as emails were sent from names I did not know. Increasingly, the names of senders became German.

There were still missing pieces of the puzzle, and I gradually realized that I had to visit Germany not only to find the crash site, but to re-trace my father's footsteps and see the places he had spoken of over the years that I was now reading about in the military archive documents, both American and German. I wondered what the surroundings looked like the day he parachuted out of the sky. I wondered where he was held. I longed to see the big fir trees of Silesia in Sagan that surrounded Stalag Luft III and to walk upon the cobble-stoned road he marched upon when evacuated from the camp in January, 1945. I felt I had to see the cemetery where the crew had left the body of Harold Flaugher, as my father had spoken of that sad moment in his life so often. And if at all possible, I was determined to find at least a small piece of his plane and bring it back to him.

I looked up more names in my father's Second Air Division Journals as I received them in the mail. I located ex-POW Tom Watt in Canada. He had visited Stalag Luft III many times with his wife, Bernice, and the two of them answered my questions on location and hotels, and whether retracing the march route was feasible. Flight Lieutenant Tom Watt had flown as a pilot with the Royal Canadian Air Force. When he was returning from a night raid on Turin, Italy, the Germans shot out one of his engines. As he flew low over Paris, the Germans shot out his only remaining engine causing him to bail out at just three-hundred feet, landing in a railroad yard in Paris in 1942. Tom was a prisoner of war held in the notorious Fresnes Prison in Paris and had been beaten repeatedly by the Gestapo. Both of his hands were broken, and he was beaten black and blue. He had been sent to Frankfurt by the Germans, but his train was bombed along the way, so he ended up in Sagan.

Once again, I saw the fierce loyalty to fallen comrades. After eight trips back to the camp, now in Zagan, Poland, (formerly Sagan) Tom's health was failing, and he was disappointed he could not return there for the 60$^{th}$ anniversary of "The Great Escape." Letters from Tom and Bernice followed advising me on the best way to get to Poland and to whom to speak when I got to the camp.

If I was to find the location of "Rhapsody in Junk's" final resting place, my research necessitated turning more to the German archives. The German KU report in the MACR had given the scant German details, but there was enough to make inquiries. With Ed's help giving me websites and interpreting for me, I contacted several German archives and waited for replies.

One day, as I was doing research and waiting for German replies to my inquiries, I saw a posting on a website. It was signed by Hanns Scharff. Surely, this could not be the Master Interrogator from Dulag Luft! He would be well into his nineties by now. I read further. The posting I noted was from his son. It stated that in 2002, The Los Angeles Sunday Times had a front page article on how the United States Armed Forces were gathering intelligence from members of the Taliban and Al-Qaida. The head of the unit told the reporters that he kept his desk stocked with copies of a book, "The Interrogator," that was practically required reading for his team. The article went on to say that the book used told the story of Hanns Scharff, the master German interrogator, who during World War II coaxed secrets from countless American pilots while barely raising his voice. The son added that he found it strange that his father's interrogation techniques were having an effect on our war against terror. There was an email address, and I typed off a quick email.

"Over sixty years ago, did your father interrogate my father?" I asked pointedly.

The reply came back immediately telling me the son had his father's old records, and he would check. Shortly afterward Hanns Claudius Scharff emailed me that his father only interrogated fighter pilots, but he could have known my father. Claudius told me he was interviewed recently about his father, and I tuned into the History Channel a few days later to watch his interview. Soon, Claudius and

I were exchanging many emails. Besides information on Germany and the war, Claudius regaled me with hilarious tales of his many trips selling aircraft around the world. He had a wicked tongue-in-cheek writing style that left me laughing many a day.

Claudius asked me about a "guestbook" his father had kept at Dulag Luft with signatures and comments from the pilots he interrogated. He knew that his father had donated it to the Wright-Patterson Air Force Museum, and he longed to have a copy of it. I called the reference archivist there, who got in touch with Claudius, and soon we both had a copy of the guestbook. Many of the downed airmen had drawn sketches, written poems and often warm letters to Hanns, affectionately known to his family as Hannsi. I continued to update Claudius on my father's condition and my research to find the crash site. What an ironic twist this all had taken.

Ed had since found one more kriegie roommate, Don Stout, living in California. I contacted him, and he sent me a lecture he gave at local schools about his war experiences. In his talks he discussed Hanns Scharff. I told him that Scharff's son was living not far from him in California. Happily, the two made telephone contact and planned to meet.

Soon an email arrived written in German from a Wulf Pingel a German archivist. Claudius translated it for me.

> "…I could find a reference to the exact crash place of the airplane of your father in the literature. In the diary of a Kiel resident…Detlef Boelck, which was published under the title "Kiel in the Air War 1939-1945" in the Society for Kiel Urban History, volume 13 in the year 1980, for June 1944, the following entry is under the date 18: "Over 70 bomber airplanes flew over to attack Hamburg. Occasionally, they were fired at by our Flak. A bomber flew very deeply over the city away and fell north of Kappeln. With that the diary entry ends. The city of Kappeln is directly at the delta of the River Schlei into the Baltic Sea, approximately 40 kilometers south of the Danish border."

I looked on a map of Germany to find Kappeln and the Schlei and traced the route from Kiel with my finger. I found an internet address for an archive in Kiel, and I emailed the Landes-Hauptstadt Archives trying to locate the crash site and also to ask about the burial place of Flaugher. I received a reply from Jutta Briel. She sent me abstracts from the day of June 18th, 1944. The abstracts showed a map where the plane went down past Eckernforde and Schleswig toward the northeast closer to Flensburg. An arrow pointed toward Sweden, Northrop's intended route. A second abstract stated that a Liberator flew low over Kiel at 10:35 a.m., and at 10:52 a.m., it was near Quern, NW of Kappeln. Nine parachutes were spotted.

"Dear Mrs. Walton,

We got your question about Harold Flaugher. In our records we found that on June 18, 1944, a bomber, Type Liberator was shot and crashes over the village Quern near by Kappeln. 9 of the crew got out by parachute. But there is nothing said about the one who didn't survived. So we ask the archive in Kappeln, we will inform you as soon as we get the answer. If you tell us your full address we want to send you copies from our records.

Jutta

Later, Jutta reported that Kappeln's archive had no information. A second email followed.

If you are sure that Harold Flaugher was buried in a cemetery in Kiel, I think it must be the "Nordfriedhof," Westring 481 c, 24118 Kiel.
I wish you good luck and a nice journey to Germany. If you have time on May 17, you can visit me and the archive in the town hall."

There were so many from so far away, who could offer pieces of the puzzle ascertaining "Rhapsody in Junk's" resting place. But world-wide input was just beginning. I found Quern on the map.

The area was more limited now but not exact. Frustrated in my ability to locate the exact location, I continued my research, hoping I would stumble on something. I asked Ed about Quern.

"....in fact, Quern is but a village and is administered by the city of STEINBERGKIRCHE."

Ed gave me an address to write to, that of Margrit Henningsen-Klein.

"From: Henningsen-Klein, Margrit

Subject: Visit to Quern

Hello Mrs. Walton,

For your research I can give you two addresses of the chronicle-group of Quern: Mr. Georg-Heinrich Jürgensen, Südsteinberg 4, 24972 Steinberg, also Mr. Hartwig Martensen, Norgaardholz 20, 24972 Steinberg. An old colleague of mine, who has lived in Quern that time, cannot remember a crash in Quern."

I chose the second name listed, Mr. Hartwig Martensen, and wrote a letter asking for his help. I also wrote letters to two German newspapers in the vicinity of Quern. Then I waited.

## Chapter 50

# *Letters from Matthias*

One morning I turned on my computer and saw an email from Germany. The name was unfamiliar to me.

"Matthias Martensen

Sent:   Saturday, March 27, 2004

Subject: Germany, 1944

Dear Ms. Walton:

You have written a letter to Mr. Hartwig Martensen who is my grandfather. I have translated your letter to him.

Meanwhile my grandfather has collected information about the plane crash of 18th June 1944. He also found contemporary witnesses remembering the accident.

We'll be telling you about that soon. I live in Iserlohn a town near Dortmund which is about 500 kilometres away from my grandfather's village.

My grandfather and I hope that we have been able to help you.

Sincerely yours,

Matthias Martensen (14 years)"

Mr. Martensen, a local historian, had received my letter but spoke no English, and thankfully, he passed my letter to his English-speaking grandson to translate. I was ecstatic and most curious to learn what Mr. Martensen had found. He had been contacted by a man at one of the newspapers I had written to about the same time I wrote to him as suggested by Margrit Henningsen. Mr. Martensen was aware of a book written by another local historian, Gretchen Bartel, and she had devoted several pages to the plane crash.

A follow-up email from Matthias quickly arrived.

"Now I would like to report on the information which my grandfather Hartwig Martensen collected with Mr. Jürgensen's help. My grandfather found out something about the plane crash on 18$^{th}$ June, 1944 in the chronicle "Zur Geschichte der Gemeinde Wagersrott." The contemporary witness Gretchen Bartel explains on page 243: 'Later, the enemy planes flew above us during the day, too. So one day we could watch a plane, which was shot down by an anti-aircraft gun and came down burning. You saw a man who opened a hatch and made a slow parachute jump. The man landed on "Schlornkjer" and was arrested by a police constable. The plane crashed into a wood in Blick next to Brückner's house.'

The location of the crash in Blick is near the village Süderbrarup in Schleswig-Holstein. (There wasn't a plane crash in Quern.) Frau Bartel would like to help you for further information."

Matthias Martensen, from Iserlohn, Germany, served as my translator and was instrumental in connecting the author with the Germans who knew of the crash site.

Courtesy of Mrs. Gerhard Martensen

Matthias gave me Frau Bartel's address in Wagersrott.

Jutta also questioned whether the crew would have returned to Kiel. All of the towns mentioned to me, even Quern, were fairly close together, but Kiel was over forty-five minutes by train, and to drive that distance entailed going around or across the many fjords taking a good bit of time and precious German gasoline which was becoming scarce. I began to doubt whether the cemetery I was looking for was in Kiel. Jutta felt the same way.

...I can't believe that the crew of the bomber was transported to Kiel after shot down, the cities of Flensburg or Schleswig are much nearer to Quern.

I emailed with the Second Air Division Library in Norwich, England, and I wrote more postings for the 8th Air Force message boards. Helpful strangers around the world came to my aid and assisted me in obtaining documents and aged files.

As I tentatively made my plans, letters written on thin paper came in the mail adorned with colorful German stamps and notations. One long letter, written completely in German, came from Frau Gretchen Bartel. My phone rang one afternoon, and Angela Goetzke, an English woman married after the war to a German, Manfred Goetzke, now a retired jeweler, was on the line from Germany. She told me she was related to Gretchen Bartel by the marriage of their children, and she wanted to tell me Gretchen had received my mail. Gretchen wanted to tell me of her experiences of June 18th, 1944! Angela would act as translator. I told Angela that I had hoped to find the cemetery, but I was unclear whether it was in Kiel, Schleswig, Flensburg or Kappeln.

Her call came several weeks later. She and Manfred had walked down row after row of graves looking for the name Flaugher on a tombstone. To search the silent and numerous cemeteries brought the enormity of the war and the waste of human lives back to her. I had pretty much decided trying to find the cemetery would be like trying to find a needle in a haystack, and I turned my attention back to the crash site.

Angela knew the terror of the war well. She was born on Edgware Road, the very heart of Cockney London. By the time the German bombings there began in the fall of 1940, she was six-and-a-half years old. At the outbreak of war her parents rented a house in Ealing, a suburb of London, in hopes that the family would be safe from the bombs. As the London bombing increased, Angela's father rented the upper floor of a semi-detached house in Marlow-on-Thames, which was considered to be far enough away from London to escape the danger. Each Friday, when school was completed, her father packed the car to the roof in the evening. Angela and her younger brother, and both parents, set off to the country retreat. The landlady was friendly and kind, and although the journey out of London was sometimes very frightening and stressful for the family, for some months they avoided danger.

Normally, the family returned to London late on Sunday night with the children sleeping in the car on the way home. One weekend, for some completely unknown reason, Angela's parents decided that they should spend the Sunday night also in Marlow and return to London/Ealing very early on Monday morning. The alarm clocks were set, and at 5:00 a.m. on Monday, the sleepy family climbed into the packed car.

Arriving in London two hours later, they pulled up to the location of their home at 11 Layer Earden. They gazed in utter horror seeing the home had received in the night a direct bomb hit. It no longer existed. An unexplained instinct had saved them, and they had to find refuge with relatives for the duration of the war.

Angela Gotzke with her mother and brother, Noel, in the yard of their home shortly before it was destroyed by German bombs
Courtesy Mrs. Manfred Gotzke

After the war came to a close, Angela visited, and later worked in Switzerland, where she met a young German named Manfred who wanted to become a jeweler. Years later, they married and had four children, one girl and three boys. All three boys served in the German Navy.

## Chapter 51

# IDPF

Max Flaugher sent me his daughter-in-law, Tracy's, email address so I could learn of the birth of her son. His name was Jack Flaugher, having taken his deceased great uncle's middle name. She sent me the baby's picture, and the resemblance to the face in the crew picture was striking. The Flaughers had a strong German heritage she told me, and her own family had had several German exchange students over the years.

My father kept in touch with the Flaugher family after the war ended. Max came to visit at my parents' home several times, and he and my father speculated on the wartime death of Max's brother. Each time they talked, my father questioned if there was not some other explanation for Flaugher's death. I think he hoped against hope that Flaugher died in some other fashion than at the hands of civilians on the ground. My father told Max that he wondered if Flaugher had not hit a building on the way down. Max also told him that Harold had had a heart condition before the war and had gotten some kind of waiver to join up. They wondered if he did not have a heart attack after bailing out. My father could no longer have these discussions with Max, so I tried to pick up where he left off. I am sure, given the opportunity, my father would have welcomed yet one more informed opinion. Over the years, he wrote letters and talked to anyone who would talk to him about the death hoping to gather more information. He would have been so happy to know that just maybe there could be a more civil cause of his death. To know that would have eased his pain over the horrible loss of his friend.

I obtained Harold Flaugher's IDPF, (Individual Deceased Personnel File) after Sam Cole, who worked with veterans' families, told me how to obtain it. He was an expert in forensics and investigated many WWII deaths in Europe over the years traveling to Europe and examining remains and graves.

I told Sam the details the crew had reported of the death and gave him all the information they could provide.

Sam's analysis raised some interesting questions.

He wondered about the lack of blood on Flaugher's body. The pressure of any weapon to kill so quickly that blood does not leave the body through the mouth or ears made him speculate further.

> "Even when the brain dies, the heart will beat enough for blood to come out of openings. Whatever happened to Flaugher also stopped his heart at the same instant to cause a bloodless death. When bailing out of an aircraft, the parachutist was supposed to count down or up from a number, first to let the aircraft fly away from them and secondly, to permit their forward momentum to subside before pulling the "D Ring." This prevented overloading the parachute and the chance that the parachutist would either be struck by the aircraft or his parachute become caught on the aircraft. The chest-type parachute worn by Flaugher quickly twisted a man so he was facing upwards toward the bomber, and the quickly deploying parachute caused him to pivot upwards as the bomber rushed back. As it did so, the right side of his head and his chest impacted against one of the two large vertical stabilizers which could

have damaged his right earphone and caused the injury seen on his head by the other crewmen when they saw his body."

Sam also said that other descriptions of men killed by striking the aircraft match the condition of Flaugher's remains identically--super pressure and body damage, but little or no blood. He had no blood on his clothing, nor was it damaged in any way. It also appeared he had no wounds to his hands which would have naturally flown up to protect his face had he been attacked. Sam continued. His comparison of B-17 and B-24 bailouts were thought-provoking.

"The B-24 had two tail booms. That is why I think he was pitched up into one. The big fear with the B-17 was going out the waist door. One had to dive down. If they went out straight, the tail could clip them before they cleared it. From the bomb bay or front hatch, the tail wheel was the big worry, as an early chute would catch on the tail wheel and take the person down with it.

Wear a chest chute, which most did, and the wind immediately rolled them over. From the front hatch of a B-17, the Bombardier of the B-17, I have been researching so long, had time to be rolled over and to see the man hanging under the tail as he fell away. Coming out of a B-24, Flaugher would not have had the same distance, it would have been a bit shorter and perhaps, he only turned part way over, which would easily explain, that if he had an early chute opening, it would have swung him into the a tail boom hard enough to do exactly what happened, instant death."

In other cases Sam had investigated he found that especially when men were afraid to jump, they held the D ring to activate release of their parachute very tightly, and then they pulled it too soon. Unlike Flaugher, some men even had their parachutes open in the plane before they attempted their jump when a plane was losing altitude as quickly as "Rhapsody" was doing.

"As the bomber rushed back" was an interesting phrase. It made me wonder if the bomber did not change direction just before it crashed, as it lost its engines and all control, and if it could have done that just as Flaugher was exiting.

I wondered what my father would have thought of all this years ago if he had been able to evaluate the forensics information. Could it have been that Flaugher was already dead on the way down?

The IDPF arrived, and one night I combed through each page. Much to my surprise I found that for years the graves in the German military cemetery were reversed. The grave marked as Flaugher's had actually been that of another airman who bailed out and drowned at Kiel that day. The body characteristics did not match those of Flaugher. For almost three years, a German cross bearing the Flaugher name had been placed on the grave next to Flaugher's actual burial place. The mistake was discovered when the two bodies were exhumed after the war to be moved to the military cemetery in Belgium, not far from Ed's home. Many of the pages gave graphic accounts of the exhumations and comparisons. Tucked away in these pages was a crude hand-drawn diagram of a German cemetery with row and section designations. One block read "American Section." At the bottom it gave a street address.

I immediately called Angela in Germany and told her what I had found. "Schleswig Military Cemetery, on Husumerstr." The street address on my diagram confirmed this was the correct cemetery. Angela told me she would find it, and she did.

I emailed Ed asking if he knew how many B-24s total had been shot down on the 18th of June.

"There were seven. B-24 -41-28733, 458BG/754BS
– (This was your Dad's plane.)"

Seven B-24s had Missing Air Crew Reports for that day, and most went down over Germany. Only one, my father's, went down in the area that I had more narrowly defined.

Matthias shed more light on the subject:

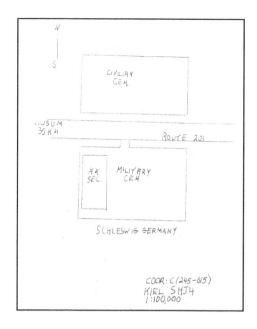

This hand-drawn map included with the IDPF provided the location of the German cemetery where the Northrop crew brought Sgt. Flaugher's body in 1944. AM designation in one section of the map indicates the American section.

"My grandfather has just phoned me. Now I would like to write you what he told me. He was in Blick and looked at the location of the crash. There you can still see a hollow today. The wreckage of the plane had been removed after the end of the war. I am going to answer the questions from your last e-mail as soon I'll be getting more information from my grandfather."

The German enthusiasm for this project seemed to be as great as mine. Updates were coming daily.

"You'll find a map on the internet (www.schleidoerferonline.de/fremdenverkehrsverein/karte.htm). It gives you a view of the surroundings in which the plane crashed in 1944. The location of the crash is near Süderbrarup (D/8). Frau Bartel lives in Wagersrott (D/8). You can also find Quern (B/8) on the map. The distance between the villages Blick and Quern is 10 kilometres as the crow flies. Kiel is about 50 kilometres south-east of this area.

You can find Kiel the general map on www.schleidoerferonline.de/fremdenverkehrsverein/

.de/fremdenverkehrsverein/fremdenverkehrsverein.html.

I will mail you the two maps. Only one plane crashed in this area on 18$^{th}$ June, 1944. Therefore, my grandfather believes it must be the plane which you search. Herr Petersen, a contemporary witness, showed my grandfather the location of the crash. It is situated in a wood. Frau Bartel's son-in-law is an English teacher, and he will be able to talk to you and translate your questions. Would you like to call Frau Bartel? Then we can arrange that her son-in-law could be there when you call."

After looking at the maps, my nephew, Tom, measured the distance between Quern and Blick and found it to be less than six miles. I contacted Darin, and with his help, determined that if the plane did not crash in Quern, it could have easily made it to Blick. He assured me it was the only one that crashed that day in the area, and it had to be my dad's plane. With such accurate information in hand, I made reservations to fly to Germany.

## Chapter 52

# *Mission Germany*

John and I flew into Frankfurt and took trains to our numerous destinations. First stop would be Kiel where "Rhapsody" almost crashed.

I told Claudius of my travel plans, and he helped me plan the trip and offered his German insight regarding cuisine, travel distances and our itinerary, particularly in Frankfurt where he was married.

> "Across the river is "Sachsenhausen" a quaint old part of Frankfurt which was not totally destroyed by the incendiary bombs during the war. The place is chock-block full of quaint pubs where "aeppelwoi" (aeppelwoi = apple wine or low alcohol cider) is quaffed in vast quantities. Other gastronomical delights are: Frankfurter Rippchen which are smoked pork chops which would rival a prime rib in size. Simmered beef in "Green Sauce." A specialty devised by Goethe containing a multitude of fresh spring herbs and chopped up boiled eggs in a creamy pale sauce. This sauce combined with the simmered beef

> and new potatoes together with good wine from the area is a fabulous treat!"

The daughter of the prisoner of war once more received help from the son of the Master Interrogator.

Across Germany, the Martensens continued their research.

> "I told my grandfather that you will be in the area of Kiel probably on 17$^{th}$ and 18$^{th}$ May. He is going to organize a meeting at which you can see the contemporary witnesses Frau Bartel and Herr Petersen and my grandfather himself. Frau Bartel and Herr Petersen still remember a lot which happened in June 1944.
>
> I just read your latest mail. I'm very glad that I have done a favour to so many people."

In my enthusiasm and travel planning, I continued to email with Matthias delighting in his replies. I hoped that we could meet. In the back of my mind I had been thinking he lived very close to Blick. I realized only later that he would have to travel eight hours by train across Germany to meet us.

> "Frau Bartel told my grandfather that the hotel in Süderbrarup confirmed your reservation. Unfortunately, I must go to school on May, 17$^{th}$ and 18$^{th}$ but I could go to my grandfather on May, 19$^{th}$. I would take the train and would probably arrive at my grandparents' in the evening. Could we still meet then?"

We would be gone by the 19th, and I felt badly for Matthias. But he was a young man with resolve.

> "My parents will ask my teacher to let me off for the 17$^{th}$ and 18$^{th}$ May 2004 that I will be able to meet you. Could you please write a few lines to my class teacher as well? Have you already made an appointment to meet Frau Bartel?"

Now, I could do something for Matthias. I immediately sent off a letter to his teacher, Herr Keese.

> "Everything went well. Herr Keese will let me off for 17th and 18th May.
>
> Thank you so much for your long letter which you wrote him. He read it with much interest. I am already looking forward to see you."

In exchange for a written report from Matthias for the school yearbook, Mr. Keese released him from school. I hoped to find a nice gift to take to Matthias to show my appreciation for all he had done for me. I asked him what sports teams he liked.

> "My favourite American sports team is a basketball team, the Dallas Mavericks. I like this team because the "German Wunderkind" Dirk Nowitzki plays there."

With an anticipated trip to Germany, I asked the remaining men of the crew about their capture. I was not sure where they were held right after capture. Gonzales tried to remember.

> "We were taken to a very intimidating place with big black iron gates. We arrived when it was dark, and it was a very scary-looking place."

He had no memory of the name or location of the interrogation center, but he told me they were taken to the basement and held in cold cells there, and they were very hungry. I emailed Matthias about the fortress-like structure and the big black gates and told him that was all I knew.

His next email proved once more he was a great investigator.

> "Schleswig is not far away from Süderbrarup. You wrote that the men were interrogated in a big fortress-like place. My grandfather believes this place could be "Schloss (=castle) Gottorf" in Schleswig. It used to be barracks, today there is a museum in it."

Not only was I finding valuable information, Matthias was teaching me German. What little German I knew was mostly derived from the words my father remembered as a prisoner. Terms like "'RAUS!" would not help me much on my trip.

I researched Schloss Gottorf, a present-day art and archeological museum. It had been home to the Duke of Schleswig between the Middle Ages and the early eighteenth century. It had also been a barracks for nearly a century up until the late 1940s. Its rectangular inner courtyard was formed at a higher level than the surrounding ground, which made the castle cellar approachable from ground level outside the foundation. The castle could have easily contained the cells where the crew was held.

With an additional place to explore, it was time to leave the United States. The date was set for May 16th for us to arrive in Germany. Matthias and his grandfather helped with train schedules. After nearly a year of preparation and research our plans were set, and we were very excited to leave on our journey into the past. Angela called several times, once asking if we minded if a German newspaper reporter accompanied us to the crash site. I assured her that we did not mind and welcomed the opportunity to speak with him.

I sat with my father all day on the 14th and into the evening. I told him of our trip and that Diane would be down to care for him and keep him company while I was gone.

The phone rang at nine in the morning on the 15th of May, as we were closing our suitcases. Diane was calling. Knowing of my departure, the nursing facility had called her believing I was already gone. Our father had had a stroke.

## Chapter 53

## *Deutschland*

With packed bags in the car, we raced to the emergency room of the hospital. My father was lying in one of the rooms, but he seemed alert when we arrived. He said he did not know why they brought him there. We waited with him as a CT scan was done, and he was evaluated. The scan did not show anything, so we were told to take him home. He seemed alert and a little confused, but we had seen that for more than a year. When the doctor released him to the nursing facility, we arranged for Diane to fly down later that day. With a heavy heart, I prepared to leave for Germany. We caught our flight and with much worry and trepidation, we flew east.

John and I landed in Frankfurt the next morning where we immediately boarded a train for Kiel. We wanted something to eat, but not too much. I walked back to the dining car and read the menu of items that could be bought and taken back to our car. A basket of German bread sounded good, although my father's wartime ration of it was not his favorite. I attempted to order the good modern-day variety with my best "brot" pronunciation. Confident I was successful in this endeavor, I was a bit deflated when I was handed two Cokes and one scrambled egg. I turned away with a smile, as though that was exactly what I ordered and returned to our car where John and I drank the Cokes and split the egg.

The train sped through Hannover and then Kassel, a name I noted. It was in a raid on Kassel that we lost so many bombers so many years before. We arrived in Hamburg to change trains. The glass canopy over the tracks arched high, and having been replaced after repeated bombings looked much newer than the station, a repeated pattern we would see at most of our train stations.

The oil refineries of Hamburg were a prime target during the war as the Allies made a concerted effort to knock out all of them. It was in Hamburg where "Rhapsody" got into trouble as German troops down below fired on the formation, and it was hard to shake the feeling of that long ago day as I looked up at the skies there.

Our hotel in Kiel, recommended by Kevin, was beautiful and sat at the edge of the estuary. We strolled down the driveway and short hill by a forest to reach the water. Though tired from our trip, we were determined to walk through the town. My father had spoken of Kiel for so many years. In a steeply declining airplane, as a smoke cover hid the city that day, his view of the estuary there was far different than mine.

We passed the small boats and huge ferries bobbing in the estuary and glanced across the water where the ships were moored at the German Naval Base. My father had told me he had been taken to a guard house in Kiel by German Marines, but after asking around we could find no trace of it and from Jutta Briel's comments, I still felt he had been taken somewhere else.

We were seeing a modern-day Kiel with our own eyes, not the eyes of enemy combatants. Remnants of the past war were hidden in the modernity, if one knew where to look. We passed a carved dedication to German Marines of WWII. I asked some Germans if they could tell me about the carving, but they said they did not know what it was. We walked past a black-stained bunker where we were told Germans fled during bombing raids. How many panicked people of Kiel must have raced here as air raid sirens screamed, and the drone of bombers blanketing the sky reeled from the crack of

Kiel's flak battalions? We returned to the hotel with a sense of what Kiel had been. It was a beautiful place.

The next morning, after a huge breakfast overlooking the Kiel Harbor—everything from sushi to champagne and fruits of every kind arranged in an artistic display, we took a taxi to the train station. Along the way, we found the office of Jutta Briel in the archive, and we stopped in to meet her and thank her for her help. We climbed the staircase that led into the rooms stacked tall with dusty volumes where Germans sat at the tables and worked. After talking to Jutta, we left to catch the 12:41 p.m. train to Suderbrarup.

Forty-five minutes later we were standing on the platform of the train station in Suderbrarup. Our trip from Kiel to Suderbrarup certainly took much longer than it had taken for the crippled B-24.

The train eased to a slow stop at the station where the group of smiling German faces greeted us. Our journey back in time together was about to begin.

## Chapter 54

# Friends We've Yet to Meet

On the train platform, Matthias tried his best to translate for us, but at times I'm sure we overwhelmed him. We all shook hands and spoke in German and English. Frau Bartel had to return to her home where we would meet up with her later. We would also meet Angela and her husband there along with the newspaper reporter.

Matthias and his grandparents walked us across the street to our hotel. We took our bags to our room, a cozy hideaway adorned with antiques. A chocolate bug sat on each pillow. We went back downstairs and joined our new friends for tea in the quaint dining room. I showed Hartwig my father's crew picture. His eyes passed slowly from face to face, as he ran his tanned gnarled finger over the old black and white photo of the youthful happy faces. What war memories these faces must have evoked. I recognized a few German words that he spoke--vater, meaning father, and flugzeug, meaning plane.

"How many are alive?" he finally asked Matthias in German.

I showed him my father and pointed to three more that I knew of, and he slowly nodded his head. His former wartime enemies

Matthias's grandfather, Hartwig
Martensen, in his German uniform
Courtesy of Mrs. Hartwig Martensen

had never been seen smiling this way. I asked Matthias to ask his grandfather of his own war experiences. Hartwig's eyes became large, and he was animated in his speech. He, too, had been a prisoner of war. He was held in Belgium by the Allies at a very young age. Membership in the Hitler Youth became compulsory in 1936 for boys between twelve and eighteen years old. I thought of the devastation to his country he must have seen there as a young boy. Matthias was only two years younger than his grandfather had been as a German soldier.

Matthias's Oma watched silently as we all spoke. I had brought her an American teddy bear with a red, white and blue sweater emblazoned with the letters U.S.A. I told Matthias to tell his grandmother she would have to give the bear a name. She smiled as he told her. At first she said nothing. As our conversation continued about the war and the crew, none of which she understood, suddenly her eyes lit up and with a big grin, she called out, "Bruno!" The bear had a name.

When World War II broke out on September 1, 1939, her thirty-six-year-old mother was alone with three children. Her mother had the sole responsibility of working thirty hectares of a large farm. Her father had died two weeks before the war started, and Ilse, age ten, and her siblings, thirteen and two, were left fatherless.

When the family's farm assistant was called up for military service, it was the children who had to help on the farm despite their young ages. Another assistant was found, but Adolf Hitler required his services also, and so he was drafted leaving Ilse's mother once more to fend for herself. As the war progressed, the farm was sent an eighteen-year old Polish prisoner of war. He was offered, and later obtained, German citizenship and was called up for military service only to later die in the war. Two more prisoners were sent, a Frenchman and a Russian, and a good relationship developed with the family and the men.

The family farm was home to cows, horses, sheep and poultry, all of which the family relied upon. Strong horses pulled the wagons and plows through fields of oat, rye and barley and along the straight rows of turnips and potatoes. A grassy meadow provided space for livestock. The turnips and grain fed the livestock, and the potatoes stored in the cellar for winter fed the family. As long as it was possible, grain was harvested and delivered to customers in town.

The children were expected to help with chores in the house and in the fields. Ilse milked the cows and fed the animals. Summer days meant longer days, and Ilse pitched in to assist with the hay and grain harvests. To maximize the crucial crops, the turnip and potato fields had to be hoed, and the young children worked beside the prisoners.

Hartwig Martensen turned twelve just two days before the Second World War began. When his father, who was an elementary school teacher, told him of the war, tears welled up in his father's eyes. Painful memories returned, and he told Hartwig of losing his brother and uncle to the last wretched war.

The spring of 1940 found Hartwig going to a boarding school in Kappeln. He had his mandatory medical examination for military service at the age of approximately fifteen. In the summer of 1944, when he was seventeen, like all the other boys, he was drafted into the HJ (Hitler Youth), and he left school. He was deployed in

Ostseebad Dahme at the Lübeck Bucht (Bay) where he looked after children who were sent to the country for protection against bomb attacks in the local towns. Hartwig later trained in Lübeck for six weeks. On December 15th, 1944, he became a soldier in Göttingen. He had a gun, but so late in the war his captain led the unit around the battles, so he did not have to fight.

As he was going off to war, Ilse tirelessly worked the farm fields. Fortunately, the farm provided a source of food for the family. Still they lacked essential products, so they were issued food ration cards for what they could not produce. Certain foods like sugar, margarine, cereal and luxury goods were scarce for the farm families as they were for other families. The family was rationed just one-hundred-twenty-five grams of butter per person each week. Short of adequate clothing and shoes, they were also issued cards for those items when they were available.

At the age of fourteen, when Hartwig was being prepared to enter the Hitler Youth, Ilse was confirmed and didn't have to attend school any more. Girls did not get a higher education. From that time on, she worked full-time on the farm. A typical working day started at 5:00 a.m. and finished at 7:00 p.m. In the open fields, Ilse froze with terror when Allied bombers flew over the planted rows and scattered the livestock. A house had been bombed in Husum, nearby, killing a German there. At Ilse's farm house, the family darkened their living room for protection in the evening. Throughout the war, Ilse's mother never mentioned Adolf Hitler to her as her family struggled to survive on the farm, suffering all the daily deprivations that war brings. They were far removed from the political dealings that initiated the war, but they were reaping the harvest of its destruction.

As the war progressed, and Allied bombers penetrated deeper into Germany, the farm house sheltered more people. When Kiel and Hamburg were bombed, families with children were sent to the country for safety. Ilse's mother took in two families trying to find room for them. Later, refugees from the east traveling on horse carts lived with the over-crowded family, as they were forced to take everyone who arrived.

Air raid sirens wailed in Kiel, and just before the war's end, Ilse's thirty-six-year-old aunt took refuge from the falling bombs in a black-stained shelter there. At the sound of the all clear, she and another woman went out to shop, but a bomb fell from the sky and killed them both. Ilse's aunt left a husband and son.

On April 8th 1945, Hartwig slept in a farm house with his unit. During the night, British soldiers made a raid, and he was taken prisoner in Westerkappeln in North Rhine-Westphalia, Germany. He was sent to a camp near Mechelen in Belgium. At just seventeen, he was detained with more than sixty-thousand other prisoners of war. It was just a little over two weeks later, the Northrop crew was liberated in Moosburg.

At war's end, Ilse had learned of an uncle seriously injured while fighting in Russia. Her cousin, fighting in Fulda, fell victim to Allied bombs and lost his right arm. Two of Hartwig's cousins died in the war having never returned from Russia. Two other cousins were loaded into a ship and brought to the United States as prisoners of war.

Eight months later, Hartwig was released from imprisonment feeling not so young as when he entered the war. He boarded a train on a cold December day to ride from Mechelen to Bad Segeberg in an open railroad car. He was trucked to Flensburg where he received his discharge papers, and he returned home to his parents and brother. The town was full of starving German refugees. Hartwig was jobless and hungry until he was hired by a farmer three months later. In November, 1946, he started an apprenticeship and became a tax consultant.

In 1948, Ilse moved from the farm and started an apprenticeship in home economics on another farm. One day, handsome Hartwig Martensen visited the farm working there as an accountant, and the two struck up a friendship. His visits became more frequent. On November 13th, 1953, they married in Ilse's home church in Mildstedt near Husum.

After her marriage, Ilse left the farm to her sister and moved away with her new husband. At that time, it was difficult to find a flat as refugees coming into the area required housing. With no place to live, the newlyweds moved in with Hartwig's parents where they had very little space. Finally, they were able to buy an almost new house in Norgaardholz, a little village on the Baltic Sea in the "Geltinger Bucht" (Bay). They raised three children there, and Hartwig retired in 1990. They stayed in the same home for over fifty years where they celebrated their golden wedding anniversary with their children and eight grandchildren.

I asked Matthias about his grandfather's involvement in the war.

> "My grandfather told me he wasn't able to imagine the meaning of war when he was a pupil. When the war started, he went to school as usual and life did not really change. Later, of course, he more and more realized and experienced what war was really like."

We had brought Matthias a Dirk Nowitzki jersey. He tried it on at the table, and it fit perfectly. We gave his grandfather an Uncle Sam figurine with comical hat and clothing, and he thanked us profusely for it.

We returned to our hotel room for a short rest, and the Martensens returned to pick us up to take us to the Bartel's home. Wagersrott, situated in Schleswig-Holstein, sat adjacent to Blick not far from Denmark. Claudius had told me Blick translated meant view, look or countenance. The view along our drive was beautiful. It was not a long drive, and we drove past more fields of rapeseed flowers brilliantly yellow in their brief May display. We passed large green farm fields and grazing tan and white mottled cows lazily ambling through the green pastures. Modern-day windmills turned their long reaching arms in slow rotation. Other than the windmills, not much had changed in Schleswig-Holstein. Time had stood still here.

The area was so different than I had imagined. I decided if my father had to parachute into enemy hands below, he could not have picked a more serene, tranquil and beautiful place. All the years I imagined him under heavy fire near the water at Kiel when he fell from the sky. I had imagined all the enemy guns firing at him on some dark afternoon amidst smoke and raging fire. But the flak guns were in Barklesby some distance away, and the tranquil cows I watched now were no doubt descendents of those kept in the same sunny fields that day so long ago. It gave me an odd feeling of peace to know that this was where he descended as his plane was blown out of the sky.

## Chapter 55

# Into the Woods

Within minutes, we drove up a long gravel and dirt road, and there before us sat the long thatched-roof home of Gretchen Bartel. She and her husband, Juergen, were standing out front to greet us as well as the newspaper reporter, Claus Kuhl, who had come to cover our trip. The Bartel's black dog, Pluto, pranced and spun like a pinwheel in greeting. Juergen Bartel greeted us with an enormous smile. He had farmed the land for many years, and his tanned face and arms spoke volumes of his hard work. Gretchen, short, blond and sprightly, once again welcomed us warmly with her dancing blue eyes.

Angela, a stately and handsome woman, approached us and introduced us to Manfred, who spoke perfect English. He had grown up in Bremershaven, a town the bomber stream had passed. He told of us of waking up one morning after a bomber raid to find a piece of shrapnel on his pillow. I had read mission reports of the bomber stream on June 18$^{th}$ passing over Bremershaven. I did not ask Manfred the date of that occurrence.

What happened next was a cacophony of excited German and English voices rapidly exchanging enthusiastic comments and a litany of questions. Matthias, Angela and Manfred struggled to keep up. Mr. Kuhl took pictures at every turn for the newspaper. I showed the group the crew picture and a picture of the plane. They marveled at the sheer size and heaviness of the plane. Gretchen looked wistful as she finally saw fully the plane that lurched and sputtered over her roof that summer day. She had seen its camera hatch open and the airman float down. The plane had shattered into pieces like a dropped glass ornament only moments after its approach and within seconds disintegrated into a smoking pile of rubble. She studied it for a long time in silence.

Adjacent to the dirt road stood a pen holding curious Nannie, the Bartel's forty-five-year-old black and white pony. Ancient and slow, she ambled to the fence to watch us. We were, indeed, a motley group assembled on this spot.

Gretchen's memories and descriptions fascinated me. Our desire to see the crash site overcame us, and after a brief burst of German conversation, we piled into cars. Our entourage followed closely as we wound past farm fields and down narrow roads, dirt flying up behind each car. We stopped midway there to pick up another eye witness, Ernst Hansen, who also spoke no English. He greeted us warmly. He was sixteen at the time of the crash and had farmed the land ever since. He had lost almost all of his family members in the war. It was becoming clear that the cruelty of the war knew no single nationality.

The cars slowed down, and we entered a narrow dirt road that ran past grazing cows. We pulled up near the woods and parked. German and English once again intermingled against the background of the soft lowing of cows in the pasture as we all trekked into the woods. Ernst Hansen, who had made the trek to the woods as a curious boy sixty years before, led the way into the cool green forest.

We walked for a short distance when he pointed to the left. Where towering trees once stood, there was a clearing of spindly young trees nowhere near the size of the surrounding massive trees. Ernst pointed to four indentations in the ground where the engines

Ernst Hansen indicates where the four engines of "Rhapsody in Junk" left indentations in the ground.
Courtesy of Mr. Matthias Martensen

hit, and he spoke enthusiastically in German. Motioning with his arms, he described how the fiery plane had slammed into the forest, and its tail twisted off and hit on the other side of the path. A glance in that direction indicated the same young branch-like trees now growing where the ground had been burned so many years ago. With fire and explosions that day, the ground shook hard, and old growth there was consumed. Young trees, resilient and strong, grew up it their places as naturally as young soldiers replace old.

We all walked quietly in the woods looking at the ground, hoping to find something. I tried to picture this area cordoned off by the young German soldiers to protect the curious public from exploding shell fragments. We poked around with sticks but found nothing.

From the woods, we went by the house at the edge of the farm field where the farmer had lived who picked up my father that day. Angela translated Gretchen's comments for me. She said the farmer had been cutting his field that day when the crippled bomber flew overhead. Gretchen repeated how she had seen the hatch open and one man float downward and land in the field. The farmer ran to him, scrambling over a small fence that was still there. From there, they walked across the field and up the narrow road to his home. This scene was all described so clearly to me as I stood so close to the field that I could visually go back in time and imagine it all. The area had changed so little since that time. It was overwhelming. Soon, we were back in cars, and our entire group turned around to return to Gretchen's home.

This is the field where Jeffers landed after parachuting out of "Rhapsody in Junk." He landed at the north edge of the field, and the farmer climbed a fence to capture him.

After being taken across the farm field on the right, Jeffers was taken down this path to the farmer's home.

German farmer, Nikolaus Claussen, who picked up Jeffers in his field and brought Jeffers to the farm house

The farm house today

Gretchen's dining room was decorated for our arrival. The dining room table was covered with a beautiful lace table cloth, and delicate china sat at each place. Coffee and tea were served to accompany Matthias's Oma's wonderful apple kuchen and Gretchen's heavenly chocolate dessert. Matthias had told them of my love of chocolate. Cheese was passed on a plate, and our group once more launched into lively conversations. It was as if we had known each other for years and sat around a familiar family dining room table to celebrate

Tea party in Gretchen Bartel's 1625 home. Left to right: Gretchen Bartel, Manfred Goetzke, Angela Goetzke, John Walton, Marilyn Walton, Matthias Martensen, Ilse Martensen, Hartwig Martensen and Ernst Hansen

a holiday. Camera flashes popped at every turn, as we took their pictures, and they took ours.

Gretchen called me into her living room. She showed me the history book she had written about the area, since she was the local historian. She turned to a marked page in the book and held it out for me to see. There was the German account of the day the plane came down that she had mailed to me. There was my father's story recorded for posterity in her book, a book that had been read by many of the villagers over the years, but now by an American with a most unusual reason to be reading it. All these years, none of the

Funeral announcement for German soldier, Karl Hans Grot whose funeral took place the day the crew was captured in the area

Courtesy of Mrs. Gretchen Bartel

crew knew their history had been recorded in Germany. Gretchen's memory took us back to that day.

> "It was Sunday morning when my sister heard the flak and shortly thereafter an airplane approached with a lot of noise. We stood at the back door of our house and looked with fear at the burning airplane. Directly above us, the door of the airplane opened, and a man jumped out. The parachute opened, and he sailed above the big house in the direction of Braupholz. We could hear as the airplane dived and hit the ground nearby, and then it was dead quiet. Our mother was not at home. She was at church as were many of our neighbors, because it was Sunday, and there was a funeral service for Karl Hans Grot, whose airplane had crashed in Lithuania on May 14, 1944, during a training exercise.
> 
> His brother, Theodore, had died in Russia in August, 1943. Three confirmed, Helmut Nissen, George Jensen and Kathi Hansen still remember the approaching, crashing airplane. They thought it would hit the church. The man who jumped from the airplane with his parachute was unhurt and landed on Schlon-kjee Kier, which belonged to the farmer, Peter Trahn. The meadow next to that belonged to Nikolaus Claussen,

and he was mowing. He approached the soldier and took him to his house and gave him some coffee to drink. Police officer Wittenburg from Norderbraup came and took the soldier prisoner. The prisoner was taken to Suderbrarup, and then he was fetched by German soldiers.

The plane crashed in a wood near Blick/Braupholz. It almost crashed onto the house of the family Ericksen who lived in Blick. The mother shrieked, "Get out, get out," and they all threw themselves onto the ground. Her cows that were grazing on a meadow near the woods stampeded and disappeared in panic. They were seriously injured in the barbed-wire fence. Our grandfather, who was draining a meadow, had to throw himself down to the ground. The burning airplane flew over his head. Grandfather Dietz was a master baker in Wagersrott. As soon as he had time, he worked on our farm, as our father was a soldier in Norway. The burning 4-engine plane drilled itself deep into the floor of the forest. For quite awhile, we could hear explosions and saw smoke. My sister and I saw this later on too when we went to the crash site. It was a veritable migration to the crash site. Everything was picked up that was lying around—tin, aluminum and Plexiglas. The crash site was secured and watched over by police and soldiers. A tent was erected where the guards slept. (This was reported by Eliza Ericksen.) The wreck of the airplane was totally dismantled. The four engines were dug out of the ground. When the guards left, everything was gathered lying around, aluminum strips. etc.

The Plexiglas of the pilot's cabin was used for jewelry and for magnifying glasses. The father of the refugee family living on the Ericksen farm used the Plexiglas to make bowls and other kitchen gear. The planes that flew attacks on German cities (Kiel) originated in England. Our area was traversed on the way back to North England. That's why several planes crashed here. The plane which crashed in Blick was shot down by flak in Barklesby. There are crash sites in Blick and other cities. On the north grave yard in Kiel are many soldier graves (military graves partly with name and date of death.) The crash site in Blick you can still see today. You can see the four indentations which the engines left. Ernst Hansen showed us the crash site. It is the forest that belongs to Thiesen Rugge. At the one end of the forest is the Bruckner house. Still many people left today can talk about the crash. There are those who are 70 years old, F.O. Jahninge, Ernst Hansen, Hans-Ludierg Peterson, and our current mayor, George Hansen."

Gretchen gave me a copy of those pages. She also gave me two metal hooks and a metal tea strainer from her museum. These were made, she said, from the aluminum from my father's plane. She beamed as she presented me with these treasures. The plane had changed form, but it was still the plane. John smiled at me knowing instantly the emotional value these simple items held for me.

Gretchen's home was the film site for a German soap opera, The Country Doctor, and in itself was a German tourist attraction. Had the fuel of "Rhapsody's" engines run out seconds sooner, the historic home, built in 1625, would have gone up in flames. Now, busloads of tourists visited weekly, and Gretchen took them on tours of her home and beautiful gardens. She had kept a museum in one wing of the home for years, and she showed us through it. The museum held a myriad of antiques, old clothing, farm implements, German helmets and German memorabilia from the area. Gretchen, dressed in costume with a crisp white apron, escorted her guests through the little museum.

Gretchen Bartel, on the left, at ten years of age, stands with her sisters, Martha and Elli, in Wagersrott, Germany.

Courtesy of Mrs. Gretchen Bartel

Afterward, we toured her kitchen where so many of the scenes from the German television program were shot. Touted as an all-around cure on the program, Juergen passed each of us a small bottle of schnapps. The label of the tiny bottles depicted his historic home. With much laughter, we toasted each other as we stood in a circle in the kitchen and took a swig of schnapps. Then we took a tour of the Bartel's barns to see the cows that had come in from pasture. For some reason the cows were timid with most of us and backed away, but they loved John, and they gathered at their wooden stall rail to lick his arm profusely with their long rough tongues. This was most humorous to the Germans, and they laughed just as heartily as they had watching me taste schnapps for the first time.

Our new friends hugged us when we left. Tears welled up in Gretchen's pale blue eyes. We were closure on a childhood experience that had terrified her decades before. In my own mind, I'd like to think we made it all better. We had lived separate lives for decades both marked by that single event. After a long interval, it was finally shared.

## Chapter 56

# *With Dignity and Honor*

The next morning after breakfast Claus Kuhl dropped by and gave me the picture of the crew he had borrowed for his newspaper article. How good it would be to see that picture in the German newspaper.

It was a warm sunny day when Hartwig dropped off Matthias to us. Angela and Manfred soon arrived, and we all went to the cemetery they had found.

Manfred drove along the waterways and into Schleswig, and we soon arrived at the Schleswig Military Cemetery, Husumerstr. The gravel crunched under the tires of Manfred's car as we slowly drove up near a gateway to the old cemetery. Birds chirped happily that quiet morning as we entered, but no one else was there. We pushed open the old short wooden gate to enter.

Up the path, were old carved German crosses marking a whole section of old burials. There were several sections in the cemetery, each with distinctive markings. I examined my diagram from the IDPF and noted the section called "American." I counted rows and graves. Starting from the first section of the cemetery, I counted horizontally. The number of graves matched the diagram exactly---section C, row

12, grave 19 the MACR had read, and the IDPF backed that up. We took a closer look at that section. All the concrete markers indicated this was a section where Hungarians were buried many years ago during and after the war. Upon closer inspection, I found that there were two newer side by side flat square stones with Hungarian names but no dates, and they were also raised higher than the others and tilted at odd angles where the ground had once been disturbed. Obviously, these were graves where Hungarian bodies were buried at a later date…..after two other bodies had been removed.

This was it. This was Flaugher's former grave.

I was momentarily overcome. All the years I had heard the story of the truck pulling up with the wooden coffin. It was a story my father could not repeat without tears. The pain he and the crew had suffered leaving such a wonderful man behind in the German cemetery was palpable. This is where they had all stood. And this is where they left their comrade behind at a chapel as they continued on not knowing their own fates.

German cemetery in Schleswig-Holstein where Sgt. Harold Flaugher was buried. His grave was just in front of the tree beside another American killed in action the same day.

The IDPF revealed that Harold had not been buried in grave #19 as the family was told, but in grave #18, second from the end of the row. For the years he was interred there, a wooden cross bearing his name stood on the wrong grave.

I had brought a picture of baby Jack Flaugher, Harold's namesake, with me. The baby had been born three-months premature, but he was a fighter and was holding his own. I carried the picture of the smiling little boy in my pocket. I patted that pocket now bringing the young face to this sacred ground where his great uncle had lain sixty years before his birth. I hoped he would exemplify the qualities of this man the whole crew loved and spoke of so highly, and it just seemed right he should be there with us.

The tragedy of the war had visited this land so many times. So many German and Allied deaths for families to contend with, and the repercussions continued for over sixty years. A young namesake would never know his deceased great uncle. At each grave lay the son, father, brother or husband of a grieving relative from a number of countries--men sleeping beneath the earth as the war continued to go on around them. Two men, whose identities were confused after death, had lain here on foreign soil never to be returned to their families. It was almost three years before Graves Registration crews disinterred them, and they were moved to the American Military Cemetery in Belgium at the request of their families.

I remembered that the IDPF revealed that Harold had not been buried in grave #19 as the family was told, but in grave #18, second from the end of the row where he had actually lain. I took a picture of the row of graves for the family correcting a long-held misperception. They were owed at least that much. The chapel was now gone, but the creaking wooden gate remained. We paused to reflect and then left closing the small wooden gate behind us.

## Chapter 57

# Big Black Gates

Manfred drove along the Schlei estuary that sparkled like diamonds in the sun. My father and others on the crew had spoken of the fear of going down in a body of water as they made their descents into enemy hands. Floating through the sky they could see many bodies of water below. We had always thought it was the harbor at Kiel, but this large estuary was more likely what some of the men saw, since they landed in or near Kappeln far past Kiel. The crystalline water could be deceptive and deadly, and other men coming down in this area had drowned. Just ahead, was Schloss Gottorf, the castle that Hartwig had found. It sat directly on the banks of the Schlei. It had been used by the German military as a headquarters and barracks during the war, and they utilized ancient prison cells in the basement. This estuary may have been where the boats had passed the night Gonzales heard them from his cell.

The car turned into a long gravel road. Just ahead, were two big black iron gates. They were just as Gonzales described them. The truck holding the crew would have passed right through them.

Walking around the castle grounds, we tried to determine how we could get down into the basement which was not open to the public. Angela and I walked to another building on the grounds where we were directed to speak with a woman there. Soon, Angela was engaged in an animated German conversation with the woman. Words like "vater" and "terrorflieger" caught my attention. Angela held her ground insisting we be taken to the basement. A call was made, and a man met us in front of the castle and then he took us down below.

Over the years, the basement was changed to accommodate the items that needed to be stored at the castle. Part of it became an art center where pieces were worked on or created. Columns and carvings sat in what used to be cells. Now the dividing walls were gone, but the low Gothic-arched stone ceiling reminded me of the Tower of London, and I could easily see men imprisoned there. Much had changed, but the damp smell and claustrophobic experience remained the same. I picked up a few rocks to bring home to the crew from this foreign place that had made such a mark on them so many years ago.

We crossed the blue Schlei and returned closer to the crash site. While my father had probably frantically pulled at his parachute to prevent landing in the water, we floated across it gently as Manfred had driven the car onto the ferry that shuttled back and forth. We would return to the woods one more time.

Once back in the woods, Angela and I explored both sides of the path where the salvage battalion from Schleswig cannibalized the plane removing the wreckage to save what the Germans could use. I could visualize them combing through the smoldering pile of rubble sorting out the burnt belongings of ten men. We found lengths of charred wood, but we had no guarantee it was old wood. Maybe there had been lightning in the undisturbed area at one time in the last sixty years.

Angela dug with a long stick. She bent over and picked up an oval black rubber patch with oddly-frayed edges. We examined it more closely. It had a vertical seam running down one side. We both wondered if it could be a patch from the plane's tire.

Matthias looked skeptical. So did our husbands. What was the chance of a piece of rubber from the tire lying there waiting for us to find it after sixty years? I bent over and picked up another small one just like it. Manfred and John speculated it could have come from a tractor tire, yet the area back in the woods was so pristine and truly undisturbed. Angela gave it to me, and I put it with the small one.

Strainer and one of the hooks that were made by the local Germans from the aluminum from "Rhapsody in Junk" The black rubber patch was found by Angela in the woods at the crash site.

    We left the woods and found a small village and had a typical German lunch. Our visit with these friendly and helpful people was more than we could have hoped for. Matthias, our faithful translator and new friend, had much material for the article his teacher required him to write for the school's yearbook. He carried many pictures in his camera back to Iserlohn. Our friends dropped us at our hotel, and we said our good-byes. We could never repay their hospitality and generosity.

    John and I walked to a grocery after returning to the hotel to get some bottled water, apples and bananas to take on the train the next day. Our limited German demanded it, and we chose not to risk another mistaken culinary encounter in the dining car. We walked to a hotel around the corner that we were told used to be an interrogation center and jail during the war. By its present looks, no one would have guessed. From Gretchen's book information, this very well could be the place where my father was first taken.

That night, I packed both the rubber patches in my bag and admired the two metal hooks and tea strainer from Gretchen. In the morning, we walked across the street from the hotel to the train station. Once again, no one was there. We waited on the platform in silence for our train, drinking in the beauty of the area and reflecting back on our productive and delightful visit.

The train pulled out of the station, and within minutes it passed Eckernforde. I had seen this town mentioned in the MACR. This was where Flaugher's body was taken by the German Marines. The area looked as serene as the farm setting we had gotten used to. The slow paddles of windmills turned in the breeze, and white puffs of clouds drifted overhead. Had it only been that way for him. Our train sped further across Germany to Kiel where we changed again as we headed for Poland.

We took the train to Berlin and changed there for Cottbus. A woman across from us sat with her little dog in a travel bag on the seat frequently speaking to it in German. I liked the idea of taking dogs on trains, and we saw it often. In Berlin, we came up from the train station just long enough to find a small bank so that we could change our euros into Polish zloty. Poking our heads out of the train station, we saw a bombed out church, the Kaiser Wilhem Kirche, purposely left that way as a reminder of the destruction of war. It stood broken and charred just across from the "Zoo" train station, its jagged steeple towering against the sky.

## Chapter 58

# *Stalag Luft III*

We arrived in Forst, near the Polish border, to wait for our next train. The closer we got to the border, the more the scenery deteriorated. Abandoned buildings, some still left in disrepair from the war, dotted the land. The farther we moved east, we could see with more frequency the remnants of years of war and of Communist rule. There were few modern structures, and old green or maroon box cars sat on sidings in many of the stations we passed. Broken windows holding jagged glass spears were more prevalent than whole ones. Drab colors on worn boards covered what buildings we saw, interspersed between tall weeds and brown fields. Non-existent were the bright yellow fields of rapeseed flowers we saw in Germany, flowers from which oil was made and sold.

The platform at our station had steps to descend to reach the other side of the tracks, so we started walking in that direction lugging our heavy bags. An old woman, who spoke no English, motioned to us with her wrinkled hand that we did not have to go down those steps with all our bags, but instead we could raise the wooden bar across the tracks and go right through to the main building. We gratefully thanked her and started across the tracks. When it was time to return to the platform to catch our connecting train, we did the same thing lifting the wooden bar and walking across the tracks. We took a seat on the platform, and within minutes three, uniformed German guards approached us.

"Passports," the first said solemnly.

I thought of all the prisoners of war who had escaped and made their way to the train stations, dressed as locals. The approach of a governmental official demanding to see "papers" must have been very similar and intimidating.

The guard examined each of our passports. He waved his hand toward the wooden barrier.

"Verboten!" he advised us.

His two companions reinforced this verboten admonition.

That was German we knew. We apologized for our misunderstanding, and no way could I come up with the words to inform him it was the old Polish woman who encouraged us to perform such a forbidden act. We assured them we would NEVER do this again, and they let us go.

We boarded the train, and sitting across from us was the woman who had given us such bad advice. She had a big smile on her face and greeted us heartily. In Polish, she offered us cough drops from a huge bag she carried with her. We politely refused, but she would not accept no for an answer. She thrust handfuls of cough drops into our laps. Periodically, during the trip she force fed us more whenever she felt we were running low. One stop before we got off the train, she departed waving to us, her new best friends. As the train pulled out of the station, chugging with increasing speed deeper into Poland, I could still see her waving on the platform.

With all the train changes and waiting, it had been an eight-hour trip. The train pulled into Zagan, former home of Stalag Luft III, one-hundred-miles southeast of Berlin. At that time, it was called Sagan, but when the boundaries between Germany and Poland were changed after the war, the name was changed. All the city signs we saw had both German and Polish names. We found the hotel Bernice Watt had recommended. Years of Communist rule had left eastern Germany and Poland frozen in poverty, and the buildings reflected the deprivations of those long years. Our hotel was old and worn but clean.

We walked across the bridge into Zagan, and we passed an ancient church. We ducked in for the end of the Mass and continued on to a restaurant called Kepler's that Bernice had recommended. It was named for the German astronomer, and murals on the walls told the story of his discovery of planetary elliptical orbits. After an excellent and very economical Polish meal, we returned to our hotel.

In the morning, we ate a breakfast heavily laden with pickles and cucumbers, and Mr. Jukubiak, who oversaw the Muzeum Martyrologii dedicated to Stalag Luft III prisoners, picked us up. He took us to the stone memorial for "The Fifty" who were shot by the Gestapo after their futile escape. The Germans had allowed the prisoners to build this memorial for their comrades sixty years ago, and yet it looked like it had just been built. Each name was clearly engraved, and I found many I recognized from reading their individual stories. At one time, all the urns of their ashes were held here but have since been moved to Pozan to the Cytadela Cemetery. All but two, whose ashes were taken home by their families, still rest in solitude there. Hitler's personal order to shoot "The Fifty" was called the Sagan-Befehl. It would take until 1947 before eighteen of the executioners were hunted down and brought to justice before the English Military Tribunal in Hamburg. Thirteen were eventually put to death.

This memorial was built in 1944 by the British kriegies from North Compound to honor the fifty men who were murdered after their recapture.
Courtesy of Mr. Duane Reed

Mr. Jukubiak next drove us to the Muzeum Martyrologii where artifacts and records from the camp were kept. The Poles dedicated the building, formerly occupied by Communists, to the memory of the men of Stalag Luft III. A wooden "goon box" was erected out front, and there were plans to rebuild North Compound and a glass replica of "Tunnel Harry." We climbed up to the museum's second floor. In the reception area, a bronze sculpture caught my eye. A man in a long overcoat pulling a sled through the snow represented all the men who evacuated the camp in 1945. It was a replica of the life-size sculpture erected by the Royal Air Force ex-Prisoners of War Association and dedicated to the memory of prisoners of war of the Allied and Commonwealth Air Forces. It was unveiled by Prince Philip in 2003 at the RAF Museum at Hendon, outside of London.

Behind the sculpture hung a haunting picture in shades of blue. Mr. Jakubiak told me Tom Watt, my Canadian POW friend, had donated the print commissioned by Myron Williams. The picture was a composite of the activities in the camp during the time of "The

Great Escape." Men underground dug tunnels as guards patrolled in the snow above. The heavy snow above the ground still looked chilling. Around the picture's four edges were the faces of "The Fifty." I could barely keep my eyes off of it, and I was determined to track it down when I got home to find if prints were still available. Glass cases in the museum held old shoes, keys, rosaries, coins, broken dishes, utensils, razors and pipes. Each of the rusted and worn items sat side by side in the cases, the previous owners' fates unknown. Knowing I would find nothing personal to me, I was still obsessed with finding some small item that could have belonged to my father. We saw the most recent find, the stove that covered the entrance to "Tunnel Harry." Mr. Jakubiak said he had found it thrown in a dump not all that long ago.

After our tour, Mr. Jakubiak took us in his small car to drive the short distance to what was left of Stalag Luft III. The camp was now part of a Polish military training area with ghosts of the past, bits of broken brick chimneys and remains of concrete foundations strewn about the overgrown forest acres. From the train station, a bumpy dirt road jolted us as we drove its quarter mile length. Tall fir trees stood as silent witnesses at the road's edge. The prisoners had walked the rutted road after disembarking from the train and passing by the wooden sentry house near the station. Farther up the road, they would have seen the rows of weathered grey huts.

General Clark had told me of the pleasant sound of the cuckoo birds that lived in the woods then. I listened but heard none that day. But in my own mind, I could hear the deep determined male voices singing mightily as the men marched out into the cold night in January, 1945. Now the songs were just a memory as elusive as the sound of the cuckoos hidden in the Polish woods. Then, the melodic tones of the men's hearty voices wafted through the air here giving evidence to their fighting spirit.

Across the road from where the main entrance gate had been, we saw wreaths of flowers from the recent celebration of the 60th anniversary of "The Great Escape" piled upon the exit of "Tunnel Harry." A plastic maple leaf had fallen from one Canadian arrangement. Red, white and blue ribbons fluttered in the breeze from all the memorial arrangements, many of which had poignant notes attached. I picked up the maple leaf to send to Tom Watt up in Canada who had been too ill to attend the ceremony.

Trees had grown up in the camp as well as at the exit of "Harry." So many years ago, the men had miscalculated the length by ten feet coming up short of the woods that had set just across the road. Now, smaller young trees had grown inward towards the tunnel's exit providing all the cover the escapers would have needed. It was easy to see the danger of popping up out of the ground with little cover in such close proximity to a "goonbox." The length of the tunnel ran under the dirt road we had walked upon. Wooden edging had been sunk into the ground, and rocks filled in between the boards that ran the full length of the tunnel under the uneven road to where it originated in North Compound. We walked its length, and I picked up a stone to give to General Clark.

Standing at the tunnel's exit, I could almost hear the guards' shrill whistles blowing into the frigid air that March night; the scurry of activity in the woods when the tunnelers were discovered by a strolling guard, the crack of broken branches underfoot, the condensed breath from panicked fleeing men, the rustle of carried bags snapping back branches as men ran through the brush and the timely fear sweat that can only come under such circumstances—in my imagination, it was all here.

We walked through North Compound past the old fire pool. The Germans had kept it filled with water in case the wooden structures caught fire, but reason dictated the supply would have been sorely inadequate.

Present-day "Tunnel Harry" running north to the exit in the woods where seventy-six prisoners exited into the woods in March, 1944
Courtesy of Mrs. Valerie Burgess

We glanced down into the remains of the theatre where so many plays and the Christmas performances had taken place. The downward slope towards the stage was overgrown with weeds and grass where Red Cross wooden parcel boxes had formed the seats. All tickets had been reserved, and the admission then was one brick of coal. The reflectors and footlights had been constructed from large British biscuit tins, and there was even a catwalk above the wings for movable spotlights. The theatre had opened one February day, and numerous musical variety shows, one-act plays and Broadway shows such as "Front Page," "Kiss and Tell," and "Room Service," had been performed. The women's parts were played, with no reluctance, by men. Fires burned in each of the four corner stoves, but their bright flames only took a small bit of the chill out of the theatre. So many years after the fact, a soft spring breeze blew across the remains of the theatre, and birds chirped noisily in the trees.

We walked through the woods to the fire pool in South Camp. Mr. Jakubiak and I communicated as best we could with the Polish language barrier.

"This is where they threw in the sheeps," he said authoritatively. I was very puzzled.

"The sheeps?"

"Yes," he said, "they raced them."

I was more puzzled than ever at this image until I remembered reading of the wooden boats, some very refined and intricate, that were made by the prisoners and raced in the fire pools.

This fire pool had been the site of chaos on Fourth of July, 1943, when Major Jerry Sage had insisted on a festive celebration. Raisins had been horded to make "kriegie brew," and plied with liberal amounts of it, the Americans and British enjoyed a day-long celebration long remembered by any man who participated. Sage, decked out as Uncle Sam, complete with a large white papier mache glove, roamed the camp in poster fashion calling, "Uncle Sam wants you!" Other kriegies recreating the painting, "The Spirit of '76," depicted the classic triad of wounded Revolutionary War patriots suitably equipped with fife and drum. Americans dressed as Indians invaded the British blocks throwing unsuspecting Brits out of their bunks. Sage took great pleasure in throwing Roger Bushell out of bed, as Sage yelled, "The rebels are coming, arise, arise! Don your red coat and fight like a man!"

For that day, the Germans did not even attempt to count the prisoners. The Brits had joined the celebration hauling out their own home brew. At first, the Germans suspected a great conflict had grown between the Americans and Brits. They hoped that the strong alliance between them had been broken. Then they watched both sides throw the other in this very fire pool and realized it was all in fun. Sage, as Uncle Sam, was the first to be thrown in. Normally sedate and very British, Wings Day, always in full military uniform, tie and medals strutted forward.

"Who will save him?" he cried "I'll save him!"

"Who're you? cried the crowd.

"Jack Armstrong of the royal U.S. Marines!" Day shouted, and with that he belly-flopped into the four-and-a-half-foot-deep pool.

The two inebriated men sat dripping on opposite sides of the pool and shook hands. Then they clasped both hands and leaned back stretching their hands across the pool.

"Hands across the sea!" they roared to cheers from the crowd.

Soon, SAO Goodrich and block commanders, A.P. "Bub" Clark, Dick Klocko and ex-Tokyo Doolittle Raider, Davy Jones, were all in the pool. They all looked down to see a kriegie at the bottom. They fished him out and got him breathing, and the celebration continued.

The party moved to the middle of the appell ground from the pool, and POW Shorty Spire riding on a "horse" consisting of two other men covered with a blanket, entertained the kriegies, goon box guards and other Germans when he instructed the men under the blanket to dump a keintrinkwasser (metal pitcher) of water from under the blanket as the horse lifted his leg for effect.

Now, sixty years later, I could almost hear the hilarity and the jubilant voices of men determined to have fun under the most depressing of circumstances. The loud splashes, the hoots and laughter were all still here—just cushioned by the passage of time. I had to smile as I walked from the pool and held onto the images.

What remains of one of the fire pools at Stalag Luft III
Courtesy of Mr. Duane Reed

Not far from the pool, we found the exact location of Building 128 where my father had lived. The barracks had been wooden then, so nothing remained but a broken foundation. Old plumbing pipes and pieces of broken porcelain from the wash house still rested in the dirt. I picked up some of the creamy-white porcelain to bring home with me.

Wild flowers surrounded by tiny delicate green ferns sprung up from the building's remains. The new fern life pushed through the broken bricks and ground where block 128 had stood, each little fern defying the consequences of war to keep it down. I picked a few of the delicate ferns and put them in my pocket. It was in the building that stood here where my father would write his three letters per month that were allowed after passing through American and German censors. It was here he would await a twelve-pound personal parcel every three months and where he would gratefully open his Red Cross parcels. Many times the letters did not come or there was a four-month lag from when they were written by loved ones and when they were received. I do not believe he ever received a personal parcel.

What a sacred place. So many brave men had passed this way. British Dickey Milne, nephew of A.A. Milne of "Winnie the Pooh" fame, had been an expert forger here. Winston Churchill's nephew by marriage, Johnny Dodge, ("The Dodger") had walked within the wire and helped dig "Tunnel Harry." Men who would become prominent doctors, lawyers, politicians, actors and teachers had all lived first among these pines.

We saw what remained of the foundation of a medical building in the vorlager, but everything in the camp had been bulldozed after the war, and only with the help of a guide and a map could the few things that remained be seen and located. We stopped at a small cemetery. General Clark had asked me to look for a war memorial there that he had always been able to see from his room when he was in North Compound. The old road ran east to west in front of the camp. At the west end of the camp, there was a little cemetery on the north side. In it was a German and French monument erected in 1815 marking the retreat of the Russian soldiers. He had sent me a sketch he drew of it.

> "Just before you get to the cemetery on the left, it has a six foot-high cross on top. The railroad station is north of the camp. See if monument is still there."

We found the cemetery, but only one other smaller monument remained. As General Clark suspected, the Russians probably bulldozed the old monument just after the war purposely destroying anything German.

## Chapter 59

## *In My Father's Footsteps*

We next drove the route the prisoners took the night of evacuation. We drove on a sunny afternoon past the same towering green trees the men had marched past. They lined the worn cobblestone road on either side for miles just beyond the camp and continuing along the curved road that ran through the small villages where the men walked. Our route would take us the same way South Compound had marched from Sagan to Hermsdorf, Burau, Halbau, Freiwaldau, Priebus, Muskau and then on to Graustein before reaching the railway at Spremberg. From time to time, the road became more modernized, but it always returned to cobblestone. These were the very stones my father had walked on. This was the road the men of Stalag Luft III spread across as they staggered along in the cold. These were the old stones that had been covered with ice that supported the frozen wheels of the refugees' wagons and where German troops periodically pushed the travelers aside to make way for men and equipment.

We stopped in the little towns along the route, and the road hair-pinned through villages with familiar names. I looked for the church where Center Compound had stayed when Colonel Spivey and General Vanaman addressed weary cold men from the altar.

We rode through Halbau and continued on, and I still had not seen the church. Soon, I remembered the church was in Halbau. I asked Mr. Jakubiak to turn around, and he graciously did. I read that Spivey's column had also reversed its direction to reach the church. History was repeating itself. We approached what was now a Catholic church after being returned to Poland. It had been a Lutheran Church during the war. We parked the car and strode up its walkway. When we tried to enter, the door was locked. The cemetery sat out back and a school was to the right, just as I read in Spivey's and other books.

We went to the rectory and found the priest. A First Communion service was to take place the next day, and the church was decorated for the occasion. The priest unlocked the door for us after we explained why we were there. I approached the right side of the church. Up near the altar, there was a plaque placed by a beautiful stained glass window, both donated by ex-POWS of Center Compound. Colonel Spivey and a few other ex-kriegies had personally delivered it many years after the march, thanking the people of the village for housing the tired, hungry and frigid troops.

> "Donated by Grateful American Air Force POWs Stalag Luft III who found shelter here during the night of 28 1 1945."

Below was the Polish translation.

Beyond Halbau, we looked for the old barns in the villages, stopping at some and at other churches along the way. Every available spot had been a shelter for someone. I had read an account of the men tramping along, and on the right there was a castle and stable where RAF prisoners were held. As they heard the long column of prisoners approaching, the RAF prisoners stuck their heads out of the stable singing and yelling to encourage the spent men. We found a small castle along the road and went inside to inquire about where a stable might be. They had no idea. Giving up, we drove down the short road leading to the castle and just off to the side was what

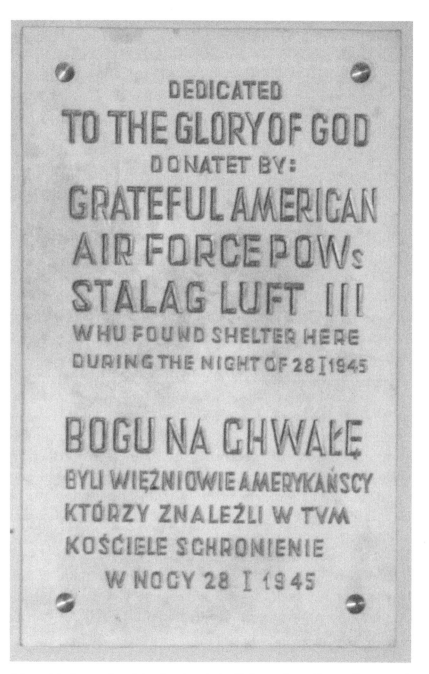

Memorial plaque placed in the church in Halbau where Center Compound spent the night in the winter of 1945
Courtesy of Mrs. Valerie Burgess

looked like the remains of an old stable. This would have been the very one those rousing English voices sang from that blustery day. Now, it was boarded up and a part of the past.

Finally, we made our way to Muskau. Mr. Jakubiak found the glass factory, and it had long been abandoned. Tall weeds grew up around it, and its windows were broken out. A metal lock held a chain to its gate to block the entrance. The two large smokestacks the men saw in the filmy distance projected from the weathered complex. The Poles had been too impoverished to remove the structure, so after all the years it still remained. The abandoned factory had welcomed the fatigued men that night---refugees from the storm too weary to go on. The warmth from its kiln was a godsend for them, and now it sat abandoned and desolate with no further purpose.

Half way across Muskau was the German/Polish border. Half of Muskau was now in Poland and half in Germany. Both Germans and Poles set up border checkpoints there. A lively trade was being conducted before the check point where Polish merchants sold food, housewares and liter bottles of soda at greatly reduced prices to the Germans who came across the border. We ate on the Polish side, ordering cheeseburgers. While we waited for our order, a Polish man motioned to me and told me he would give me $15 for my new digital camcorder. I politely refused. Cabbage and cucumbers smothered a questionable grayish patty of meat. My father had spoken of eating cabbage during his confinement, and it was the one thing he would never eat afterward. Evidently, the cabbage patches were still thriving in Poland.

We showed our passports at the border and drove back into Germany. Once across the border, the shabbiness of that area of Poland was behind us. The shops and streets were more upscale. Many of the towns on the way to Spremberg still showed the results of Communist neglect when they had been part of East Germany, but Spremberg was beautiful.

## Chapter 60

# *Spremberg*

Our trip of over sixty miles ended in Spremberg where the prisoners of war had boarded the boxcars to leave for Stalag VIIA in Moosburg. Our guide dropped us at a stylish hotel in Spremberg since it was too late to go on to Munich. The escalators in the building ran only when they were turned on by those wishing to ride. Our key in the door turned off the lights when we left, and lights were programmed to turn off and on in the hallways. I washed my white slacks that were now pretty dirty and put them on a towel warmer to dry. There were no tissues, bar soap, shampoo or shower caps again, but we were comforted by the fact we had the matches and shoe horns we'd grown accustomed to seeing in the hotels. With great difficulty, I called the United States, and I spoke with Diane who updated me on my father's condition. So far, he was still holding his own.

After a good night's sleep, we made our way down for a lavish breakfast. Special tea pots that strained and held the tea leaves, juice pitchers with built-in ice holders and what looked like miniature wastebaskets with swinging tops sat upon the tables. A little forethought allowed us to have perfectly strained tea and constantly chilled juice, and in return we cleaned up our own table and put napkins and papers in the small container on the table. It was German efficiency at its best.

We went to the train station to buy tickets to Munich, and the woman in the ticket office spoke no English. I communicated to her where we needed to go.

"Ja, Ja," she said, and handed me the tickets.

We had awhile to wait, and once again, we were the only ones at the small station. I walked back inside and in my fractured German tried to tell the woman why we were there. I told her my "vater" had been a prisoner of war, and he had been brought to this station in 1945 by the Germans and was given "zoop." She pointed to her arms and indicated she was getting goosebumps as she understood what I was saying. She shook her head up and down and smiled. In our own way, we had a pleasant conversation, and it helped pass the time.

"Your vater, your vater," she kept repeating, as she held her face in her hands and shook her head in dismay, and I knew that through all the distance and years that a stranger my age in Germany understood.

I sat on the bench on the platform gazing across the grassy fields covered with row after row of rails. The German Panzer Divisions had trained near here. Young intrepid tank commanders had loaded tanks on flatbeds and headed east. Steam engines had huffed in and out, and audible German commands had rung though the air as a desperate and nearly-defeated nation tried to hold on. The Germans had doled out what nourishment they could provide, and cold anxious hands held steaming cups of hot barley soup. Far across rows of rails farther down, the men had gathered in bunches to board. Men in frosted heavy greatcoats and tattered blankets helped each other up into the Forty and Eight cars here. The masses of men so long on the road and so far from home crowded in determined to endure and to survive another day.

# Chapter 61

# Munich

In far more comfort than the prisoners had ever hoped for, we caught a local train from Spremberg to Cottbus and then a regional express train to Leipzig. We changed trains in Leipzig, which had been a prime target during the war. The railway station must have been obliterated, and what stood in its place was an ultra-modern two story-mall. Activity bustled on the platform, as a woman cooked crepes, infusing the station with a delicious aroma. Upscale clothing and electronics stores sat beside a vast array of eating establishments. I wandered into a busy shop and got an order of deep-fried zucchini with apricot sauce and savored each bite. I looked down the tracks and tried to visualize the bomb crater that swallowed up Hanns Scharff's files and typewriters as he raced to board the train here.

We took the ICE train (Inter City Express) known for its speed to Munich. We pulled our luggage aboard and sat across from a well-dressed business woman who told us about the storks in the area that migrate to Africa for the winter, and once more people with friendly dogs boarded the train.

Our hotel reservation was lost in Munich, so we were forced to take what we could get. The manager apologized for not having a room for us, but he called another hotel he insisted we would love. It was walking distance to the train station, and that was a big plus for us.

Unfortunately, we found upon arrival it was on a tawdry street and was very run down. Our dismal room was upstairs, but the wooden shutters at the head of the bed just at the tops of our pillows opened out onto a walkway where, day or night, anyone could walk around the top of the building. With no screen on the window, they were literally walking inches from the tops of our heads. The room was very stuffy, and we had to keep the shutters open to get some air. We hoped for the best. A small television hung in the corner of the room, and the only thing we could get on it was static. The hastily-installed bathroom, not much larger than an airliner's, was painted a bright coral color, and a dimly-lit bulb dangled from the ceiling to cast dismal shadows around the dark room and out onto the dirty carpet. Despite the assurances we would "love it," we found that we did not. The room was on par with Dulag Luft's "cooler," no doubt complete with fleas.

A cool rain fell as we made our way to the famous Hofbrau House that evening as we looked for a restaurant for dinner. This is where Hitler had gotten his start holding meetings and gathering crowds in the early 1920s. Now, it rang out with German drinking songs and the clinking of foam-dripped glasses. The blue-and-white-checked Bavarian flag was painted on the ceiling, and four flags grouped together were swirled into a swastika. Who would have guessed that the seemingly innocent design would be incorporated into the Nazi flag and portend such evil? We walked through the misty night in the town where Hitler had gotten a foothold, resulting at the end of the war in its almost total destruction. Behind us, the gaiety and exuberance of the Hofbrau House faded, and the rain came down a little harder as we walked back to "our cell."

## Chapter 62

# Frankfurt

It was with great haste we left the hotel in the morning and made our way to the train station in the rain. In three-and-a-half hours, we were in Frankfurt meeting the parents of a German student, Tim Klaws, we once "adopted" while in our country. He had been in high school then and was now finishing law school in Germany. I had been corresponding with Tim's father, Wolfgang, and using far from adequate translation services on the computer. Thankfully, he spoke excellent English. I found that the computer translation website translated the name Walton literally into Whale Sound in German much to our amusement.

Now, we stood at the kiosk in the Frankfurt airport, our pre-arranged meeting place, and a gentleman approached me. "Family Whale Sound?" he said with a broad smile. It was Wolfgang.

He and his wife Katie drove us to our hotel. The hotel prided itself on its bakery on the premises and its homemade chocolates. They could not have found a better place for us. Our room was decorated in bright orange and yellow, with plump pillows covered with crisp white pillowcases that sat above the plush featherbeds atop each bed. The bathroom had an elaborate and large shower, and there was a lighted magnifying mirror on the bathroom wall. And there was soap! It was a pure joy after our stay in Munich. The dining room had a gourmet cook, and white asparagus was in season.

The hotel molded chocolate maikaefers, (June bugs) that were said to bring good luck that time of year. So those were the bugs on our pillows in Sudebrarup!

For two days, the Klaws family hosted us taking us on a tour of Frankfurt with two friends of theirs where we saw all the places Claudius had recommended. We walked through the Roemer town square, which had been heavily bombed during the war. We peeked in the former church where President Kennedy had spoken on one of his stops through Germany, the year of his "Ich bin ein Berliner" speech. We passed the city hall where Claudius and Monika were married. We strolled on Frankfurt's equivalent to Fifth Avenue, and we tasted fresh figs, Indian tea and warm breads from open stalls in the marketplace. Both couples had brought their small dogs along, and they trotted along happily behind us. We walked across the river to Sachsenhausen for apple wine in a small restaurant with a gnarled tree pushing up through the roof. The dogs slept beneath our table. We toasted each other and our friendship. We had a delicious German dinner, and in the morning, Wolfgang took us to the train station so that we could board a train to Oberursel.

## Chapter 63

# *Dulag Luft Revisited*

The prisoners of war had taken the train from Schleswig in the north western part of Germany to Frankfurt in the southwest corner. From there, they had boarded a train to Oberursel for interrogation and transfer to permanent camps.

The train station in Oberursel, from pictures I had seen, had not changed at all. The trolley the men often rode from Frankfurt to Oberursel still ran, but it was not in sight the day we visited.

We got off the train and walked up the hill the men would have climbed. New housing stood in the place of the old buildings at the foot of the Taunus Mountains, green with mighty beech, pine and chestnut trees. Claudius's father, Hanns, would have walked up into these mountains with the Allied fighter pilots.

Some of the buildings from that era were still standing but were dilapidated. I compared the one left standing with the pictures I had brought. The high slanted roofs and the series of three small windows high on the ends of the building were identical to the pictures I held in my hands. We creaked open the door to one of the abandoned buildings no doubt soon to be destroyed or renovated and walked inside and upstairs. The old wooden floor creaked under our footsteps. Most likely, the building was an administrative building, but there were bars on the windows that sat at ground level. Phones no longer rang in this room, and papers cataloging thousands of men were now gone. It was desolate and empty and what exactly took place in this room we would never know.

The U-shaped cooler where the men were held in isolation was long gone. As we walked back down the hill, we saw a woman walking her dog and asked her a few questions. She directed us to a large wooden carving that appeared to be the floor of an outside basketball court. We had no idea what it was. Entitled, "Never Look Back," it was a memorial carving and statement addressing the events of the past decades. In one corner, we saw the carved picture of Hanns Scharff holding his little daughter, Claudius's sister, Della! Behind him, was a building where three prisoners of war were being taken. One could see "POW" on the roofs of the carved replicas. I wondered if Claudius or his family knew the carving was there and later found out they did not. I took pictures of what we found to pass along to him. Although much of Dulag Luft was gone, there were still reminders whispering its past, if only in the form of a wooden carving reminding everyone what had happened there.

After our day in Oberursel, we returned to Wolfgang and Katie, visiting their beautiful apartment and walking through their village to a quaint restaurant for dinner with their friends. We dined on pork covered with the German green sauce, so tantalizingly described to me by Claudius. Accompanied by fried potatoes and in-season, German white asparagus, it was a most satisfying meal. After toasting with the obligatory peach schnapps, we walked back to the apartment and returned to our hotel.

The next day we drove on the autobahn with Wolfgang at the wheel cruising along at well over one-hundred-miles per hour. Along the way, Katie told me of her mother's plight during the war, about which her brother had told her.

In 1939, at the time of the German invasion of Poland, Herta Erna Glienke, Katie's mother, and her two children, Eva and Peter, hid from the invading forces. There was no food for them and no milk for two-and-a-half month-old Eva. The baby became malnourished, and Herta took her to the hospital in Graudenz. It was far enough from Herta's home that she could not visit her baby often in the wartime conditions. The battles raged on, and at one point the Germans gained a foothold against the Poles. With this small break, desperate Herta rushed to the hospital. Her baby was gone. The nurses explained that they thought Herta had been killed during the invasion, and they had given the baby to foster parents. It would take two-and-a-half years and the intervention of the Red Cross to find Eva and return her to Herta.

On Christmas Eve, 1944, Peter Glienke sensed something was about to happen. He was now eight-years-old and living in Graudenz on the east side of the Weichsel River in West Prussia. Herta was then twenty-eight-years old, and the returned baby, Eva, was five. They were joined by a new baby, six-month-old Klaus. It was a bitterly cold winter, the coldest winter on record in Germany in fifty years, and the war had taken a turn, causing the residents of the area to consider their safety not only from the Allied bombings but from the Russian troops moving in from the east. With each day, the troops moved closer, and the tenuous grasp the families had on their homes slowly loosened.

Herta Glienke with Peter and Eva

Courtesy of Mr. Peter Glienke

Herta's husband, Herbert Erich Glienke, a 32-year old farmer, was now a soldier in the German army at the Kurland Army front. The front stretched from Estonia at the Gulf of Finland over Latvia and through a part of Lithuania to the Baltic Sea. As the family struggled, he was captured at Gomel, in the middle of Russia, in Weissrussland in 1945. He was not wounded, but his fate was held in the hands of the Russian Army. Herbert had the advantage of speaking Polish and understanding Russian, so he was able to translate the orders given by the Russian guards for his fellow German prisoners. His translation skills afforded him and his fellow prisoners enough to eat, and the German prisoners grew tobacco plants convincing their Russian captors that it was needed to protect against diarrhea. By using the tobacco to smoke and offer to guards or barter with, he and his men were given preferential treatment only slightly increasing their chance of survival.

Back in Germany, Herbert's family anticipated Germany's defeat. Daily, his family watched a procession of refugees pass through the streets. Open carriages filled with despondent Germans rolled past young Peter's home. The half-broken wagons loaded with straw, featherbeds and frightened people were drawn by tired horses towards the west. A few of the travelers were lucky enough to have covered wagons so that their occupants were afforded some protection against the cold. Buckets jangled at the sides of the wagons, and full sacks and spare wheels attached in random fashion swung back and forth as the wagons ground along through the countryside. Sometimes, many wagons clustered together; other times they came alone. Most were filled with old couples and young women with many frightened children. The men of the villages were gone off to war, so many to never return. It was an endless line that snaked its way through West Prussia each day until sunset with no one knowing what would lie ahead. It was too dangerous to continue in the dark, so weary families sought shelter along the way.

As she heard the wagons pass, Herta threw open her windows. Soon, rickety wagons pulled up in front of Peter's house. He watched as the weary passengers passed bedcovers and blankets through windows into the house. Quickly, the floor was covered with refugees who had come in from the cold. The home was turned into a refugee camp for transients, and Peter felt great sadness as he peered out the frosted windows to watch the tired, often wounded, horses. They stood in exhaustion, great breaths of vapor from their mouths visible in the moonlight. Some had frosted tattered blankets covering their backs, but many went without.

In the morning, the treks through the snow continued. It was Christmas night, and Peter's mother made a dinner of schwarzsauer. The concoction was made from the head, neck, wings, stomach, heart, feet and blood of a goose or duck combined with dried fruit, potato dumplings, vinegar, sugar, salt, marjoram and clove. Peter could smell it cooking. As it cooked, excited neighbors called loudly for the family to come outside. The group of neighbors standing in the cold scanned the dark sky.

"Bomber! Bomber!" they cried.

Peter could hear a big boom, but he saw nothing. The scare was over, but it was a further indication that the area was becoming increasingly dangerous for the family to remain.

In early January of 1945, Herta decided they could no longer remain in Graudenz. She packed up her children and loaded them into an awning-covered wagon. The lumbering wagon was pulled by two horses toward the home of her father-in-law, Friedrich Wilhelm Glienke, on the east side of the Weichsel River. The small family of Glienkes, past hosts to so many, had now also become official refugees.

Early one morning, Friedrich Glienke's house was hit by gunfire and was engulfed in flames. He led his terrified family into the cellar immediately. When it was safe to come up, they saw the smoky ruins. The house was not destroyed, but it was too dangerous to stay there, so they moved to bigger accommodations. There was a hotel directly behind the dike on the river. All the rooms were occupied with soldiers and refugees. In the garden, behind the hotel, stood a field kitchen, and in the yard in front of the kitchen, cows and pigs killed by pistol shots were cut up on the tables in the restaurant to feed the hungry people.

One frigid day there was a low-level attack near the hotel, and the occupants of the hotel raced to the cellar. Peter's grandfather ran to the meat-smoking chamber in the basement. When the attack was over, he stumbled out of the smoking ruins, and Peter grinned seeing the black soot on his grandfather's face and hands. The family stayed for a few more days. Curious, Peter wandered over to the dike to look around and visit a stable of horses nearby. A loud explosion rocked the area. Before he knew it, Peter was violently thrown through the air and landed on a haystack. Simultaneously, the iron railway bridge across the river exploded and burst upward into the sky. The explosion blew window panes out of the hotel, and panicked Herta ran to look for Peter. She found him unhurt. He was quite excited to see the action around him, far too young to realize the seriousness of it. The only bridge still intact was a wooden one, and when the German Army opened it to civilian traffic, the wagons rolled across and continued on their journey. For those who did not want to wait, they precariously eased their unstable, loaded wagons down the riverbanks and onto the frozen river to continue westward.

Since it was no longer safe for anyone to stay at or near the hotel, the surrounding farmers organized a caravan of refugees, and Peter's long journey began. The adults were prepared for the worst, but the children, being children, did not recognize the dangers. Day after day, the group walked and rode frequently encountering the German Army whose equipment jammed the roads. At night, the refugees sought shelter in vacant homes, farm houses, barns and stables. Hour after chilling hour, they plodded along against the biting wind through Danzig and Stolp.

Wagons broke down, and the journey became more difficult. Peter sat between the featherbeds and straw in the open carriage watching his mother. Eva and Klaus watched ahead as roads closed permitting only military traffic. The long line of wagons detoured through the frozen farm fields causing many more to break down on the bumpy terrain. In the ditches, and along the frigid roadsides, lay damaged household items cast aside to lighten the load. After traveling many miles, the family lost its wagon. Often, forced Polish workers served as drivers, and when given the opportunity, they left with the horses and/or wagons of the refugees. Peter's family was forced to flee on foot. All they owned was gone except the clothes on their backs. Peter's mother carried a rucksack and a small bag, and Peter carried a small rucksack stuffed with clothes. His grandfather carried a jute sack, and Peter was curious about its contents. He peered inside. It was filled with harvested tobacco from his grandfather's garden. As his grandfather dug through the sack, sometimes eggs would drop out.

Herta was a determined woman, and she flagged down a truck and loaded her children and father aboard. They made their way to Koslin by truck near the Baltic Sea where Peter celebrated his ninth birthday on February 27$^{th}$ in the cellar of a government building. There was little to celebrate that cold day, but the family offered him their warmest congratulations.

Bombs fell on the building briefly in the afternoon, and the family once again boarded the truck and rode all night toward Kolberg. They approached a large farm house, and the owners prepared meals for the hungry refugees. They spent the night in a room with a tiled stove. Herta put some sugar and milk in a little cooking pot wanting to make the children caramel sweets, but she needed some pieces of wood for the stove. Eagerly, Peter dashed outside and carried in some pieces of wood he found. The farmer's angry wife reprimanded Peter for taking her wood. Only days later, the farmer's wife joined the caravan in their trek west.

Many miles had passed before the refugees reached a railway. So many stations had been bombed. Boxcars normally reserved for cattle were filled with straw and were reserved for women with children. The big crowd waited on the railway platform at the station to board, when ice and snow blew over them in a storm. Peter began to cry, as his feet were very cold. His mother looked at the bottom of his shoes and found they had no soles, and he had been walking on the cold ground with only thin socks for protection against the bitter cold. There was nothing his mother could do to fix his worn shoes. She fastened the children together, tying a cord onto their tiny wrists to keep them at her side. Along the rails, the train was strafed from time to time by Allied planes. When the roar of the planes engulfed the train, Herta bent her body over the children and held them tightly.

The hissing steam engine pulled the boxcars into a village station. Herta got out of the cattle car to search for some water for the children to drink. Peter watched his tired mother leave. Suddenly there was movement! The train started moving! Peter was panic-stricken, fearing the train was leaving without her. He sobbed loudly as the rickety car slowly moved along. It eased to a stop only having been separated from the other cars. With great relief, Peter saw his mother return and climb up into the car with water, and she soothed the frightened boy.

The train rattled on through the city of Swinemunde where the refugees could see it lying in ruins. The railway embankments they passed were lined with refugee possessions of all kinds—household articles, boxes, suitcases, bags, clothes, featherbeds and much more. When the train stopped on the open track between stations, Peter could see dead babies buried into the frozen ground as best as the families could improvise. The train rumbled on past streets filled with damaged wagons and dead horses creating bleak and terrifying images in the little boy's mind.

The box cars clattered on through Greifswald, Stralsund, Rostock, Lubeck, Luneburg and eventually into Bremen-Blumenthal where the exhausted family was taken to a factory. Wollkammerei was a wool processing plant being used by the Red Cross. For the first time in weeks the people could take warm showers. They were deloused and received clean clothes provided by the Red Cross. Peter and his family were taken into the big house of the Hager family which doubled as a household supply store. Peter's grandfather was accommodated nearby.

In the following weeks, air raid sirens blared. Peter had never heard them before. The war was following them. With the others, the family raced to the air raid shelter both day and night to drop down into a hollow in a nearby hill.

Soon, the Glienkes were assigned three rooms in a hut. It had been occupied by German soldiers of an anti-aircraft gun emplacement unit who were gone now, leaving behind chairs, tables, wardrobes and a bedstead. Their long trek had begun in January, and they were finally settled in March of 1945.

The weather was warm in the spring, and one day dust flew up from the road outside. As Peter played there, he heard adults shouting.

"Everybody into the houses-- the Americans are coming!"

Down the street, Peter saw a big dust cloud and heard the sound of a tank. He peered from the window and saw two Jeeps side by side pulling long iron chains which created the flying dust. He saw a machine gun in each Jeep and two Negro soldiers. It was at that moment that Peter knew that World War II was over for his family.

Near the make-shift home sat a large underground fuel depot used by the German Army. In the following weeks, columns of United States' trucks filled containers with fuel. Large tank trucks arrived frequently to take the much needed fuel. The German children watched for the trucks and became friendly with the drivers. The drivers learned to bring along chocolate, candies, oranges, cookies and chewing gum for the children. Thankful for the treats, the German children brought the drivers home grown onions and carrots.

Herta was still worried for her children and needed to support her family. When an American barracks sprung up near their home, she washed the soldiers' uniforms by hand and pressed them as best she could with no electric iron. No dollars changed hands, but the soldiers paid Herta with cigarettes, coffee, clothes, shoes, butter, sweets, oranges, soap, chocolate and canned food. Once, when Peter went exploring near the barracks, he found a piece of white bread with butter and cheese, and after a quick taste, he decided it was the best thing he had ever eaten.

In September of 1946, wracked with malaria, POW Herbert Glienke was released by the Russians. Tired and hungry, he made his way to Leipzig where he lived in a camp and took work in a factory. He made contact with the Red Cross and asked them to find his wife Herta. In December, 1946, fourteen months after his release by the Russians, the Red Cross sent Herbert a cable that they could not find Herta in Bremen. But later they sent her a cable that said they had located him in Leipzig. Herta cabled him and asked when he was coming home. When he arranged for a permit to come to Bremen and to stay with his family, he headed north. So many lives had crossed through the train station at Leipzig.

In January of 1947, a man in a Russian quilted jacket walked slowly down the road near the family home in Bremen. Peter watched him coming.

"Do you know where the Glienke family lives?" the tired man asked after some moments.

"Why do you want to know," Peter asked.

The man knew him at once.

"Because, I am your father," he said.

Herbert Glienke, a prisoner of war of the Russians, had finally made it home. No longer a farmer, he found a job doing road construction and later a job with the municipality's construction and greenery unit. A year later another son, Harry was added to the family. Katie and one other child followed.

The war had taken its toll on German marriages. With their husbands gone to war and missing for years, German wives became very independent and self-reliant. They fought for their own survival and that of their children. After the war, they were no longer subordinate to their husbands, and many marriages ended. But through their difficulties, Herbert and Herta stayed together, branded as refugees but determined to remain a family. They died within three months of each other in 1978 and 1979 having raised seven children.

Years later, Peter and Katie mused that it was nothing short of a miracle that their mother was able to bring the children to safety. Over sixty years later, Peter never forgot the bravery and love of his mother. The moment of terror in the moving train for a nine-year-old-boy never left him, and over sixty-years later his emotions of that moment remained the same.

"She brought us out of chaos, dirt, fear, coldness, thirst, hunger and danger," he said. It was a superhuman deed, and she did it with responsibility, sense of duty and with care."

Katie's family remained in Bremen where Peter grew up and later became a civil servant until his retirement in 1991. Katie, born after the war, remembered her mother kindly, as a woman whose nightmare influenced her to always provide food and warmth to everyone, long after the war. Only a woman who had known such deprivation, Peter told her, could realize the importance of such necessities.

Story told, we arrived at the University of Heidelberg to visit Tim, the German student who had come to the United States several years before, whom we had not seen for several years. Together, the families ascended the steps up to the picturesque castle and enjoyed the view down the Neckar River. As the war wound down, this location had been chosen for Allied Headquarters. Knowing the plan, commands were given that is was not to be bombed. Downstream cities suffered from the bombs instead. It had been in beautiful Heidelberg where

General Patton died in the hospital after a car accident at the end of the war and ironically never lived to experience post-war Germany.

We sat with the Klaws family on the sunny cobbled town square having tea and apple strudel with vanilla sauce. We spoke of the war and what the German people had suffered at Hitler's hands. Their pain was as deep as ours over their parents' war experiences, and the war had left scars as much for them as those of us on the other side.

We had one last meal on the campus devouring roast pork, spaetzles and potato dumplings, and washed it down with cold German beer.

The next morning, we stood in the hotel lobby waiting for Wolfgang and Katie, when a young man came in with a gorgeous and friendly Irish setter named Tango and arranged for a room for them. Tango's nose went up in the air at the smells of fresh bread and chocolates. The man told us they were staying there for the night. He was an actor from Hamburg and said they both had been in jail there the night before, because his dog was running more than twenty feet from him in a park, and that was illegal in Hamburg. He said the dog liked South Africa better, and soon they would return there. He did not like to keep a dog confined.

After taking a few pictures the next morning, Katie and Wolfgang took us to the airport. Knowing my passion, Katie thrust bags of German chocolate candies into my hands for the trip. With many hugs and European double kisses on our cheeks, we left our friends and left Germany.

## Chapter 64

# *Our Hero Stumbles*

I checked bags filled with a rubber tire patch, aluminum utensils and hooks, broken Polish bath porcelain and priceless memories. The brown, green and yellow checkerboard squares of German soil shrank to minute faded patches behind us as we lifted up into the clouds. Below, lay a land my father and his crew had known well. It was a land we were still getting to know. Our journey into the past would continue with more research and more people to ferret out the facts, but the faces of the people of Sudebrarup, Blick and Schleswig-Holstein would long be remembered. We had all bonded in our memories, and the information they gave me was a gift.

The local Germans could put human faces to the tragedy that enfolded in their village that day. The men of "Rhapsody in Junk" they got to see for the first time were not terrorfliegers, but young men far from home on a dangerous mission to fight a tyrant who had engulfed the entire world in the madness of his war.

We flew into New York on our return, and there were messages on my cell phone from two of my sons, John Thomas and Scott. The news was not good. My father had had a major stroke two days before and was hospitalized in very bad condition. My sons had been at a Cincinnati Reds game when my sister called them. They rushed to the hospital and stayed with him, and then Scott followed the ambulance at 3:00 a.m. when they moved him to a Cincinnati hospital for urgent care. The brothers took turns staying with him until Diane arrived driving from Michigan where she had just returned.

Back in Ohio, we went immediately to the hospital. Diane had promised him I was coming. I did not know what to expect when I entered his room. The stroke had left him drawn, and his eyes and facial expression reflected the reality of the stroke that had impaired his speech. He could barely swallow. He still recognized me, but he looked vacant and said nothing.

Diane and I monitored his progress for days as decisions were made where to move him now that he would need more care. We chose a facility close to my house. We wanted to return him to the familiarity of where he had been living, but he needed more care than the facility could provide. Their Hospice unit was full, and we would have to move him from the good people who cared for him and knew him well. The new facility could not take him for a week, so we moved him temporarily to the hospital Hospice unit near his old nursing home.

He was still in emergency care there when my nephew, Tom, drove from Michigan to place his Marine dog tags in my father's hands, and as quickly as he came, he drove back home. The other Michigan grandchildren drove down to see him and kept watch over him on their visits. One morning, Scott drove over to see him and wheeled him outside for fresh air. Ohio was in the seventeen-year cicada cycle, and the buzzing insects flew everywhere in massive clouds causing those who encountered them to jump and scream. For weeks, the insects swarmed covering cars, buildings and people.

Together, Scott and his grandfather sat quietly in the hospital courtyard enjoying each other's company and watching in amazement as the strange loud creatures hummed in unison overhead and flew around them and the trees. They noisy insects amused my father greatly. Their life cycle was nearing its end. Shortly, they would be gone.

I packed up my father's possessions from his nursing home room carefully putting his hats and gloves in a box. I packed the penguin and the picture of my mother and then took the cherished wartime pictures off his wall. My parents had celebrated their anniversary at that facility and had danced to 1940s music wearing their jackets from their wedding during the war years, and the staff had planned a party for them. My father and I had celebrated Halloween there, he dressing up as a gorilla and I as a witch, and at Easter, he volunteered to dress as the Easter bunny for all the staff's children who were coming for a party. He did so quite willingly, enjoying seeing the young children and holding them on his lap. After all the children had gone home, we both sat outside on the front porch in the tall rocking chairs. Still in his Easter bunny attire, he happily waved at all the cars that went by honking their horns. And it was in this building that even in his confused state he would still hold me in his arms and let me rest my head on his chest, if I was upset.

While we waited to move him, John and I took the rubber patch from the woods in Blick to Wright Patterson Air Force Base, where there was a B-24 on display. Darin, whom I had not met but felt that I knew well through the paternal bonds of war, was visiting there that day from Kansas to reunite with his father's crew. We were able to meet them and talk to the pilot who told me he had also flown "Rhapsody in Junk" before my dad flew in it. We showed him and Darin the patch, and together we found the B-24 inside. I held the weathered piece of history against the tire of that plane, and the long seam running its length matched exactly. It was then we knew we really had a piece of my father's plane. He had always told me his plane was aptly named, and the baldness of this aged patch proved it.

With his release from the hospital after several days, we moved him to the nursing facility five minutes from my house. I told him there was a park very near the new facility, but I could not guarantee we would see deer there like we had in the other park. In all the times I had walked in the new park for some reason, I had never seen even a small one, even though it was surrounded by woods where they could hide. Later, it turned out he was really too ill to even take him across the street to visit the new park at all. He would have really loved it there.

My father came by ambulance to the new facility, and I paced anxiously at the curb until he arrived. When he was settled into a room, I placed the picture of my mother across from his bed in his line of vision. For the first time, tears came to his eyes when he saw it. He was finally fully understanding her death. I quickly put the picture in a less visible place.

He was having difficulty swallowing, and we tried to feed him very slowly, but he wanted little to eat. While we sat with him for days in the hospital, Matthias, Gretchen and Claus Kuhl, all sent a copy of the German newspaper article Claus had written. There on the front page was the crew of "Rhapsody of Junk." A picture of the German investigators and witnesses and me talking in the woods was juxtaposed beside it. Angela graciously translated it for me, so I could read it to my father.

German newspaper article published after our visit to Germany
Courtesy of Mr. Claus Kuhl - Schleswiger Nachrichten

"Gretchen Bartel, owner of the county museum in Wagersrott remembers: It happened on the 18th of June, 1944, a Sunday morning, as my sister and I first heard the anti-aircraft fire over Barklesby, and shortly after the roar of a damaged plane. We watched anxiously from the back door of our home, as the burning plane flew directly over our house and a man jumped out and his parachute opened and carried him in the direction of the nearby Braup Wood. We heard the howling plane crash into the ground and then followed total silence.

The man who had jumped from the plane was Thomas Jeffers, the father of Marilyn, who wants to document his experiences in a book which is the reason for her visit to the original scenes of his time spent after the crash in Kiel, Berlin, Zagan in Poland, and Schleswig-Holstein. Her father is now over 80 and so could unfortunately not travel with her. Walton's original assumption was that her father had landed in Quern (about 40 kilometers away from Braup Wood.) but Hartwig Martensen from Nordgaardholz (near Quern) found this not to be the case after studying the chronicles, and by a chance contact with Gretchen Bartel found the solution: date etc. fit in perfectly with the memories of the then nine-year old Gretchen's description of the crash, and so began a lively email contact with the U.S.A. Bartel found help in an English relation, Angela Gotzke, and a meeting was arranged in the Hollanderhof (Gretchen's home.) Mr. Martensen met the American lady and her husband at the train in Suderbrarup and found her to be charming and warm hearted, and she repeatedly asserted her peaceful mission. She had brought photos of her father's B-24 plane with her, nicknamed "Rhapsody in Junk." The war-tired plane was susceptible from the start and had already lost the first motor over Hamburg. Before the crash, only one propeller was working. Nine from the ten crew members were able to survive the crash. Jeffers was the last to jump out.

Sixty years later the path led back to Blick in Braup Wood where the holes which the four plane motors had made in the earth are still to be seen. Ernst Hansen who also witnessed the crash and who led the interested group into the wood, was then at the time of the crash 15 years old and one of the first to arrive at the scene. Later, many more people arrived and began to collect the metal and aluminum and Plexiglas pieces that were strewn over the surrounding ground, until the police arrived to cordon off the area.

The thoughts and words of the small group returned again and again to the time of the crash, when all lived in fear, and when those tiny fragments of the tragic crash had been made into kitchen implements of aluminum or pieces of jewelry from Plexiglas. Marilyn Walton's visit brought back vivid memories to those who had lived through this most unhappy period, and for the younger generation, she aroused a healthy curiosity. Now, all will be anxiously awaiting the Walton book to read about her visit and her father's war memories."

My father did not respond, but he seemed to hang on every word and study the crew picture gracing the German front page. I had hoped that the German newspaper would mention Matthias who had traveled so far across Germany at our behest.

A newspaper reporter from the Cincinnati Enquirer, Howard Wilkinson, came to my home to write up our journey to Germany. He planned to run the article on June 18th, on the sixtieth anniversary of the plane's loss. We spent a good bit of time talking about the war. I asked him to contact Matthias in Germany who had been so instrumental in making our trip happen. True to his word, Howard did, and much to his delight Matthias was quoted in the American paper.

A photographer from the newspaper came and took pictures of the tea strainer and hooks and the rubber patch sitting beside my father's WWII Army/Air Corps hat. Its golden eagle insignia reflected off the glass table the items sat upon. His crew picture and a picture of "Rhapsody in Junk" were tucked in the display. The items on this small glass table represented such an integral part of his life. These few items told the story of war and suffering, history and redemption and the kindness of a former foe. The photographer and Howard and I drove the short distance to the Hospice facility where my father now rested. I placed the rubber tire patch and the hook and the tea strainer in his eager hands.

"Here is your plane," I remember saying to him. "It has come home to you in a different form after sixty years."

He twisted the tea strainer in his hands and rubbed his fingers over the rubber patch. How much he understood, I will never really know, but his eyes seemed wide with interest, and they followed all of us as he held the tea strainer tightly. Howard approached my father's bedside before we left and looked into his vacant eyes. He thanked my father for his World War II service to his country and told him how pleased he was to meet him. Tears glistened in the hardened reporter's eyes.

My phone rang the night before publication, and one of the employees at the Cincinnati Enquirer said he was looking through all their resources to find Blick, Germany, to pinpoint it on a map for publication.

"We can usually find anything in the world," he said, "but we can't find Blick."

Evidently, air and sea rescue had the same problem.

I told him where it was, and he was satisfied. The next day the story ran on the front page. The crew picture accompanied it as well as a map of Germany with Blick clearly marked. Once again, the crew of "Rhapsody in Junk" smiled from the pages of a newspaper.

The article's publication triggered emails and phone calls from people I had never met. Don Ebding, a model airplane builder, emailed me and asked my permission to build a model of "Rhapsody in Junk" as a tribute to my father.

Model of "Rhapsody in Junk" made by Mr. Don Ebding who matched every detail exactly, right down to the identical shade of paint

He wished to give me the model, and like so many others he asked me to give his thanks to my father for his sacrifices in the war.

## Chapter 65

# *Our Hero Falls*

For two weeks, we kept vigil at his bedside. The penguin rested on the pillow never to be thrown again, along with a little stuffed dog brought by the supervisor at the previous facility who had become very attached to my father. Often, she drove fifteen miles after work to visit and care for him on her own time. Day by day, he declined. We spent hours praying for him and caring for him and watching him. Restless, he often threw the sheets off, and I could not help but notice his feet--how many miles they had walked in his lifetime, and I thought of how cold they had been marching through Germany. I held his warm foot in my hands. It would take no more steps.

There was much time to look back at our family's life together. Long after the war, my father would still refer to eating something good as a "bash." In researching his history, I found the same terms he had used over the years were also used by his crew and the other men of his era. He talked of people who were "sad-looking apples," a term that I had read in war journals, as the writers had described forlorn prisoners. "Eager beavers," which he called us from time to time, were the most prone and anxious to escape the prisoner of war camps. He spoke of "flubbing around," which planes often did for a full hour as every wing man looked for his element leader, and bombardiers looked for their squadron leader as pilots jockeyed for position to get into formation. Seeing something good we had to eat, he would smile reaching for it and tell us he thought he would "liberate it." If my sister and I argued, he yelled, "At ease!" to end the "flap" we were in. Oftentimes, he would be more amused at it all, and say to us, "Let's you and him fight." These are words he heard in his camp when tensions of crowded men rose to a pinnacle, and onlookers watched other men settle their differences physically and bystanders received the benefit of the resolution. He never changed the "him" to a female version. He preferred using the phrase the way he had learned it.

The camp was the place where "there I was," stories were told, as each new prisoner told and retold the story of his descent from the sky and capture, ad infinitum. After so many retellings, the men found themselves without an audience. There were tales of planes "giving up the ghost." The men became "sack loggers," sleeping away the day from pure boredom. They "logged many sack hours" instead of recording flight hours in a pilot's log, counting out the days they would come home. Broken items were "kaput," and "raus" and "raus mit euch" became their alarm clock and invitation to daily appells or barracks inspections. They cooked in a "communal pot," and they spent hours dividing a special treat evenly during a bash. Growing up, we always went by the rule if one person cut a piece of pie or cake, the other person chose first. He spoke of "stooges" and "ferrets," the guards specializing in escape detection. The vocabulary of the time and place stayed with a man for a lifetime. Everything did. Sixty years after the war, my father still drove a car using both feet on the pedals reminiscent of his experience in the "heavies" of the era.

Diane and I were warned to give him no "duff gen" (bad information). He urged us to move along faster with a cry of "Hubba, hubba," telling us we were "tail end Charlies." It is only now that I understand that was a bad luck of the draw in the formation placing a ship at the end and most vulnerable position unprotected and most likely to be hit. It was always time to "hit the rack," at bedtime. A semi-stern protective figure would ask for a "time hack" before we went on dates, or if we were to meet him somewhere to make sure all our watches were synchronized, just as important to him then, as it was before a mission. "After You Alphonse," he would say mimicking the French cartoon character in the New York Journal News, as he held a door for us. Continually bowing, Alphonse and Gaston were the symbols of a politeness so unctuous that it prevented anything from ever getting done. I saw the phrase so many times in the books of other prisoners of war.

My father spoke of "sweating it out," reminiscent of the days of waiting for the planes returning from a mission, and from time to time he spoke of "Big Stoop," a man so notorious that those who were not assigned to Stalag Luft IV, as the enlisted men were, still knew of his brutal reputation and the reign of terror he generated there. We never thought to ask where all these terms came from as we grew up. Now, it was abundantly clear. The more I read veterans' journals and books, the more such phrases leapt off the pages. They were terms firmly planted in his mind and theirs at a formative stage of life never to be forgotten. They were the familiar phrases that bonded men during a time of danger and crisis, and afterward, they were the words and phrases my generation grew up knowing but never questioning.

As I sat beside him reading a new book about a man who had been a prisoner of war, one of the paragraphs stunned me. The man described the hunger of the men in the camp and wrote of how they helped to assuage that hunger and to kill idle hours by keeping notebooks recording favorite restaurants they would visit after the war. The men went around the camp finding men from different states he said. Each man was asked the best place to eat in his home state or city, and the answer was recorded in the book. These were all the places the men dreamed of visiting when they were free, and the list gave them some hope. Now, I knew what the little black notebook from my father's bedside drawer was. I think he kept it all those years to remember how hungry he had once been, and he never took anything for granted.

Now, ice cream was the only thing he could swallow without choking or aspirating, so we fed him all that he would take. We prayed the rosary with him, played soft music for him and when he would watch, we watched animal shows on television. In days, he was refusing food and sleeping more. Our old soldier, true to MacArthur's quote, was truly fading away. While he slept, we took breaks and visited the park to let our dogs run. Scott, the closest living grandchild, took the day off work to stay by his grandfather's side. At night, he slept on the floor next to the bed. The other grandchildren, farther away, called to stay apprised of their grandfather's condition.

I sent the Enquirer's newspaper article to Matthias to share with the people of Blick.

> "I read the newspaper article and I'm very glad that the report mentioned me in detail. . ."

Simultaneously, a letter arrived from Gretchen Bartel. She sent me a picture of the farmer who had picked up my father that day. He was standing beside his home which we had seen there. It was too late to show it to my father and ask if the man was familiar to him. Gretchen had chosen the day of the anniversary of the plane's loss to write. She had not yet realized we found Flaugher's burial place.

> Dear Marilyn,
>
> Today is June 18, and our thoughts are with you and the plane crash which took place sixty years ago today in our surroundings and which caused us great fear. If you had not come to find what happened to your father, this plane crash would have been forgotten, because only those who are at least seventy years old could remember it. I have been approached about this now quite often because the newspaper article by Herr Kuhl. It stirred everything up again. Please let me know where your father's friend was buried. I will then try to find the gravesite. I hope that your father

is still in good health. Angela told me about your telephone conversation. Please write to me again. My grandchild can translate the letter.

Many dear regards,

Gretchen Bartel

Six days later my father would be dead. His health continued to deteriorate. For another week we kept vigil at his bedside. As the days of June rolled by, and his death was imminent, priests came and went praying final prayers with him and giving him Holy Communion. Family members took turns going in to say their final good-byes to him, each spending a few moments alone by his bedside. We held his hand and whispered in his ear telling him we loved him and what a good father he had been while secretly hoping he would never leave us.

Late the night of June 23$^{rd}$, Diane left to get some sleep. I stayed until 3:30 a.m. the morning of the 24$^{th}$, and my father's vital signs improved. I told the Hospice nurse I was going to run home, just five minutes away, and take a shower, and I'd be right back. Shortly after I stepped out of the shower, I heard the phone ring.

"You'd better come right now," the nurse said.

I tore from the house, jumped in the car and sped the short distance toward the care facility. Peeking out from the trees along the way stood a small female deer watching and waiting in the woods at the edge of the road. I swerved to miss it, barely slowing down. I raced into the parking lot, threw the car into park and ran into the building and down the hall. The nurse's somber face greeted me.

"He died at 4:25," she said.

I looked at the large clock on the wall above his bed. It was 4:26 in the morning.

We waited for him to take one more breath, but he did not. She said he had opened his eyes, looked at the ceiling, breathed a labored breath and was gone. She told me so many times in Hospice she had seen patients wait until everyone was gone to die as they chose to do, by themselves on their own terms, sparing the family they loved those last agonizing minutes. As in life, he was always thinking of his family. Knowing my father, I'm sure this would have been his choice. He did his work on this earth, and folded his tired wings. Now, he was gone from us but resting in God's hands.

On that sunny June morning, the funeral director arrived, and we watched as the van took our hero away. I wrote his obituary and told my friends of his death. His struggle was over.

## Chapter 66

# *Saying Good-Bye*

The next morning, I took my dog to the park across from the nursing facility. I could see my father's former room and window. It was very early, and there was a morning mist that covered the green grass and swept and swirled up the embankment of a small hill where I walked. Even on this summer morning, there was a light breeze that cooled the awakening park. It was deserted, except for just the two of us. As we approached the small hill shrouded in morning mist, I glanced up and stopped where I stood. A beautiful giant buck stood at the apex as if posing for a picture. In the quiet stillness, it watched us for a few seconds standing very still, and then slowly lifted its regal head and turned to run into the woods. I never saw it again.

I returned to the room where my father died and collected his few things. With his stuffed penguin tucked under my arm I left the building and knew I could never return.

As we made funeral preparations, there was one more person I wanted to inform of my father's death--Claudius Scharff. His father had passed away some years ago, but the pain of his loss was still evident. With much sorrow, I typed out an email to him:

Claudius,

At 4:25 this morning, my hero passed away. It has been a long struggle this week. We are so glad he is now at peace. We were so lucky to have him for 83 years. His link with your father so long ago has led to a wonderful relationship with you. Fate takes so many twists. Keep us in your prayers over the weekend as we lay him to rest.

Warmly,

Marilyn

Although he may have expected the news, it still caught him emotionally off balance.

"Dear, Dear Marilyn,

Our hearts are with you and your family right now. You have lost your hero, and that is sad. But soon it will become uplifting.

We lost our hero sometime back. But we still remember what it was like. Confusion of emotions. An internally produced drug to dull the actual physiological and psychological pain which helps acceptance in the short and long term.

You did more at the twilight of your father's life than many a son would have done. Your trip, perhaps a little too late, still brought more home to your father than you had anticipated. Bringing the hand wrought tea sieve back to him was an ultimate means of telling your father that you understood what he had endured and who he was to you. To him - his war years - were probably the most important part of his life, and his daughter (who should have been a son) brings back full circle, the defining moments of his life. His eye movement and recognition of what he held in his hands must have sent a message of overwhelming recognition of what you had done for him and, of course, in his eyes, what you had turned out to be. He was so proud, and had he been physically able, he would have burst around in joy at what you did for him.

Remember him this way, and the remembrance shall endure. I see my father as a natural extension of what he was. He is in our minds daily. We talk about his opinions on the subject matter. We opine about his feelings on another matter etc. He is always there for us.

So, you too Marilyn, will always have your father near to you, even though he is gone, his presence will never leave you. And I hope that you may be comforted in that.

Yes, I think a special relationship has grown among us, and I too hope that that will endure. It reminds me of the special relationship my dad had with a pilot he had saved from a death sentence. The son of the ailing pilot called on the eve of his father's death and asked my father to visit once more. That was the dying man's wish. My father humbly and awestruck complied. The family Weisel will always be in our hearts.

You and your family have joined those ranks, and we are inexorably linked from the past into the future.

We pray,

Hanns-Claudius and Monika Scharff"

I was incredibly touched.

Comforting words poured in from my research friends and the remaining crew. From around the world, via hand written notes or email, the Germans and the Americans offered their prayers and consolation. My new German friends felt they knew my father through me, and their genuine sorrow was evident. No one had to tell them the depth of my loss.

"Marilyn,

We were so sorry and sad to learn about your father. It seemed so strange to think that when the article was written he was still alive, and although I have never met him, we've talked about him so much during these last weeks that I feel I know him very well. He has found his peace now.

Fond wishes to you both, Angela and Manfred"

Howard Wilkinson called from the Cincinnati Enquirer and asked to write a special obituary. Then I heard from Matthias.

"I should like to offer you my sincere condolences. I will phone my grandfather to tell him about your father's death. I'll ask him to inform your friends in Blick, too."

It was good to hear from Matthias. He sent one more:

"I phoned my grandfather and told him about your father's death. My grandfather talked to Frau Bartel so that your friends in Blick know about it. My parents and grandparents offer you their condolences, too.

Last weekend we especially thought of your father at a church service in the Catholic Church "Heilig-Geist" in Iserlohn. Me and my twin brothers are altar servers.

Some days ago I got to know my English mark for this term. I got a one (Author's note --- one is an equivalent of an A.) in my report in English for the first time. I think it's because I have been improving my English through the contact with you."

The funeral director called me and said he had the clothes he needed but asked that I bring a pair of socks. Socks---my father never seemed to have them when he needed them. I pulled into the parking lot of Meijer and quickly walked in the door. We had shopped there so often, and now all that would change. I bought him the best and warmest pair of socks I could find. I turned to look behind me when I took them from the basket at the cash register. The sudden and devastating loss of that gentle figure wrapped in coats and multiple shirts and socks who dug through my basket to place items on the conveyor belt was not looking back at me. The void, now permanent, almost took my breath away. On the way to the funeral home, I drove past the nursing facility where my father had spent his last days with my mother. The tall empty porch rockers, almost ghostly in their appearance, rocked gently in the breeze--devoid of one tall and gentle white rabbit.

A video Claudius had recently sent arrived, and as I waited to leave for my father's visitation, I decided to watch it. It was an old copy he had just found and had never seen himself until recently. The Master Interrogator was being interviewed after the war about his interrogation techniques used at Dulag Luft. I was captivated by the humor and repartee between the participants as he addressed some young military officers. It was strangely comforting to watch this man, whom I'd never met, who so long ago had been linked with my father in a different time and place. I was grateful to his son for sending it.

At the conclusion of the video, it was time to go to the visitation. My father was dressed in his black Air Force dress uniform he had worn to my wedding. Battle ribbons were displayed proudly on his chest, and the American and United States Air Force flags stood at either end of his shiny wooden casket. In the corner, rested a triangular American flag. I approached his casket and for one last time laid my head on his chest feeling the cold medals press into my cheek.

My father had a full military funeral. The back of his funeral folder featured a B-24 banking into the sky and disappearing into the clouds. I think he would have liked that.

His grandsons carried his coffin from the funeral home. Five of his grandchildren had served or were serving in the Navy, Army and Marines, and finally one of them, Alex, represented the Air Force. As they carried his coffin from the funeral home, we played the theme from "The Great Escape," the movie about his former prisoner of war camp. Little Jack, his great-grandson, marched behind with a bouquet of small American flags.

After a Latin rite Mass of Christian Burial, which he had known so well as an altar boy, we began the long drive to the cemetery in Springfield. There had been such a void for him after my mother died, and now they would be reunited.

An honor guard from Wright-Patterson Air Force Base met us at the cemetery and carried his casket to his gravesite. How youthful their faces looked. The strains of "Taps" echoed from the bugler that warm, June day, and military rifles cracked out a 21-gun salute. One of the guards handed me the shell casings. The triangular folded American flag from his casket was presented to me with words of appreciation from the President of the United States, and our hero was laid to rest beside my mother who had been at his side for sixty-two years.

An old soldier and patriot had lived a noble life. We each took a rose from the funeral spray to remember him by and drove away.

## Chapter 67

## *Remembering Yesterday*

I drove back to the funeral home to pick up some flower baskets, and as I drove I noticed the sky was criss-crossed with dozens of contrails, brilliant stripes of white against the brilliant blue sky. I called Scott, who was driving from the opposite direction.

"Do you see the crosses in the sky?" I asked him.

He saw them too, and we were both humbled by what we saw.

Once again, all seemed right with the world.

After my father's death, I comforted myself by wearing his sweater and playing his 1940s war era music he had loved so much whenever I drove him anywhere. "The White Cliffs of Dover," "There'll Always Be an England," "Boogie Woogie Bugle Boy" all delighted him and blared from the radio. When he could remember nothing else, he remembered the words to these songs that had been so meaningful in his life. I vacillated from happily singing along on some days to almost pulling off the road to mourn for him on others. Daily, as I took the dog to the park, I passed the room where he died.

Now, came the unbelievably sad task of going through his possessions. I held his shirts and coat to my face. His smell was still on them. The socks that I had labeled with Jeffers were stuffed into a bag. His baseball cap emblazoned with a picture of a B-24 that he wore constantly rested on my dining room table. In the bottom of the box was a note I found on his bedside table a week or so before he left the nursing home.

---

*I LOVE YOU MARILYN*

*I LOVE YOU DIANE*

*Thank you!*

*Mr. Jeffers.*

The note my father wrote a few weeks before he died. Written in bold pencil strokes, the note read, "I love you Marilyn; I love you Diane. Thank you! Mr. Jeffers."

He surrounded me, but he was gone. How would I ever be able to sort though all that he owned? I found a million reasons not to do it as the weeks passed. One day, the Vietnam Vets left a brochure, and they requested clothing. In my heart I knew he would want his clothing to help others who had none. The time was right. I packed most of his clothes into the bright yellow bags. I held up the beige winter coat with the worn elastic button loop. That old coat was such a part of him. He had many much better, but he preferred that one. So many times, I had stretched that elastic loop over his top button when he could no longer do it himself. I knew he would want the coat to warm someone who could not afford a coat, but parting with it was like abandoning an integral part of him. I held it in my arms one last time, slipped the elastic over the top button and gently put it in the bag. Then I put the bags at the curb. I arranged to be away from the house the day of the pick up. When I returned the bags were gone.

Knowing one of his roommates in Stalag Luft III was named McDarby, I typed the information into the computer. I found a McDarby in Indiana, and that night I made a call. The voice that answered was the right age. He was the right one. He remembered my father, and I told him of his passing. He had been a pilot from Missouri in October of 1943, when his B-17 sent to bomb a ball bearing factory in Schweinfurt, was shot down by FW190s. Bailing out near Maastricht, Holland, he sprained his ankle upon landing and was captured by the German infantry. Names like Schweinfurt and Ploesti even after so many years would bring a chill to the men who flew the missions to those cities and to historians who chronicled the war.

McDarby told me my father was a terrible bridge player, and he said that the roommates played bridge often to pass the time of day. They played a lot of poker also, and during the games the comic-strip nick-names Downing had given the men in their group contributed to the enjoyment. I asked him if he remembered the names. He did not miss a beat and repeated them to me as if he had used them yesterday.

> Tribbett was "Uncle Raffe," a hillbilly.
> 
> Newcomer, Jeffers, was "Dead End Kid"
> 
> Tall, McDarby was "Earthquake Magoon"
> 
> Beatty was "Mr. Chips," a school teacher from movie fame.
> 
> Roberts was "Robbie"
> 
> Don Stout was "Hose Nose"
> 
> O'Neil was H.P – "Hot Pile"
> 
> Downing called himself "Trigger"
> 
> Kauffman was "Snow Shoe," and
> 
> Morris Jones was "Available Jones"

I laughed each time he told me one. I told him I was writing my father's story he was never able to finish.

In writing my father's story, I went over mission records and archive records, journals, letters and first-hand accounts from men who were with him. Each trip to the mailbox was a new revelation. For weeks I tried to find out just what the target was that the crew was bombing in Germany that day. No matter where I looked, I came up empty-handed. I could find the cities but not exactly what it was in Fassberg they were after. I told Dean's daughter, Brenda, how the information had been impossible to find. Then she remembered a Christmas card my father had sent to her father many years ago after they had run into each other at a 458th dedication at Wright-Patterson Air Force Base. She scanned it to me.

> Lawrence,
>
> I'm real happy that we could get together after all these years. Regarding our last mission, the name of the plane was "Rhapsody in Junk." Very appropriate, since our problems started when we lost two engines due to poor maintenance. SN was 41-28733-P. It was one of the original ships flown to England in January, 1944. Our target that day was Fassberg, Germany, near Hamburg, a V-1/V-2 missile launching and storage site. We went down on the Danish peninsula and spent our first night in jail in Schleswig (which by the way is my wife's grandmother's home town!) I think I told you that. Harold Flaugher is buried in the American Cemetery near Liege, Belgium. My wife and I visited there several years ago. Hope to see you again some time.
>
> Jeff

There it was in my father's own handwriting, he clearly described their target that day, a V-1 rocket research and storage station. It was as if he was communicating directly with me, and the answer to my question came in his own handwriting.

I continued to write as a tribute to my father. In doing so, it kept me in contact with so many who had shown interest in him. Matthias was no exception.

> "Thanks for your long email last week. It was exciting to get to know something about the way a funeral for fallen officers takes place in the U.S.A. I think your father had a very festival funeral. . ."

I once more turned my attention to finding Butler's family. Through persistence and help of researchers who traced obituaries, I finally found not just the first daughter but two more, and middle daughter, Kay, had a son at the Air Force Academy. Until I made contact with Butler's daughters, I did not know their father was quite an artist in his prisoner of war days. Kay sent me a picture, one of many her father had sketched sixty years before. It showed my father reading a letter to her father telling Butler he had a daughter.

Drawn over sixty years ago at Stalag Luft III, Dee Butler captured the moment fellow prisoner, Jeffers, told him he had a daughter.

Courtesy of Mrs. Kay Gamble

I had not known this treasure existed. I wondered if my father had ever seen it. I'd like to think he did. Later, she sent me her father's complete journal with numerous accounts and pictures he had drawn. Sadly, the Butler girls had also lost their mother, Miriam. I passed on the materials I received from Kay to each of the other crew member's daughters. I sent her pictures of her father holding Kay's sister just after the war from my father's photo album. For years, we had all grown up hearing the stories of "Rhapsody in Junk" and seeing our fathers' war mementoes. Jointly, the combining of all of them painted a more interesting and full picture. How strong the bonds were between all these men.

Thinking of that bond, I thought back to a day I attended a reunion with my father where for the first time I met General Clark. It had been a day of watching old friends and comrades reunite at Wright-Patterson Air Force Base, and I took it all in with great joy and admiration for them. A man had approached my father that day and read his name tag. Giant tears welled up in the man's eyes.

"Jeff?" he said incredulously, "I thought you were dead."

My father's eyes and mine misted over as well as the man recounted the event of June 18th, 1944, when the Northrop crew went down.

"I came back to the building," the man continued, still experiencing the pain of that moment so long ago, "and you were all gone."

He had left on his own mission and had not returned believing they had all been killed in action. I never learned the man's name.

For silent moments these two men stared into each other's eyes in disbelief as the man comprehended this discovery. No more words needed to be spoken. Thinking back on that moment, I decided to visit the Academy. It was time for another reunion, this time of my own.

## Chapter 68

# The Good General

Eighteen years had passed since I had spoken with General Clark. It would be good to see him again.

The outline of purple mountains in the distance, as I flew in, signaled my arrival to Colorado Springs. The Air Force Academy lay just below. My mother had told me how handsome a man General Clark was during the war years when she knew him. I called him, and he agreed to pick me up at my hotel near the Academy so that we could have lunch. I watched from the lobby as a car parked in the lot, and I watched the general walk slowly in, aided by the use of a cane. Dressed in a navy sport coat with an American flag on the lapel, ninety-one year old General Clark was still a dashing figure.

We seated ourselves in the hotel's atrium restaurant. After a hearty lunch, he took me to the Academy library. We drove into the gate on a clear day that made the mountains at the base of the Academy look like a painting. He was saluted sharply, but still insisted on showing his i.d. We wound slowly through the curved roads, and he slowed and pointed to the right.

"That is where my wife is buried," he said.

Portrait of former superintendent, Lt. General A.P. Clark, which hangs in the McDermott Library at the United States Air Force Academy
Courtesy of USAFA McDermott Library, Stalag Luft III Collections

*Rhapsody in Junk* ✷ 391

As a very young Lt. Colonel, handsome Albert P. Clark had his picture taken by the Germans for his POW identification card. He became one of the longest-held prisoners of war at Stalag Luft III.

Courtesy of USAFA McDermott Library, Stalag Luft III Collections

Lt. General A.P. Clark – U.S. Air Force Academy - 2006

Courtesy of USAFA McDermott Library, Stalag Luft III Collections

He had lost his dear wife just two years before.

"And that's where I'll be buried."

It was a beautiful area.

We rode the elevator up to the sixth floor and entered The Colonel Richard Gimbel Aeronautical History Collection. The Gimbel Collection boasts an amazing array of items pertaining to the history of flight. General Clark was proud to show me the five-thousand-year-old seals carved from semi-precious stones that document man's earliest dreams of flight. Within the room was the Clark Collection commemorating Stalag Luft III. We walked between the glass cases and long rows of books. In an adjacent room, a glossy polished table held his famous scrapbooks, opened and ready for us to examine. We pulled up our chairs, and he took me back in time. I had not realized what an excellent artist he was, and his pencil sketches from the war depicting camp life were stunning. He turned the pages with his careful hand. A West Point ring adorned one finger. I asked him about his ring, and he told me it was a second ring. He had taken off a glove at an airport several years before, as he tried to help an elderly man, and the original ring that he had worn throughout the war flew off, never to be found.

As we looked at the scrapbooks he had pulled through the snow on the long march, he spoke of a woman he remembered seeing on the march… "a young well-dressed woman wearing a fur coat and hat sitting in a fancy pony cart. She was not the typical refugee, and she had just begun her long journey." He wondered what happened to her, and still did after all the years that had passed.

The librarians brought out a BBC documentary about "The Great Escape." He dimmed the lights, and just the two of us watched it. I was amused that the good general knew all of the men who were interviewed. Soon, they spoke of the horror of the boxcars, and he turned to speak to me.

"How awful it was," he said sadly. "Those dirty boxcars held prisoners and Jews—and it was terrible what they did to the Jews." I could see the pain of that memory returning, and we turned the movie off.

I told General Clark I would love to see one of the original compasses from the camp if they had one. In a glass case we found a kriegie compass boldly stamped on the back that it had been created at Stalag Luft III. Next to it was an Army Air Corps jacket of the era. General Clark explained how the men hid maps in the linings of their clothes. That particular jacket had been sent to the cleaners before it was placed in the collection he told me, and the cleaner found two more maps hidden in the epaulets that until that time no one knew were there. He smiled impishly recounting this story to me. His boys had been immensely clever.

We had spent hours in the library, and it was time to go.

We stopped at a gas station, as he needed to refuel his car. I offered to pump the gas for him, and at first being the gentleman he was, he would not hear of it, but I told him it was the very least I could do for him. I was humbled and honored to do such a small thing for him. General Clark drove me back to my hotel, and I took a picture of him capturing that wide still boyish grin I had seen in the picture from Moosburg as he sat high atop the liberating tank. I told him how comforting it was for me to see him and how much I enjoyed my time visiting with him. Then I kissed him good-bye.

I spent the next day at the Academy as there was a dedication of the C-46 Commando that the Hump Pilots flew during the war in the Pacific. The brave men who transported fuel and oil over the Himalayas from India to China after the Japanese closed the Burma Road were there for the unveiling of a bronze sculpture of their plane that would stand on the Academy's square. The men who "flew the Hump" had lost many comrades on the treacherous air route as the United States supplied the Chinese Army, the U.S. Army 14$^{th}$ Air Force and the China Air Task Force.

A small band of cadets broke into "In the Mood," as I walked across the sunny, but windy square. My father had taught me to dance to that song when I was small enough to stand on his shoes. I buttoned my coat against the wind. As I looked at a B-24 sculpture there, several of the men and their wives beckoned for me to join their group for the ceremony and took me in as one of their own. The sculptor of the plane spoke, and I realized I had spoken to him on the phone just weeks before and ordered folded flag pins that he made for our family members to wear in honor of my father to an upcoming 458th/RAF dedication. I had no idea he also was responsible for the bronze sculptures at the Academy.

It was good to see all of these men getting the credit they deserved for flying difficult missions and helping to win the victory over Japan. I missed my father very much that day.

As I drove to the airport the next day, a glider sailed gracefully through the sky casting a shadow on the purple and grey mountain. The morning was tranquil and glorious. I boarded my own plane and settled into my seat, and we too soared into the air. As I watched the majestic mountains fall behind the plane, I wondered if I would ever have a chance to see General Clark again.

## Chapter 69

## Behind the Wire

When I returned home, I found that General Clark had written to his friend, Arnold Wright, in Arkansas and asked him to contact me. Arnold had published the ledgers of Lt. Ewell Ross McCright. Now entitled "Behind the Wire," the book was instrumental in authenticating information that enabled men to receive the proper medals they deserved including Purple Hearts. Many, including my father, had lost all their military records in a fire in St. Louis years ago. The ledgers also allowed people like me to research and document information reading the first-hand accounts. I called Arnold and ordered a copy of the limited-edition book. When it arrived, I read the entries of each of the incoming officers of "Rhapsody in Junk" as dictated to McCright after the men's arrival at Stalag Luft III. Each entry had been carefully transcribed. (Author's notes in parentheses)

>Jeffers, Thomas F. 2 LT – USAAF 128/5 (building and room assigned in the camp) Bombardier. Springfield, OH - 6128 (POW #) B-24 6-18-44 Dulag Luft 6-20 to 6-23 Stalag Luft 6-27-44. No. 1-4-3 engs.

failed. Oil pressure dropped. Bailed out landed near Schleswig. Captured Imm by Luftwaffe. Hamburg, Germany (target) M- (married) – C – (Catholic) - 2-1-21 (birthdate)

Butler, Dee J. 2Lt – USAAF 129/16 - Pilot (He was co-pilot) – Ogden, Utah, #6097 - B- 24 6-18-44 – Dulag Luft 6-20 to 6-23 Stalag Luft 3 6-27-44 - Same as ledger # 1531 (Jeffers). Landed 10 M from Schleswig, Germany. Feet injured on landing. Airfield Hamburg 733 ("Rhapsody in Junk's" #), M – (married) M. (Mormon) 8-11-20.

Deimel, Frank C. 2LT – USAAF – 126/7 Navigator – Chicago, Illinois - #6104 – B-24 – 6-18-44 – Dulag Luft 6-21 to 6-24 Stalag Luft 3 6-27-44 – same as Northrop (#1438). Cuts on face. capt. Imm by civilians. Left shoulder dislocated in air - came back in place when landed. – Air Field, Hamburg – S (single) C (Catholic) – 8-7-16.

Northrop, Henry H. 2 LT - USAAF - 128/17 Pilot - Batavia, N.Y. #6152 – B-24 – 6 – 18-44 Dulag Luft - 6-20 to 6-24 - Stalag Luft 3 – 6-28-44 – Eng. No. 1-4-3 failed. Bailed out-landed in vicinity of Kiel, Germany. capt. by civilians. Airfield - Hamburg, Germany – S – P (Protestant) 3-28-17.

Brodek, William J – USAAF 125/7 – Armament Officer – Jamaica, N.Y. - #6096 – B-24 – 6-18-44 – Dulag Luft 6-20 to 6-22 Stalag Luft 6-27-44 – No. 1-4 engs. Failed. Straggled No. 3 destroyed by flak. Bailed out – landed 10 M from Schleswig, Germany. Capt. Imm by home guard. Flying as gunner. Airfield South of Hamburg #733 – S-C (Catholic) – 8-19-16.

I referred to the book many times as I researched. Every now and then I gratefully took a request from Ed in Belgium to check for a name in the book for someone he was doing research for. He helped me far more than I helped him.

I read my father's entry over and over trying to glean any small bit of additional information about his capture. The remaining crew and my father had mentioned being held at a guard house in Kiel, yet after visiting the area we found it would have been almost an hour's drive back to Kiel that night, only to be brought back to the castle in Schleswig the next day. I read Butler's journal again. He stated Flaugher had been picked up within a military facility. I pulled out the MACR again and read the German reports. They were signed by a German officer in Schleswig, not Kiel. The MACR said Flaugher was picked up in Eckernforde which is adjacent to Schleswig. I wrote to Matthias and asked him to ask his grandfather if there was a naval facility nearby then.

> "I asked my grandfather if there was a German military base in Eckernförde. He told me that there had been a research institute for torpedoes."

So, there was a navy base at Eckernforde. I wondered if the crew could have been taken to a guard house there, which was much closer to where they came down. They had been briefed on Kiel before the mission, and from the air the subs at Eckernforde would have made the area look very much like Kiel that they had already flown over. Cardenas had been picked up by Marines, and my father had told me he had been picked up by a farmer and then eventually taken by Marines. The base at Eckernforde had been so secret that no one knew it was there.

My father's Military Officer magazine arrived in the mail that day. On the "In Memoriam" page, he was listed in the" Sounding Taps" column. I ran my finger over his name still in disbelief he was gone. When his Second Air Division newsletter came, he was listed under "Folded Wings." His death was slowly becoming a reality.

The author and son, Scott, before boarding the B-24 for a memorial flight

## Chapter 70

## Flight into the Past

When a B-24 from the Collings Foundation, one of the few operational wartime aircraft that fly today, visited in our area, I was determined to fly on it. Darin emailed me that it had just been in Kansas, and he had the flight of a lifetime simulating his father's B-24 experience. I scheduled a ride and took my son Scott, a licensed pilot, with me. Before leaving home that day, I found the bombardier wings my father had made of pitch and metal from Spam cans at Stalag Luft III that he had given to me years before, after they were shown in a POW display near my home. I pinned the wings on my 8th Air Force sweatshirt and felt ready to board.

At the airfield, the "Dragon and His Tail" sat on the runway, its silver body gleaming in the sun. A crowd had gathered to view it. After a short briefing, Scott pulled me up into the belly of the plane through the bomb bay, the same place the crew used to enter. We sat on faded green cushions on the long bench my father had sat on for take-off, tucked just below the cockpit. My legs straddled a yellow oxygen container, and I was warned not to let one of the moving cables nearby touch my leg. We were wedged in tightly, and the plane rattled and shook when the engines thundered to life. We had to yell to each other to be heard. We looked down the narrow fuselage to the open camera hatch. Both the hatch and the bomb bay doors bore signs warning that stepping on the doors during flight would cause them to open, as they were made to double as escape hatches. I tried to imagine my father parachuting from that relatively small camera hatch in the panicked moments before the crash. The hatch doors then closed, Scott and I held hands, and we took off.

After take-off, the pilot rang the bail out bell, our signal to unhook the military-style lap belt and move around. We crawled on our hands and knees through the narrow bomb bay area to reach the nose. It was difficult to go through even without the five-hundred-pound bombs they had carried in the racks. I poked my head in the cockpit where the pilot and co-pilot sat in incredibly close quarters surrounded by tons of instruments. Through the Plexiglas of the nose in front of the bombsight, we got an idea of the spectacular sweeping vistas my father saw as bombardier. The bombardier and navigator's quarters there were unbelievably cramped. We crawled back and stood by the open hatches where the waist gunners had stood firing at the enemy. We looked down to the river and the edge of northern Kentucky as the wind blew through our hair from the open hatches. How cold it must have been standing there for the waist gunners when the temperature was fifty below zero. We pushed our way through the narrow passages that led to the tail gunner position where Clifford had been so far removed from the crew, and we scanned the skies from that vantage point. After half an hour's ride, the bail out bell rang again, and we hooked our seat belts and roared back down the runway to land. The flight made me wonder how any crew could survive thirty to thirty-five missions in the extremely confining interior and in such noise and frigid temperatures.

A month later Diane and I, along with our two eldest sons, returned to England for the RAF/458th Bomb Group Dedication at Norwich. How my father would have loved to have been there. He had visited the Second Air Division Museum in Norwich some years before. A fire had burned it after his visit destroying many of its records, but many remained. I took his obituary, pictures and copies of his journal and letters to donate, and I took Darin's father's navigator log book to add to the library's collection.

I thumbed through the Books of Remembrance there. There were the names of all the Morley crew listed with hundreds of others who did not come back from the war. Years before, when my father saw one name was accidentally omitted, he made sure it was included.

We wandered through the town past the cathedrals and pubs and streets that were so familiar to the airmen. Then it was time for the ceremony. Elderly British airmen had assembled near the runway they had used during the war. At every turn, colorful medals splashed bright colors against navy blue blazers. The aging warriors seemed anxious to talk to us.

"This chap here, won the whole war for us," one told me proudly as he pointed to his friend, who stood covered by an impressive array of medals. He saved our whole regiment."

"What did he do?" I asked in astonishment.

"He killed our cook." he said smartly with his English accent.

Soon a large assembly of people gathered near the edge of the runway at the top of a small hill. With great pomp, bagpipes and music from a band, the shiny black granite monument was unveiled.

The visiting Americans stood with the members of the RAF and their families as the monument, draped with American and British flags, was unveiled. British war planes flew over. Speeches were given and hymns were sung, and those who did not survive the war were remembered.

The schedule of events we were handed indicated we were to sing "God Save the Queen" and then "The Star Spangled Banner." After singing "God Save the Queen," the program jumped to the next event. My nephew, Tom, politely asked the organizers what had happened to our national anthem. It was explained to him that the band had forgotten to bring the music for the anthem, but if we liked, we could sing it a cappella. The announcement was made with an added plea to the British attending to help out, and all the

Americans in the group strode up the small embankment to the monument. There, about twenty-five of us joined together and with the musical attempts of the British, loudly sang "The Star Spangled Banner." Just as so many years ago, the British/American alliance saved the day. We sang for our country, and we sang for our victory, and most of all we sang for our fathers and grandfathers.

The author and son, John, with her sister, Diane Stamp, and son, Tom, standing at the 458th/RAF Memorial in front of the airstrip at Horsham St. Faith where "Rhapsody in Junk" took off in 1944

Afterward, two men approached me and seemed to know who I was. They identified themselves as the British father and son who were excavating in an area where a B-24 had crashed, and they were finding many personal artifacts. They showed me a few they held in their hands including buttons that had come from American uniforms, all found in the wreckage. The men were Trevor Hewitt, and his father, Derek. It was Trevor's father and grandfather who had saved the airmen in the crashed B-24, "Belle of Boston" so many years ago. They were e-mail friends of Darin's, and he told them I would be in Norwich. They, too, came to see the ceremony. We took pictures of each other, as Darin had been emailing with them after finding information on the crew of "Belle of Boston," but he had never seen them. We congratulated ourselves on locating each other in the crowd, neither of us knowing what the other looked like.

Much of Norwich and Horsham St. Faith had changed, but the dance clubs and some hotels were still there, and the Norwich Castle and its history still attracted visitors. This had been my father's home for a few months during those troubled years. This had been his base. And because it was a part of him, it was now a part of us.

## Chapter 71

## *An Unexpected Gift*

The following February 1st, the day that would have been my father's eighty-fourth birthday, I received a gift. In the mail was a letter from Mexico from the long-lost Cardenas for whom I had been searching for more than two years. Mail had been extremely slow to Mexico, and he had only just received my letter to him mailed months before. He was excited to be found and assured me he would come to the United States for the sixtieth prisoner of war reunion in April in Arizona that all of us had planned to attend to reunite with the men on his crew. The timing could not have been better.

I called Deimel to tell him the good news. His wife, Marian, answered and told me he had been in and out of the hospital, and he was having very serious health problems. I told Marian that with great sadness, I would notify the remaining crew. I called back a few days later, and Marian told me he could hear but not respond, and their daughter was on her way to Texas to be with them. The scenario sounded so familiar.

I found Risko's son, and he promised to send me all the pictures and records he had on his father who had been frostbitten and did not fly with the crew that fateful day. Very shortly thereafter, it all arrived. I spent the afternoon sorting though everything and reading his father's journal. I was anxious to see what he wrote on June 18th after his stay in the hospital for frostbite.

> "On the day I went back on flying status at 9:30 a.m. sick call, my crew went down on a raid to Hamburg, Germany. They left at 4:30 a.m. and an armament officer took my place. Reports say that two of the crew airplane's engines were on fire, and they were headed for Sweden. No word from crew, and they were officially missing. On June 21st their personal belongings were sent home. I moved in with six other fellows whose crews also went down."

Among the pictures his father had kept was one of Jack Gonzales and his brother. We were all puzzled as to why he would have had that one. Finally, we decided Risko must have found it after Gonzales's personal possessions were being shipped home and kept it all the years not knowing how to return it. In addition, there were pictures of all the gunners during their training days. He sent a crew picture of "Rhapsody in Junk" I had not seen before. On it, "Salvo Kid," was written artistically under the crew. I was totally mystified about the name "Salvo Kid."

It was February 9th, and my phone rang that evening. Frank Deimel, the eighty-seven-year old navigator who at one time longed to be a priest, had died at 3:30 that morning from a stroke. It was Ash Wednesday. He had lived to see his face in the German newspaper, and we had wonderful telephone conversations about the trip to Germany, and I was thankful for those.

"I'm going to write my story one day," he had told me every time I called him, "but hell, you've got all this written, and I still haven't written one page."

Then we would both laugh. He had been such fun to talk to.

"You are something," he would repeat to me when I told him of some new fact I had found out about his mission, plane or crew.

But it was really he who was something.

I read his obituary, and I was surprised to see he had relatives from the east coast named Jeffers. When time permitted, that would be one more thing to look into.

My father's newly-discovered POW roommate, Ed Stout, was excited about the reunion. His wife emailed me, and she said they were also planning to attend, and we would all have a nice talk out in Arizona.

About that time Matthias's article for his school about our visit was published in his school's yearbook. He sent me a copy. There was the crew, surrounded by German words written by a young man just learning about the war in the most personal of ways. I copied the yearbook article and sent it to General Clark, and he placed it in the Clark Collection. Matthias was very excited when I told him that, and he was delighted to tell his teacher that his writings were in the United States Air Force Academy library.

## Chapter 72

# *Dresden*

I monitored Darin's 458th website, and one day saw a posting from a man name Zedeker. The name was very familiar. I had worked with a woman named Zedeker thirty years before. We had been friends and had our first sons about the same time, and over the years we lost track of each other. I emailed him asking his wife's name. It was, indeed, my friend. Her father-in-law, as it turned out, was a prisoner of war with my father, and they had been on the long march together.

When Mara Zedeker's family emigrated to the United States, they brought the memories of war-ravaged Germany with them. As immigrants from Latvia, the family had fled to Germany and settled in a town one hour from Moosburg. Just two days after Mara was born there, her future father-in-law, 2nd Lt. Robert L. Zedeker, was liberated from Stalag Luft VIIA along with my father. We will never know if the two men knew each other.

In the years I had worked with Mara, I remembered she said her family was from Latvia. Neither of us had reason to mention the war, so the fact that my father and her father-in-law were on the same march from Stalag Luft III and were liberated together in Moosburg never came up. Neither did the fact that her fleeing family had suffered one of the worst of the war's catastrophes and lived through it—the bombing of Dresden. Her family had been evacuated from Latvia as refugees. Mara's mother had been pregnant with her, and Mara's sister, Regina, and their parents had the untimely misfortune to be in Dresden.

On February 13, and 14, 1945, the rain of terror fell from the Dresden sky. Fifteen years after Mara's brother-in-law, Hugo Purins, arrived in the United States after the war, he wrote his first-hand account, so that all that came after him would never forget. He entitled it, "The Night Old Dresden Died."

Hugo and Regina Purins in happier days shortly before the bombing of Dresden

Courtesy of Mrs. Mara Zedeker

Veterans of the bombing of Dresden, like other bombing victims, suffered the effects long after it was over. Many feared standing with their backs turned to windows at night. They jumped at the screech of low-flying aircraft or the screams of night-time sirens. The memories were too close and deep.

Dresden was the capital of Saxony and royal residence for the kings of Saxony. Centuries of extraordinary cultural and artistic splendor were evident there, and it was famous for its historical buildings, monuments and classic architecture. It was a city of spirit and cultured fine arts. But on February 13, and 14, 1945, all of that changed.

On that day, Hugo wore a German uniform as a war correspondent for Latvia and had been sent to Berlin. Hours afterward, he was to return to his military unit in Latvia. Wanting to see his wife, Regina, who had moved to Dresden the previous summer after escaping the Soviet regime in the Baltic States, he tried to arrange a route that would take him through Dresden.

With high hopes, Hugo stepped up to the German corporal in charge of issuing travel documents. As he started to write the order, Hugo offered him some cigarettes and asked that he be put on a train route home via Dresden.

"Sorry," the man said, shaking his head, "Dresden is out of your way. You'll have to go via Stettin."

Hugo handed him the entire pack of cigarettes and received the order he wanted promptly and properly stamped and signed.

After arrival in Dresden, Hugo and Regina sat in the landlord's library speaking with him and listening to the radio. He was a retired lawyer plagued by arthritis and was quite crippled. Another tenant, a disabled man in his late twenties, Herr (Mr.) Baumann, also sat and talked with them. He was an ex-Wehrmacht officer who was permanently injured during winter battles in Russia. As they all talked, the radio station suddenly interrupted its musical program. A calm voice from Civil Defense made an announcement:

"Achtung! Enemy aircraft over northwestern part of Great Germany. Stand by for further developments."

"Here we go again," said Herr Baumann. "Just when are they going to get tired of this?"

"What else can we expect?" asked the lawyer. "He, who sows wind, harvests storm."

"What do you mean by that" Baumann asked.

"You know what I mean," the lawyer said. "We started it didn't we?"

At 10:05 p.m. came the second radio alert:

"Enemy planes are keeping their course. Dresden is a possible target."

All conversation stopped. The landlord's housekeeper brought hot coffee. As the group sipped it slowly, their attention turned to the mahogany radio console in the farthest corner of the room. It sat in eerie silence. Hugo asked Regina where the nearest public bomb shelter was, and he suggested that she get her suitcase ready.

"There is no public shelter in this neighborhood," she said. "In case of an emergency, we would have to go to the cellar of our building."

Regina assured him that would not be necessary as alarms in Dresden were nothing but routine as a consequence of so many flyovers.

"They drop plenty everywhere else," said Hugo, "Why not here? Is Dresden some kind of taboo?"

Herr Baumann had been listening to the exchange.

"Now let me say this," he said, raising his voice. "If you and thousands like you would only stay in your battle stations and fight, we might not have to worry about what is going to be bombed and what is not."

He looked at Hugo suspiciously.

"By the way," he said, "What exactly is your business in Dresden? Nobody gets a furlough at times like these, and I just wonder…there is nothing here for a war correspondent to write about."

Just then the radio came to life.

"Achtung! Achtung! Enemy bomber formations in three separate waves approaching Dresden from the northwest. This is an attack. Take Cover! Take cover!!"

Suddenly, the whole darkened city was filled with screaming sirens, but not in the long intervals the citizens were accustomed to. Now, they blasted through the night in a short rapid staccato warning of the imminent attack. At that, the group ran five stories down towards the basement, or Luftschutzkeller, as they heard the low-flying roar and grind of the first wave of approaching planes. The first impact of the bombs rocked them, and the ground shook with each successive hit.

Thirty tenants, mostly older people, huddled in the cellar. Only a few held suitcases, briefcases or plain cartons of their valuables and necessities. Hugh and Regina were empty-handed. The pale frightened people were calm, and there was no panic. Herr Baumann stood with his fists clenched and lips tightly pressed, standing close to the door. Hugo observed his face. It seemed that every single explosion outside found its echo in Baumann's face and body.

The noise of the explosions grew louder and louder, and the ground shook with the violent pounding. The planes were right overhead. Then slowly, the deadly thunder rolled farther away, and the terrified tenants caught their breaths.

In the brief interim, no one spoke. A voice cracked from an old man's portable radio and gave an up-to-the-minute informative message:

"The first wave of enemy bombers, strength approximately one thousand, has flown over. Phosphorous bombs and light explosives were sprayed. Second wave is on its way. God save Dresden!"

"One thousand planes!" Helpless Regina's voice broke the sudden horror. And they have only lit the targets for the others..."

Regina was frozen with fear waiting for the bomb that would end it all. Hugo was glad to be with her. He tried to reassure her.

"They can't hit every house," he said soothingly. "They'll hit some, but not every one of them. Remember that. This is a big city. They won't hit our building, say that in your mind over and over..."

"But what if they do? she asked. "What if they throw a carpet?"

Carpet was a well-known expression referring to the bombing technique by which a close-flying formation released its bombs simultaneously. Such carpets could cover one to three city blocks. Destruction was absolute.

Hugo held her hand tightly.

"We won't die here, Regina," he said. "We have lost too much already...we have lost everything but our lives, and God knows that. He will be with us. Just pray, forget everything, just pray."

Seconds later, death started to rain from heaven. The carpet bombing began. Hugo knew the sound of it having heard it before. Some of the bombs were set to detonate at timed intervals. Calculated to do the most damage, they usually hit the roofs and slid through the stories of a brick building exploding in the cellar or close to it. Hugo had lived through such bombings in Berlin and Cologne and felt confident then that he would live. Now, he was not as confident. He heard the deep-hollowed crash of collapsing buildings all around him, and he became so nervous that he bit his own hand to suppress the involuntary shake which took command of his whole body.

It felt like the floor was the deck of a rolling ship. Periodically, people arose from it and clasped their hands in prayer. Some moaned, some cried and others whose senses were paralyzed by fear, just stared at the ceiling, seemingly not fully understanding what was happening. The lights went out, and soon after, there was a terrifying crash and explosion. Hugo was thrown across the room and against the wall. People around him shrieked in panic and pain. Loose bricks flew in all directions, and Hugo could smell smoke. A rush of cold air blew through as the building opened to the ravished skies. He staggered in the blast and rubbed sandy dust and grit from his mouth, nose and eyes.

"This is the end," he thought, but he realized that through it all he was still alive.

Gasping for air, and coughing and choking simultaneously, he fumbled around like a blind man. He reeled through the thick darkness desperately calling for Regina. He found her on the floor near the door. She was not hurt seriously but seemed numb and in a state of shock.

Surfacing from the debris, Hugo found a bomb had barely missed their building but had landed in the backyard causing a large portion of the cellar wall to cave in. Two people were dead, and a few others suffered broken bones. The old lawyer, his housekeeper and Herr Baumann were unhurt. They helped the injured by placing them in more comfortable positions, and they pulled two bodies from the debris. Then they waited.

By 1 a.m. it was over. The sirens did not work, nor did the radio, but there were no more bombs, and they could hear no more planes. They cautiously arose from the cellar with wet handkerchiefs over their faces.

Their entire surroundings, except the building they were in, and the one next to it were ignited. As far as they could see, the glow of snapping flames swept upward from the rubble. Hundreds of tall apartment buildings, or their ghostly remains, were burning, and they could hear the fury of the flames all about them. Sparks burst from the damaged city into the night sky, and clouds of biting smoke teared their eyes. Everything felt hot around them as they climbed out, and smoke-induced tears ran down their cheeks.

Up at street level, there was unspeakable horror. Partially-dressed women ran along the street clutching babies in their arms. Older people and children screamed, and their faces were distorted by fear and smeared with blood and soot. They ran for their lives to one of the city's parks a few blocks away where there was still hope of escaping the flames. Hugo's group was pushed along in the crowd.

"Doomsday," the old lawyer muttered, "Oh, God, Oh, God, I can't believe it—Dresden is dead… a dead town, think about the people…hundreds of thousands of them and why? Why? What for? What have we done? This is not a war. This is murder!"

Hugo had other ideas.

"This is retaliation," he said. "The price this nation has to pay for London, Warsaw, for the concentration camps, for the ghettoes and for the civilian mass-graveyards all over Europe. It's a price for waging a total war…a price a nation must pay for lulling itself into the hands of dictator."

"Be quiet, be quiet," Regina whispered in fear, "Somebody will hear and report us."

Regina was thinking about Baumann who was nearby, but he had not heard. He was staring across the street where the structure of the Technical College of Dresden stood engulfed in solid, red and blue flames.

"After our victory, we'll build a new Dresden," he shouted frantically, shaking his fist. This is not the end of it. We'll build a new one, a better one, brick by brick."

After the terror of the night, day broke. Regina and Hugo left the park. He wanted to see the downtown. They walked for twenty minutes. All they saw was smoking or flaming ruins, upended, demolished vehicles, streetcars off their tracks burning furiously and worst of all, corpses. The street was two-hundred-fifty-feet wide, and yet there was not a tiny clear path on it. They climbed over smoldering debris all the way to the main railway terminal at the edge of Oldtown Dresden.

Koenigstrasse, the main street through Dresden's heart, was filled with smoky debris. Hugo peered from the Bahnhofplatz (train station square) and saw nothing but ruins. Beneath it, two-hundred-thousand people had met their sudden and violent ends. Regina's place of employment, the Loewenapotheke, (Lion's Drug Store) was right in the middle of the district. If he had not come to Dresden to meet her, she would not have gotten off two hours early as she had. She would have been among those that perished.

Gas-masked, white-helmeted Civil Defense workers carried bodies from a shelter underneath the terminal and put them side by side on the sidewalk. Within minutes, there were more than one-hundred corpses, some burned beyond recognition. They brought up more and more.

Hugo and Regina walked back on another street. At one of the intersections, right in the middle of the street, lay a child. It was a little girl all alone. They went over and knelt beside her. She was three or four with blond hair and rosy cheeks. Dressed in a dark blue overcoat with white trimmings, she looked like a girl from one of Renoir's paintings. She lay on her back peaceful and still. Her blue eyes were wide open, as if she was wondering about something. Hugo touched her cheek. It was stiff and cold like the pavement her small body was resting on. He carried her to the sidewalk, gently laying her down next to a group of dead women and men.

He could keep control no more. Loudly, he burst forth and began to cry. During the past four years he had lost relatives, friends and people he knew on a daily basis. He lost them to the torture chambers of the Soviet NKVD, (Narodnyi Komissariat Vnutrennikh Del – People's Commissariat Internal Affairs) through mass deportations, to slave labor camps in Siberia and later through the bully tactics of the German Gestapo and their camps in Germany. He had lost some in action against Communism and some at the Eastern Front. He never shed a tear. The war would not permit it. But the tiny lifeless child—a broken porcelain doll in the rubble, broke the dams inside him. The war was ugly and senseless and could be so merciless to spare not even this innocent baby.

Hugo made an immediate choice as he walked towards Regina's apartment. The landlord there must have read his troubled mind.

"If civilian clothing can help you..." he said.

"It can," said Hugo. "Thank you."

Regina and Hugo packed two suitcases. Then he changed into civilian clothes. Regina was sobbing knowing what would happen if he was caught. As they raced out, they saw Baumann in the corridor.

The next thing Hugo knew, he was looking into the barrel of Baumann's 9mm Parabellum gun.

"I should have guessed that!" Baumann snapped "A deserter! A traitor! Put your hands on your head!"

"Wait a minute," said Hugo raising his arms over his head," Let's talk this over."

"No explanations!" I am taking you to the Fieldgendarmery. Both of you. Do you know that I can shoot you right here? Move!" Baumann ordered.

He motioned with his pistol towards the stairway.

Hugo thought for sure Baumann would shoot him on the street. There were already so many dead bodies there. It was possible too that a crowd could lynch Hugo and Regina. Their German had an unmistakable foreign accent. He felt they would be executed at the gendarmerie if they ever got there, so their prospects of survival were very slim.

I am not going anywhere with you," Hugo told Baumann calmly. And you won't kill me. You are not a murderer, Herr Baumann, not you."

"Face the wall," Baumann shouted.

His hand was trembling.

"No," Hugo shouted back in desperate anger. "You know why I am leaving. Because what is going on now, is not my war; because I was fighting for my country, not Germany, and that battle is lost. Latvia is under Soviet control and far away from here. I can't help her anymore, not right now. What happened here last night has convinced me of that."

Hugo talked fast and continued on his way. Herr Baumann did not pull the trigger. After awhile he lowered his gun, and Regina and Hugo lowered their arms. Hugo told him about the allegiance he was forced to swear to Stalin, and later to Hitler, both times against his free will. He told Baumann that when German troops liberated Riga from Communists in 1941, people received them with mountains of flowers, and that crowds were kneeling before the first troops on Riga's streets shedding tears of gratitude. But, soon they all realized that the old terror and humiliation still existed, and that only the big boss's name was changed from Joseph Stalin to Adolf Hitler.

When Hugo finished, there was a moment of silence.

"And where do you want to go now?" Herr Baumann asked his voice under control.

"West," Hugo said. "Towards civilization. If it is somewhere in this world at this time, it must be there, because it cannot be found here."

"Have you your pistol with you?" Baumann asked.

"It's lying in Regina's room on the table, on top of my uniform."

Herr Baumann said, "Better take it along. You might be needing it."

"No," Hugo smiled, "I have always hated firearms. Keep it as a souvenir."

The two men looked at each other for a long minute and shook hands.

Thus, ended Hugo Purin's story. In all my research about the war, I had never read a first-hand account of the Dresden bombing. It was a chance encounter on a website guestbook that not only reunited me with a long-lost friend, but also provided witness to the horror and savagery that was Dresden. My father and his fellow prisoners had missed being in the midst of the firestorm by just eleven days.

## Chapter 73

# *A New Family Found*

I had found where to order the print of Stalag Luft III that had hung on the museum wall in Poland and ordered it from a Canadian ex-POW. It came in the mail from Canada and will serve as a constant reminder of what happened to "The Fifty."

Claudius emailed me that he had heard from a Jennifer Schwartz who was writing a WWII book. He put her in touch with me knowing I had just returned from Sagan, as she had also visited there. She was hoping to find ex-prisoners of war to interview, and I told her about the prisoner of war reunion. She made reservations to attend.

A few days before I left for Arizona, I was contacted by Don Stout's wife. She told me my father's old roommate had just passed away, and she would not be able to meet me as planned in Arizona. I was so sad to hear her news and realized what she was facing. Claudius had not yet gotten a chance to meet with him in California, but they were able to speak on the phone a few times. The oft-given statistic of fifteen-hundred World War II veterans passing away each day was becoming a reality to me.

Lawrence Dean, Marilyn Walton and Jack Gonzales at the Prisoner of War Reunion in Arizona in 2005

Within days, I left for Arizona, and Scott came with me.

Meeting with the three remaining men on the crew and their families was the culmination of two years of work for me, and it could not have been more satisfying. Butler's daughter, Kay and her husband came representing her father, and Gonzales's grandson, Robert, Scott's age, came after serving and being wounded in Afghanistan. The whole extended Gonzales family including early contact, Jack Whetstone, arrived. When Gonzales looked at Scott, he remembered my father. Tears came into Gonzales's eyes.

"You look just like him," he said, and the two hugged.

My nephew, Tom, flew in, and Dean and daughter, Brenda, arrived. Cardenas and his wife would arrive the next day.

Within the first twenty minutes of meeting, we all felt we were long-lost family. Together, our new extended family spent several days exchanging stories and pictures.

One other person came up and introduced herself to me. It was Becky Lawson, daughter of Morris Epps, whose errant page had ended up in my father's Missing Air Crew Report. Receiving the page about her father had initiated much research on her part and resulted in her attendance at the reunion. In a Christmas program Dee Butler had saved from Stalag Luft III, there was a picture of Butler and his friends as members of the Holiday Harmonies Chorus. Just down the row was Morris Epps.

There was a knock on my hotel door, and Claudius' contact, Jennifer Schwartz, stood there. I invited her in, and we talked to the early hours of the morning. All the people I had known just by email addresses for so long became real.

Before Cardenas and his wife, Estela, arrived, the ex-prisoners visited the Pima Air Museum. Dean and Gonzales told us all about the B-24 that was on display there as they relived their experiences before our eyes.

Lawrence Dean and Jack Gonzales had not seen each other in six decades when this picture was taken.

"Right there is where your father dropped down on his knees to pray," Gonzales told me as he pointed up to the bomb bay.

A television crew arrived, and Dean, Gonzales and I were interviewed for the Phoenix news. Under bright television lights and fitted with microphones, the two men told what it was like to be reunited there. Brenda watched in tears.

The high point for all of us was to witness the reunion of Cardenas, Dean and Gonzales who had not seen each other in sixty-one years. We all waited in the hotel lobby near the elevator for Cardenas and his wife to emerge. Anxious faces turned into broad smiles as Cardenas exited the elevator into the waiting arms of his former friends.

Jack Gonzales, Alex Cardenas and Lawrence Dean reunite after sixty-one years.

The men picked up right where they left off so many years ago. When family introductions were over, pictures and journals were passed around. I showed Cardenas the obituary of his good friend, Risko, who had died years before. He studied it for a long time and told me what a good man his friend had been.

The next day Scott, Tom, the Cardenases and I went to Mass at an ancient church near the hotel. Estela, a still beautiful blue-eyed senorita, now plagued by a bad hip started on our walk to the church pushing her walker. Tom and Scott took over pulling down its seat and converting it into a seated walker. In seconds, they were racing down the street with her at top speed. Cardenas and I followed behind them and laughed at the sight and the sound of her shouts. Inside the stone walls of the church, we shared the solemnity of the moment during the service and the wonder of three generations, days ago unknown to each other, worshipping in this place.

We had one last dinner arranged by the reunion organizers. The Cardenases had not gotten tickets. We were trying to find them two tickets when a man stopped by where we sat in the lobby, and he said he had two tickets he was not going to use. He explained he had planned the trip with his father, and he came alone having just lost his father a few days before the trip. My heart went out to him.

We had one last breakfast together, and cameras flashed as we took our final group pictures of the "new family."

I had one further question for Cardenas. I asked him if he knew the meaning of "Salvo Kid" which was written on the crew picture where the men had each signed it. At one time I had asked Darin if he had ever heard of a plane by that name, and he said no.

"That was your dad's nickname," Cardenas said with a laugh.

Then he told the story of training in Casper, Wyoming, when one day Northrop was going down the runway for take-off, and my father accidentally stepped on a floor control and salvoed all the bombs. My father's only reply, he said, was "oops." From then on, he was known as the "Salvo Kid."

When we had finished breakfast, we said our good-byes. I hugged my elusive Cardenas who was so hard to find and so much fun to be with.

It took so long to find Cardenas, but soon it was time to bid him farewell. This tearful picture was taken the final day of the Prisoner of War Reunion.
Courtesy of Mr. Scott Walton

"I love you, baby," he said.

The reunion was scheduled to be the last, but so many people attended that it was decided that in two years there would be one last reunion. We all agreed to meet again there and bring even more of our families.

Next, Gonzales went up to Cardenas to say his good bye.

"Look into my eyes," Cardenas told Gonzales with much authority, holding both of Gonzales's shoulders in his hands.

"I love you."

Gonzales hugged him, and then they parted.

I had enjoyed the animated Gonzales, full of stories and so youthful for his age. It was so easy to see why my father had enjoyed these men so much.

We found Dean in the lobby, and more hugs were generated as we bid farewell to the kind radioman I had come to know as quiet and unassuming, but with a wonderful sense of humor I enjoyed so much. Early on, he and Gonzales were a constant source of information for me as I asked them to go back through the years to remember so many details. They never let me down.

Three generations of the "Rhapsody in Junk family"

Two weeks after I returned from Arizona, I got a call from Emmett Cook, one of the first prisoners I had contacted when I started my research. He was calling to tell me all about the reunion he had just attended and all the wonderful prisoners who were there, and how much I would have enjoyed it. I never knew he planned to attend. I told him I'd see him at the next one.

## Chapter 74

# Return to the Woods

John and I planned one more trip back to Germany the next month. We flew into the Frankfurt airport noting that our gate number was B-24. Once again we visited our German friends near the crash site. Before traveling there we took a cruise up the Rhine stopping to stay overnight in a castle, and then on to Remagen to see what remained of the famous World War II bridge of movie fame. After a stop at the cathedral in Cologne, we took the train to Iserlohn to spend a few days staying with Matthias and his family. It was wonderful to see their town and finally meet Matthias's parents and brothers. We took an overnight train from a station near their home to Flensburg. Throughout the night, the train made many stops, and at each, I could hear German-speaking men calling to each other in the rail yards. My father must have heard similar voices on his war-time train journey to Moosburg.

In Kappeln, near Flensburg, we stayed with Angela and Manfred. Manfred had gotten a metal detector, and the four of us re-entered the woods in Blick and started to dig on a cool misty day. Soon, we were finding broken Plexiglas from the windshield, wires and melted rubber pieces. For the first time we saw the wide scar on the bark of a tree where the plane had hit. A local man who saw us there brought me a fifty-caliber shell casing he had found. It had been fired, so unless the fire set it off, we know they went down fighting!

A large horizontal scar can still be seen where "Rhapsody in Junk" hit a tree in the Blick Woods.

Gretchen Bartel, eyewitness to the crash of "Rhapsody in Junk," holds a picture of the plane and the crew she was just coming to know sixty years after the crash.

Angela and Manfred drove us to Matthias's grandparents who had arranged an elaborate tea in our honor with Gretchen and Juergen Bartel. Bruno the Bear sat on the back of the couch. We gazed from the back yard of the Martensen's home across the Baltic Sea. Clearly visible was Denmark. The crew had been so close to Denmark that day. Hartwig Martensen spoke of the U-boats that had been there and around the north of Germany that Hitler had sunk with political prisoners and undesirables aboard, many of whom were German. The tragedy for the area was enormous, and the pain of that memory was evident as he and the others spoke of the incident at the close of the war. He had written a book about the U-boats and gave me an autographed copy. No wonder he knew of the secret base at Eckernforde.

We had dinner at Angela's with Gretchen and Juergen later and showed them what we found in the woods. Juergen spoke of the trek he had taken as a child from Graudenz and how he had lost one of his brothers in the extreme weather. That city's name rang a bell with me, but I could not remember for what reason.

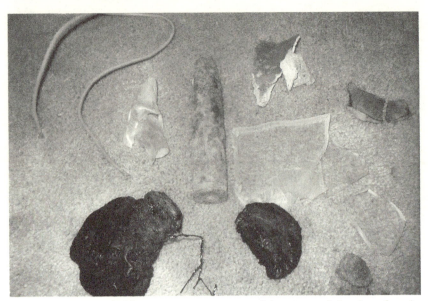

Sharp Plexiglas and old wires are among some of the pieces of the plane found in the woods.

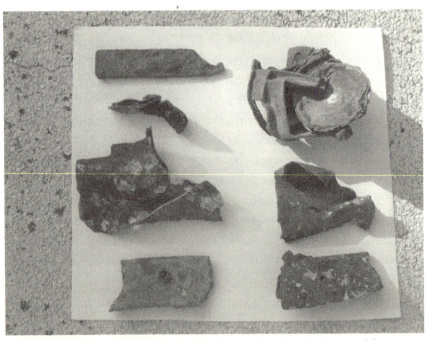

Matthias Martensen's family returned to the woods to dig. Using a metal detector, they unearthed these pieces.

Courtesy of Mr. Matthias Martensen

Angela and Manfred drove us to the train station in Eckernforde the next day. We got our first look at the German naval base there where her sons had been stationed. It must have looked so much like Kiel during the war. We took the train to Frankfurt on the final leg of our trip to visit once again with Tim's parents. I told Katie of our dinner with the Bartels up near Denmark, and that Juergen had told me of his trek from Graudenz during the war. It was then I remembered that her family had been on that trek. I asked her if she knew the name of Bartel, and she said she did, and there was a huge family of Bartels in that area during the war. Time and distance from the war was still creating some very unusual coincidences. At a later date, Peter would call Juergen.

After a stop in Berlin to see Tim, our former student and now a lawyer, we went to Moosburg where I had arranged for a tour of what was left of Stalag VIIA where the men were liberated. We arrived on the same railroad track the box cars had used and walked to our hotel, and then to the newspaper office where my father had once told me to go, as he had once done. The editor, Horst Mueller, took us on a tour of the camp just as the previous editor had once done for my parents. We drove the short distance to the remains of the camp.

Many of the old beige stucco barracks were now used as low-income housing. Some barracks were abandoned and sat in disrepair. The melody of "Don't Fence Me In," and "At Last" had long faded away. Sorrow and misery had lived here, and jubilation beyond anyone's comprehension, replaced it. Gone was the building with the showers my father had spoken of that they had all initially feared. No curling black smoke rose from the primitive cookers, no deep voices in all languages bartering for cigarettes and no crack of guns or rumble of tanks remained. The bridge over the Isar River was long gone. Young children played in the streets oblivious to what had once been there.

We looked down Sudetenland Strasse, the main street that led into the camp. The wooden tower there was gone where the column of men would have moved to the left of it to enter. We saw the cheese factory, still operating, where the SS troops held out on its roof, and across the green fields, I could picture the tanks as they approached. We were taken to a cemetery off of a road past the camp where close to one-thousand prisoners from the camp were buried. Of those men, seven-hundred-and-fifty were Russian, and eleven were American. It was a grass square within a chain link fence with no markers, and it was hard to believe so many could be buried there. I wondered who the eleven Americans were, and if their families knew where they now rested. All nationalities had been buried here, and now only scattered yellow rapeseed flowers dotted the grass, and a small plaque marked the men's passing.

We entered St. Kastulus Catholic Church through the ancient door where my father would have entered, and when we left, we glanced upward towards the two steeples that had flown both the Nazi and American flags. This very ancient church had witnessed so much in the turbulent days of World War II.

We strolled through the town and found a monument dedicated to all the war dead of the area. Up ahead, through narrow curving streets, was where the final battle was waged and where newly-released prisoners rampaged through the town. I could only imagine the fear the people of Moosburg had during those terror-filled days.

# Chapter 75

# *Through the Generations*

    My father's story took me west two months later to surprise Gonzales who was finally presented his prisoner of war medals in California at a ceremony on the 4th of July. I spent the night at the beautiful home of Claudius and Monika Scharff at their invitation, who lived up on a hill in the Santa Monica mountains. We walked in the morning on their terrace to pick fresh citrus off their trees, and then Claudius and I walked up the hill to a serene spot that overlooked the canyons and mountains. Here, high above the city on that quiet morning Claudius showed me the sheltered spot where the ashes of his father, beloved "Hannsi," were interred. One generation removed from an insidious war, we were both missing our fathers very much.

    Monika showed me her mosaic studio where so many stunning works had been created by her and her late father-in-law, and Claudius took me on a tour of their home. The view from one window overlooked the rolling hills and a myriad of varied homes below. And sitting on the pink marble window sill there sat the tiny

Prussian sergeant in command of his three marching soldiers that Hannsi had brought from Germany.

The Scharffs showed me the sights of Los Angeles. We toured the Getty Museum and enjoyed a lunch and dinner together. Then they graciously drove me to Cerritos to surprise Jack Gonzales.

Linda picked me up at my hotel, and together we entered Jack's home where he was still working on his acceptance speech. He was stunned I was there and greeted me with a hug.

"You don't think I would miss an occasion such as this, do you?" I remembered saying to him.

I showed him the rubber patch from his plane's tire. Soon, his whole extended family arrived, photographers from the newspaper came, and afterward we all left for the park where he was to meet his Member of Congress. Jack was dressed in his World War II uniform and escorted by grandson Robert. What a proud moment it was for Linda to see them together on the stage. After the medal presentation, Jack gave a short but wonderful speech. Afterward, strangers came up to greet him, and Boy Scout leaders wanted their boys to shake his hand. The family made me so much a part of their day, and we ate out front at Robert's home and watched the fireworks. It was my most memorable 4$^{th}$ of July.

I returned to Ohio and went somewhere I had never gone. On one nostalgic day, I visited Dayton and found the rooming house my father had moved to from New York when he worked at Wright Field before the war. I went in the church where my parents were married looking toward the altar where they had stood for their small wartime wedding. Within walking distance was their first apartment. My mother had spoken of running downstairs in the winter without coats to duck into the movie theatre that was right next door. The shiny red and blue wall tiles of the theatre were still there, but it had become a mission of some kind. Their front door had been so close. This was the door my father had walked through to go off to war, and where he no doubt said his final good-bye.

Claudius and Monika Scharff, son and daughter-in-law of Master Interrogator Hanns Scharff

After sixty years, Jack Gonzales finally received his medals. Proud grandson, Robert Waddington, wounded in Afghanistan, stood by his side.

## Chapter 76

# The Missing Documents

As I wrote the final chapter of this book, I received an email from Darin who worked with a researcher at the National Archives. I asked Darin if he thought the man could locate any kind of a War Crime's file that might give any information on Flaugher's death, since I knew many of the crew made reports after the war. Those judged to be valid for prosecution were assessed, and Darin told me he would request that his researcher friend check the archive for me. Shortly thereafter, Darin notified me a file had been found.

"...There are 17 pages, mostly accounts of Deimel, Butler and your father's detailing the events of June 18, 1944, involving Harold Flaugher."

Darin forwarded me three depositions from the officers. The letter to Northrop requesting a deposition was there, but his deposition was missing.

With some amazement I read my father's deposition given just after he got home in 1945. I recognized the familiar blocky handwriting at once.

> "Killing Kiel – Harold Flaugher S/Sgt. USAAF. It is my belief that this man was killed after landing in Germany. He was in perfect physical condition when on bailing out and other members of the crew picked him up later in the mine room of the navy yard at Kiel, he had a head wound and his chest had been crushed. His parachute had definitely opened as I examined it myself. The Germans present claimed ignorance of English language but suggested that the chute did not open.
>
> On June 18, my plane was shot up over Kiel, Germany, and no member of the crew was injured prior to the bail out order. Myself, and three other officers were captured and taken to the Kiel Naval base and upon entering a small mine room we saw the body and placed it in a coffin. It is my opinion that Sgt. Flaugher was killed by a blow from some person or persons. His right temple was crushed and his chest badly mangled. No one spoke English, but when I asked if his chute opened, one naval official shook his head and said no. His right earphone had been crushed, but his left earphone appeared to be in good shape. His helmet was on the floor, and I picked it up, and it was in good shape but there was no blood on it."

It was interesting to note my father's mention of being taken to Kiel. All the German records I had found thus far said that the body was picked up at the Eckernforde Naval base, and, again, I can only attribute this discrepancy to the fact this was a secret base that the men were unaware of. It was much closer to where they bailed out than Kiel was.

Butler added even more in his typed deposition.

> "We were ordered into a truck and driven to a city the name I can't remember. At the time an ordinary black coffin was in the truck but none of us thought much about it as being meant for one of the crew. The truck finally pulled into a military installation which was definitely

*navy and stopped before a long supply warehouse. The guards ordered all of us into the warehouse and motioned towards a body lying on the floor with a covering over it. We hesitated long enough so that one of the guards who was impatient ran over and jerked the covering off. We then recognized that it was Sgt. Flaugher, and we could plainly see that he was dead. The guard motioned to me to take off Sgt. Flaugher's ring and dog tags and also to take off his parachute harness. He used a chest chute and the chute had already been detached from the harness. None of his legs or arms were broken, and the only sign of damage was a discolored area covering his right temple. His chest had also been crushed, but none of his clothes were ripped or torn and the buttons on his shirt were still intact. We then put Sgt. Flaugher in the coffin, placed it in the truck and buzzed away to the town cemetery.*

*The other officers who witnessed the same thing belonged to our crew. They are Lt. Henry H. Northrop, Lt. Thomas F. Jeffers, and Lt. Frank Deimel. The Germans were quiet at the time we were removing the articles mentioned from Sgt. Flaugher. If Sgt. Flaugher had hit an obstruction before landing on the ground, I don't see why his clothes were not torn or ripped; or why there were no broken bones other than his chest caved in and his bruised area on his right temple."*

Butler's deposition raised the same questions regarding the condition of Flaugher's body. Had he been killed instantly resulting in no blood? Wouldn't his hands be scratched up from trying to defend his head from striking blows? Could his parachute have gotten hung up as he exited the plane resulting in a blow from the tail assembly as it kept flying? Could that have crushed his chest? Could someone on the ground have jumped on his chest? What crushed the earphone and discolored his temple? A blow from a rifle butt? When Butler saw the parachute descending, could Flaugher have already been dead?

The third officer who was deposed was navigator Frank Deimel who recorded his thoughts in his own elegant handwriting.

> *"Following our parachuting and being captured, we, that is all officers of our crew, were put in a truck and placed under guard. There was a wooden box which the Germans used as coffins on the truck with us. We drove for some distance and finally arrived at what appeared to be a small navy yard. We were instructed to take the coffin and follow two officers who had appeared. We were led into a room which seemed to be a warehouse of some sort. There on the floor lay Sgt. Flaugher. His head and chest were crushed although his chute had successfully opened. What had happened all of us could only conjecture. He was dead when we found him, and as far as we know, there had been no violence. Upon taking his class ring from his finger and his watch from his wrist, and turning these over to the German officers, we placed him in the coffin. After getting on the truck, the Germans picked up the other crew members. Then we were driven to a church with a cemetery attached where the body of Sgt. Flaugher was left. These are all the facts that I know with regard to the death of Sgt. Flaugher. All else I would say is all conjecture. We know his chute opened and he was alright as he floated to earth. What caused the injury to his head and chest I do not know. The others who were present were Lt. Hank Northrop, (pilot) Lt. Dee J. Butler (co-pilot) and Lt. Thomas Jeffers (bombardier)"*

It is interesting to note that Deimel assumed there had been no violence at a time during the war when an enraged Hitler wanted downed airmen to be surrendered to public fury.

Until now, none of us knew these documents existed. It was too bad that Northrop's was not included. I doubt any of the officers ever saw each others' depositions.

As I continued to ponder the varied analyses of Flaugher's fate that day, I requested the opinion of a person well-qualified to objectively analyze the facts. Ed Woods, a retired thirty-year FBI agent, former Green Beret and paratrooper, had jumped from vintage WWII aircraft in the sixties and was a present-day corporate jet pilot. He provided yet another opinion.

> "If the last of your father's crew, the co-pilot and Flaugher, bailed at eight-thousand feet, it would seem to me that the bomber was under control, in that it was still flying, I'm assuming in pretty much of a level attitude until impact. The pilots would have trimmed it for level flight, as best they could, or used the auto-pilot if it was available. Even assuming it was descending because of the dead engines, it would have remained level enough for them to bail out.
>
> So it seems that without the aircraft in a spin, which would require the controls to be held in a full rudder, full-up elevator condition or more likely in a "graveyard spiral," or rotating rapidly (or possibly in a flat spin) caused by a missing control surface (a piece of the tail or wing blown off causing the other surfaces to continue to do what they're supposed to do and thus rotating the aircraft), then they should have been able to bail out and fall away from the aircraft. Any aircraft descending at five-hundred feet per minute is still in a pretty stable condition. So the scenario seems to indicate that (even given the war-time horror of it all) it should have been a normal bail-out situation with no one jumping out of the bottom of the aircraft and somehow defying the physics of it all by going up and hitting the tail of the bomber.

> The co-pilot could have seen a chute but 'maybe' not Flaugher's. My bet is still on the chute not opening. I agree that, as stated in the depositions, there would have been more visible damage if the locals got to him."

Gretchen had told me the plane was level flying over her home that day, but unfortunately, she did not know of anyone who saw Flaugher land. She did not know if he hit the hard ground, if he had hit a building, as his brother speculated, or if he had hit a tree. Some airmen who bailed out in farm country hit haystacks, which minimized their injuries. There was any number of possibilities regarding his landing. I had found many written documents, but not nearly enough.

I was to find one more.

I wrote to the commander of the Naval Base at Eckernforde who promptly forwarded my letter to a contact he thought would be helpful. I received an envelope from Germany with a letter from the mayor of a small municipality of Rugge which was very close to Blick. He had found a written account of a school teacher who recorded the events of June 18th in a school yearbook. I immediately sent it to Claudius for translation.

> "On June 18th at 12 o'clock in Brarupholz an enemy four-engine American bomber coming from Kiel was behind the home of Farmer Erikson. Two in parachutes jumped over Kappeln, one dead because the chute didn't open. Four were taken into custody in Wagersrott-Gangerschild and another two in Mohrkirch-Osterholz. (Claudius indicated that these were very tiny villages since their names were so long.) One assumes the ninth man perished in the crash. The plane flew in a circle over Suederfeld and then straightened out over Fraulund towards Helleberg and raced toward the village of Rugge. It would have crashed on the Moellgaard property next to the school but lifted once more and turned

towards Rueggesgaard. There the plane circled the dwelling and farm yard where the Rasch family thought they were being attacked, but one of the engines was restarted, and the plane again started to climb with the wings at an angle and in a steep curve. Then it finally crashed into the forest of Braupholz in a ball of flame.

There were no exploding bombs, but the machine gun ammunition kept exploding up until evening. Up to that point, fire fighters and the militia kept guard until the military came and took over the remains of the completely destroyed aircraft. After days of the military collecting all the remains and transporting them away, the local school children were able to collect 337 kilos of pure aluminum and a lot of brass and iron which they sold to the scrap dealer Hoffeins in Brunsholm for sixty Reichmarks."

Yet, another document surfacing after decades. So the plane really had changed direction and curved around just before it crashed. This is what the forensics people had suggested. The German mayor sent a map indicating the flight path that day, and I could clearly see how the plane curved as it headed for Blick just before it crashed. The two men mentioned bailing out over Kappeln had to be Flaugher and Butler who went out of the hatch together after the others had jumped. The "ninth" man, who most likely was the one picked up by a farmer in his field had to be my father whom this teacher assumed went down with the plane. Wagersrott was the location of Gretchen's home, so it appeared many of the crew jumped very quickly before the plane crashed in the woods near her. The men on the crew I spoke with could not tell me the names of the towns where they landed, but here it was in black and white—the very places where I visited. The information on Flaugher's parachute not opening has always been a source of debate. One wonders if the Germans examining the shroud lines of my father's parachute were discussing Flaugher's case, speculating on what had happened and already knowing he was dead. It is hard to say where the teacher got this information. My father's deposition said he had checked the parachute carefully, and all the men arrived at the same conclusion. The document confirmed that my father did, indeed, salvo the bombs. All of Flaugher's frantic fuel transferring that my father had described must have paid off enabling Northrop to restart the engine. I could almost picture the German children that were saved that day combing through the woods as we had done. Northrop's expert flying saved many Germans on the ground, especially the school children. I think Sgt. Flaugher would have liked that very much.

Chapter 77

# Their Legacy

There are those who will always speculate on the death of Harold Flaugher. Some researchers and military forensic people I spoke with felt adamant about their conclusions. Other military researchers say the accidental death could not happen so easily in the B-24 as the B-17. In the final analysis, I value the opinion of the remaining crew. They were the men who were on the ground in Germany that day to suffer the loss of their crewmate. They were the men who flew with him, and they were the men who took him to their hearts. In conversations with them even after six decades, they still mourn for their crewmate whom they believe was killed by civilians on the ground when terror and fury were a hallmark of that period of German history. The crew and their experiences were fascinating to research for me. Without the cooperation of so many, I could have never done it.

My return to Germany was a tribute to my father. He had told us some, but not nearly enough of his war experiences, the essence of which shaped him. Our visits to Germany filled in the gaps. The peaceful farmlands of Blick gave me great comfort. Incongruously, my visit gave me the feeling of being there with him in a time of great peril so that he would not be alone. The peaceful cows in the field adjacent to the woods where the plane crashed, the lush green grass, the trees and the wild flowers on a bright summer day are all an intrinsic part of the land today, just as they were sixty years ago. They did not paint a picture of a war-ravaged land. The scene could have been the same as farmland in the United States. Only the language and circumstance were different in 1944 Germany.

My father never held a grudge against Germany. He returned many times during his lifetime. He saw the damage of Dresden which is still being rebuilt today. My father was a man who had seen the brutality and stupidity of war and always, despite his own experiences, understood that people the world over, no matter what nationality, were for the most part good people. He believed that until the end. He was amazed that during this tragic time for Germany that their captors fed the prisoners at all when their portions and Red Cross parcels could have easily gone to a starving German citizenry and losing army. He felt the Germans tried their best despite the war to maintain some civility and care for the men in the camps as best they could as staggering numbers of prisoners, far more than could be accommodated, were sent their way. Not all would agree, especially those who were held in the brutal SS camps or who had experienced the wrath of sadistic guards. Each man must judge from his own experience.

In characteristic modesty, he and his crew never believed themselves to be heroes. We gratefully gave that name to them when we became aware of their immeasurable courage facing the vicissitudes of war in those flak-riddled skies. Like so many veterans of the era, my father would not want to repeat his experience, but in his patriotic youth, he would not have missed it for the world. For him, this was the most exciting time of his life.

Our meeting with the people of Schleswig-Holstein reinforced everything my father had taught me. Their generosity and hospitality enabled me to close a chapter of my father's life. His war experiences came alive for me, and I learned the majority of Germans swept up in the terror and chaos of 1939-1945 had suffered greatly. The war set in motion the trek of twenty-million refugees in eastern Germany and Prussia trying to cross the Elbe River. Three-and-a-half-million Germans marched off to Russia. Half were never heard from again. Data from prisoner of war reunions indicate fifteen to seventeen million war dead. Such is the brutality of war. So many of the Germans were not Nazis, but human beings caught up in Adolf Hitler's madness. They had the same love for their families that we had for ours, and they suffered their losses just as deeply. No one remained unscathed by the war.

For the American prisoners, it is said, it was the "longest mission," beginning in an English airfield just after dawn and ending years later as they streamed from the German camps. I have read of crews being described as "ten men huddled in sheepskin and leather gasping rubber-tainted oxygen while scanning skies for hostile fighters." I think that is an accurate depiction. These were the men of the Libs and Forts who bought our tomorrows by giving up their yesterdays.

During my research, I spoke with, interviewed and read about so many POWs in the European Theatre of Operations who were located the same places my father was. It is striking the selective memories they still hold. I found there were four things these men mentioned that they will never forget: the ships floating below them at Normandy after the D-Day invasion, the American flag going up on the flagpole in Moosburg, the taste of white bread and the sight of thousands of bare-bottomed men squatting in the field as their boxcars stopped outside of Moosburg. There were few that did not mention these incidents to me, but not always in that order.

As the interminable missions ended at the close of the war, the men who had been captive became a statistic of a war that resulted in a staggering 292,130 American deaths.

Data indicate that over a million sorties were flown during the war, and in their 89% effectiveness, over 30,000 enemy aircraft were destroyed. There were 94,565 American air combat casualties with 30,099 killed in action. Beyond that, 13,360 were wounded and evacuated, and the remaining 51,106 were missing in action, prisoners of war or internees. Allied prisoners of war were many with 139,000 Americans and 217,000 British adding to the toll.[21]

I will never know how my father tried to escape from Stalag Luft III as he had noted in a debriefing document after the war. He never once mentioned this to us. He had written that a German guard had "thrown a barbed wire gate" at him. I wondered if this could have happened during an escape attempt and wondered how a gate could have been "thrown." His simple words left no clues, but he did say the gate injured his upper leg. I will never solve that mystery, but my own research turned up other interesting facts. I believe he was taken to the same church where the funeral of German Karl-Hans was taking place the day my father was shot down, but he never would have known that. He assumed it was a normal Sunday service. And he never would have known he was taken to Eckernforde Naval Base and Schloss Gottorf castle. Nor would he have known his deceased crewmate, Harold Flaugher, had been confused with another man who died that same day, and their identities in the German cemetery had been switched for nearly three years. Only recently have I found out that the second man buried there had trained with my father as a bombardier. Not only did my father not know he had been killed in action, but he had no idea the day he and his crew left Sgt. Flaugher's coffin there, that he was steps away from the grave of his fellow bombardier who had been buried there the same day. And certainly my father never would have known he was only clicks away on a computer from finding his long-lost crewmates and opening up a dialogue with researchers around the world. How he would have loved that.

My father was one of many who passed through the eye of the needle, "that indescribably small window between life and death that virtually all downed fliers squeezed through on their brutal journey from cockpit to prison camps,"[22] and he had survived it.

To me, the legacy of that day in June of 1944 is analogous to the Phoenix rising from the ashes. Despite such tragic losses, often good does come after evil, and the forging of international friendships such as we experienced indicates much good and understanding can rise upward out of tragedy even sixty years later.

As this book is brought to a close, a picture of the crew of "Rhapsody in Junk" rides along in a Humvee in Baghdad, Iraq, put there by my nephew, Lt. Col. Stephen Hogan, who tells all his men about this brave crew. No better guardian angels could be watching over the men of the 18th Airborne as they transverse the desert sands.

Lt. Col. Stephen Hogan, nephew of John and Marilyn Walton, proudly displays the crew of "Rhapsody in Junk" in the window of his Humvee where the picture stayed for the duration of his tour of duty in Iraq.
Courtesy of Lt. Col. Stephen Hogan

At this writing, Cadet 1st Class Chris Gamble, grandson of co-pilot Butler, has connected with Lt. General Clark at the Air Force Academy where Chris is studying to make the Air Force his career, and Scott Walton, grandson of bombardier Jeffers, has earned his pilot's license, making flying his chosen career.

Cadet 1st Class Chris Gamble, grandson of "Rhapsody's" co-pilot Dee Butler, at the U.S. Air Force Academy with General Clark

Pilot, Scott Walton, grandson of "Rhapsody's" bombardier, Thomas Jeffers, continuing his grandfather's love of flight

Courtesy of Mr. David Sorcher    Cin Weekly

Having located the children of the crew, we have become the "Children of 'Rhapsody in Junk'" united in the love of our fathers. During the war, the crew could never have imagined that sixty years later their children would connect in joy and tears and hang on each others' words for the smallest shared memory of the men's experiences. I think the entire crew would smile broadly at the thought. The legacy they left to us is the gift of each other. We are now bonded in a way few are, and that bond began on a farm field in Blick, Germany, six decades ago.

Not only the children, but now the grandchildren of these brave men have taken much interest and like young Matthias in Germany, we leave it to the future generations to remember.

※※※

# Epilogue

**Martin Allain** – whose American flag graced the Nazi flagpole at Stalag VIIA, returned to his home in Louisiana where he became a much-beloved pediatrician. Besides treating his patients, he was on call for twenty-eight years, twenty-four hours a day, at Holy Angels School for the handicapped. He had the reputation for treating all children whether they could pay or not.

**Douglas Bader** – the British double amputee removed from Stalag Luft III, later escaped from Lamsdorf Medical Facility and finished the war at Colditz, the castle that held the most notorious and determined escapers. Bader was freed at the end of the war, from Colditz as he was planning another escape. He left the Royal Air Force in 1946 and became managing director of Shell Aircraft until 1969 when he left to become a member of the Civil Aviation Authority Board. Paul Brickhill, author of "The Great Escape," wrote a book about Bader entitled, "Reach for the Sky," which was published in 1954 and was later made into a movie. Bader, who was knighted by the British government in 1976, died in 1982 at the age of seventy-three.

**Robert Beatty** – Jeffers' blockmate from Stalag Luft III died in September, 2006 at the age of eighty-eight. Although I had not met him and only had telephone conversations with him, his long letter to me describing my father's attempts to lift his fellow prisoners' spirits during bleak days will always be remembered by me.

**Gottlieb Berger** - who had summoned Colonel Spivey and General Vanaman from Spremberg to Berlin was summoned himself to be tried in Nuremberg. Spivey's support of Berger saved him from hanging. When Hitler decided to use thirty-five-thousand prisoners of war as hostages, it was Berger's failure to deliver or enforce the order that saved the lives of thousands of the prisoners. He was arrested and put on trial in the Ministries Trial in 1947 and was convicted in 1949 for his role in the genocide of European Jews. He was sentenced to twenty-five years in prison. The sentence was reduced to ten years in 1951.

**William Brodek** – who flew with the Northrop crew that fateful day returned to Jamaica, New York, where his interest in mathematics continued. He married his wife, Jean, and they had one son, Bill, Jr. Brodek became a physicist for Hughes Aircraft after he studied engineering at Columbia University. An avid reader and learner, Brodek spent his days at Stalag Luft III immersed in education. He later worked with William P. Lear in Ohio, who had an eighth grade education but invented among other things the auto pilot system and first car radio. He also, with the help of Brodek, designed the Lear Jet. Just before a scheduled move to Japan, Brodek died at the age of fifty-eight of a heart attack.

**Dee Butler** – settled down with wife, Miriam, after the war and had two more daughters, besides Julie--Kay and Sue. He was a career officer in the Air Force after the war, and his assignment in Germany allowed him to travel widely with his family. After arriving home on June 9th, he wrote to Dean that he was playing with his new baby daughter and doing much sleeping and eating, and he regretted not having the opportunity to talk to Dean in Germany or France. Thirty-one years later, he reunited with Woody and Gunn and shared their memory of that moment on the march when Woody could not go on. Butler enjoyed the outdoors and took his family camping, fishing and hiking. Besides being an excellent artist, he was a talented wood carver and writer. As the years passed, he was a well-respected leader in his church and community. Butler died of a heart attack in Utah at the age of seventy-two, leaving letters to his family about his love of God and how he was sustained by that love through the war and his entire life.

**Alex Cardenas** - returned to Texas and worked in airplane sales before moving to Mexico. He became an airline pilot after the war and flew for over fifty years, many of them with Aero Mexico. He found and married his blue-eyed senorita, Estela, and he had three daughters and a son, Angelita, Laurita, Estelita and a son, Alex, who is also a pilot. In 2005, his entire town and government officials turned out to celebrate his life and the publication of his autobiography. He currently resides in Torreon, Coah, Mexico.

**Albert P. Clark** – returned to Texas to his wife and three children, racing through lawn sprinklers to fall into their arms. Before he arrived, his treasured scrapbooks beat him home necessitating the pay off of his scotch bet. After liberation, when a friend from Willie Lanford's old bomb group brought Lanford much-needed food and clothing, Willie gave him the books and Clark's home address and asked that the books be mailed. A check was issued for $75.00 by Clark to obtain the scotch when it was next available. A lieutenant colonel at just twenty-eight during the war, Clark served a distinguished military career in the United States Air Force culminating in his appointment as the sixth superintendent of the United States Air Force Academy in Colorado Springs, Colorado, where he currently resides.

**Charles Clifford** – divorced before his enlistment, returned home to California. He was never heard from again. He died with no family to claim him in August, 1985, in Fresno, California, at the age of sixty-three.

**Charles Davis** – Jeffers and Butler's roommate in England perished June 17, 1944, with others on the Morley crew. His brother later fought at Normandy. Weeks later, the mayor of Caen told his brother of the crash of Charles's plane. All nine bodies were so badly burned that they had to be identified by dog tags. The Morley mission was the third that day, and the lead navigator, probably due to fatigue, led the formation off course and over a German panzer division in Caen, France. Davis's mother received mostly personal items that were not her son's after the war. He was brought home and buried in Charleston, Missouri.

**Lawrence Dean** - stood outside a "Tent Revival" smoking a cigarette as Frances McCurry listened to a Baptist preacher inside. When she saw him on her way out, it was love at first sight, and she told her girlfriend she would marry him one day. He left for war, completing gunnery school in Harlingen, Texas, and went to Sioux Falls, South Dakota, for radio school before joining the crew. During the war, Dean's promises to Frances for the future were predicated on the ever-present thought, "if I ever get home." Waiting at home, Frances's hopes for the future revolved around "if he ever gets home." A few years later he did. They married and had two children, Steven and Brenda. On Valentine's Day in 2002, their church presented them with a plaque that read "Champion Lovers Award." It was given to the married couple who was most admired, loving toward one another, devoted and by their efforts in and out of church, set the best example of a good Christian couple. Sadly, she died two weeks later, having been grateful for his return from war for fifty-six years. Dean worked as a turbine engineer for Meade Paper Company and retired after forty-three years. He presently resides in Kingsport, Tennessee.

**Frank Deimel** – made his way back home to Chicago and eventually settled in Texas. After years of bachelorhood, he married Marian, a widow, and adopted her 14-year old daughter, Anna. The Deimels were married for forty-four years. Frank was very devoted to St. Francis and loved animals. When he visited his wife's family's hunting lodge, he could not bring himself to kill any of the animals. For years, he put out dishes for stray animals, and on many occasions approached the meanest of dogs trying to befriend them. He suffered more than one dog bite, but he never stopped trying. He worked as a sales representative for the midwest for Scalandre Silks dealing in high quality silk fabrics. One of the places he supplied was the White House as well as numerous famous museums. He retired after over thirty years and became a doting grandfather to his three granddaughters. The "old man" on the crew lived a long and happy life, dying from a stroke in 2005 at the age of eighty-nine.

**Dulag Luft** - The Intelligence Center in Oberursel where top fighter aces and bomber crews were interrogated, was renamed Camp King and later became the headquarters of a transportation company. After the war, the United States Military held Goering, and other famous Nazis and interrogated them in Oberursel in preparation for the Nuremberg trials. They were held in the same cells as the former Allied prisoners.

**Harold J. Flaugher** – was interred in his final resting place in Belgium. He rests in Plot C, Row 7, Grave 24, Ardennes American Cemetery, Neupré, Belgium, (Neuville-en Condroz) just beside the town of Liege where Jeffers began his journey home.

**Jack Gonzales** – was released from the hospital after the war in October. A month later, he dined in a restaurant with friends, a pleasure he had been deprived of for so long. He looked up to see the most beautiful blond he had ever seen in his life. His friends introduced them. He immediately broke up with a girl he had been dating, and shortly thereafter, married seventeen-year-old Marie. After the war, he became a truck driver in a family trucking business delivering pipes. He had two daughters and a son, Linda, Jacqueline and Bryan. He lives in Cerritos, California, and has been married to his beautiful blond for fifty-nine years.

**Trevor Hewitt** – and his father, Derek, were instrumental in excavating the crash site of the "Belle of Boston" near his English home in Frettenham, England. As late as 2005, the Hewitts found pilot Kingsley's identification bracelet a few inches down in the soil. It was engraved with a message from his wife. With a joint effort of many people, nine of the ten crew families were located, and crew relatives traveled to England to meet the Hewitts and finally learn their loved ones' fates. In 1979, Trevor and Derek Hewitt, with a mechanic, Peter, were in Derek's workshop one-hundred yards from the plane's crash site when they heard a terrific bang. They ran onto the road and could see a car on its side at the roadside exactly at the "Belle" crash site. Two cars had a head-on collision, and when Trevor and Derek looked inside, they discovered that both drivers had been killed. The police came and asked Derek to remove the wreckage with his tow truck after they had finished their investigations. The men collected the bits and pieces lying on the edge of the road in the hedge. Trevor found a piece of aluminum three-feet long by two-feet wide in the hedge. Since aluminum at that time was at a premium price for scrap, they put it on the truck with the other bits and sold it for it scrap. Only then did they realize that it was a piece of the "Belle" that had been hanging in the roadside bush for thirty-five years. The author visited the Hewitt family in 2006 visiting several crash sites and touring Norwich and what remained of the airbase, and saw the runway where "Rhapsody in Junk" departed on its fateful last flight.

**Bennie Hill** – the sole survivor of the Morley crew was held prisoner by the Germans in a hospital run by Catholic nuns. He was repatriated to the United States as the Allied troops closed in. The stain of war covered Bennie for years to come. Before returning to his home in Minnesota, he went directly to West Virginia where he stayed for three years for treatment of his burns. He returned home, and when he approached his house, his mother turned him away. His burns had disfigured him so that she said he was not the son she sent off to war. It took her years to accept him. His wife, Delores, divorced him, and later, Kenneth, the son he had with her, died. Bennie took a job at the VFW as a bartender, and later he worked at the Post Office. He married Elna and had another son, who died at birth. Eventually, Bennie had nine sons, the baseball team he always wanted, Benjamin, Barry, Brian, Blaine, Bradley, Brent, Barton, Blair and Brooks. He successfully raised nine young men to adulthood while always mourning his nine crewmates that never came home. War experiences had taken a severe toll on him, and Bennie died at the age of sixty-four from liver failure. Bennie is buried in the Summit Cemetery in Morris, Minnesota, across from Baby Hill, his first son, "The Tenth B.

Hill," as his brothers call him, and also next to his own twin brother who died at birth.

**Thomas Jeffers** - returned to Phyllis and to Springfield, Ohio. He had enlisted September 29th, 1942 and called to active duty at Sheppard Field, Wichita Falls, Texas. He went on to the Northwestern State Teacher's College in Alva, Oklahoma, and then San Antonio, Texas, to the Aviation Cadet Classification Center. From there he left for Ellington Field, Texas, to pre-flight training, and on November 18th, 1943, received his bombardier's wings in Big Spring, Texas. He went to Salt Lake City, Utah and Casper, Wyoming, to phase training and on to Topeka, Kansas, to the Staging Area there. He was in the reserve from 1947 to 1951 when he was released from active duty. He reenlisted in November, 1952, and became a career Air Force officer. He had another daughter, Marilyn, to join sister, Diane. After the war, he earned his business degree from Rutgers's University and later an MBA from the University of Chicago. He served as a procurement officer working on missile systems and the M-16 rifle, both in the United States and in Bangkok, Thailand. He retired from the Air Force as a Lt. Colonel after thirty years of service and became Director of Purchasing at Riverside Hospital in Columbus, Ohio, where he started their first credit union. During the post-war years, he often attended prisoner of war reunions. Frequently, the German guards were invited, and he enjoyed his conversations with them. He never stopped trying to find out what happened to Sgt. Flaugher. Jeffers died of a stroke June 24th, 2004, at the age of eighty-three. He wrote one last page in his journal in 2001 after the June 17th entry as he sensed his memory starting to fail:

> 22 June, 2001 - We did fly a mission the next day, June 18, 1944 & unfortunately got shot down over the Kiel Navy yard in Germany. All bailed out and spent the rest of the war in a German prison camp.
>
> T.F. Jeffers
>
> Harold Flaugher was killed on this last mission. I

visited his family in Ohio upon my return.

T.F.J.

I assume that last entry closed that chapter of his life.

**The Lido Club** – in Norwich, as well as two others, are now Bingo halls. Andrew's Hall is still in use today.

**James Rhea Luper** - later went on to become Commandant of Cadets at Maxwell Air Force Base preflight school. Novelist, David Westheimer, a B-24 navigator and ex-POW shot down over Italy, authored "Von Ryan's Express," in which the character of Colonel Joseph Ryan, played by Frank Sinatra, was modeled after Luper. James Luper died on a snowy night in 1953 at Offut Air Force Base, Nebraska, when his plane crashed.

**The Marine Dragon** – was a freighter of the C-4-S-B2 type that carried Jeffers, Dean and Clifford home to Boston arriving June 17th, 1945. It was built in 1944 by the Sun Shipbuilding & Dry Dock Company. The ship was renamed "HAWAIIAN MONARCH" after the war and bought in 1965 by the Matson Line, which renamed it "MAUNAWILI (#2)" in 1978. It was still active in 1980.

**Matthias Martensen** – returned to the crash site several times with his family to find more parts of the plane. At age sixteen, he came to the United State as a visiting high school student.

**Dennis McDarby** – Jeffers' blockmate from Stalag Luft III died in June, 2006, at the age of eighty-three. Weeks before he died, he had two toes amputated, residual damage from the frostbite he sustained on the march over sixty years before. After being widowed, he married his wife Julie.

**Francis "Red" Morley** - pilot of the doomed flight on June 17th, had a daughter, Karen, born after his death. She was adopted by a step-father, and fifty-four years later, both daughter and mother died from cancer within a week of each other. Three weeks later both of Morley's brothers died. Morley is buried in Oak Grove Cemetery, Logan, Ohio. Morley's mother received a box after the war, but it contained very few of his belongings.

**Morley Crew** – were quickly buried and most remain in France. At the Normandy American Cemetery Colleville–sur mer/St Laurent-sur-mer (Calvados) France are the sacred graves of Sg**t. William Rickert** – Plot F, Row 27, Grave 333; **Henry Hier** Plot F, Row 27, Grave 30, **Sgt. Earl Dunaway** Plot F, Row 27, Grave 32, **Sgt Paul Dulmage** – Plot F, Row 27, Grave 3.and **Sgt. Wesley Darden** - Plot A, Row 2, Grave 33. **Max Detty** was brought home by his family and is buried in Jeffersonville, Ohio.

**Henry Northrop** - returned to marry Billie Conners, the student he had met in Utah. They married on February 9th, 1946. He continued to make the military his career. Twenty days after his officer's separation from the USAAF in 1946, he signed up as a master sergeant and made the Army his career. He served for twenty years. Northrop never got over the feeling he was living on "borrowed time." He had a daughter, Marielaina, and three sons, Hank H. Jr. (Sonny), Michael and James. Michael remembered his father throwing the fastest baseball he'd ever seen. Northrop died in 1997 at the age of eighty.

**George S. Patton** – On December 9th, a day before he was due to return to the United States, Patton and his Chief of Staff went on a day trip to hunt pheasants outside Mannheim, Germany. Patton was severely injured when, in the early morning haze, his car was struck by an Army truck which turned left in front of his car. He was thrown forward, broke his neck and was paralyzed from the neck down. He died in a hospital in Heidelberg, Germany on December 21st, 1945 and was buried in Luxembourg American Cemetery along with other members of the Third Army after a simple soldier's funeral.

**Hugo and Regina Purins** – After surviving the bombing of Dresden, Regina and her husband came to America in 1951, sponsored by an American church. They settled in Dayton, Ohio, and raised two daughters. Regina became an LPN and later worked in payroll at a department store. Hugo, who had a background in drafting and engineering, eventually received an MBA and worked for General Motors. His boss had been an airman in the Dresden airstrikes. Hugo wrote several books and also articles for a Latvian newspaper. He died of leukemia in 1977 at the age of 56. Regina never remarried and died of kidney cancer in 2005 at the age of 82.

**Joe Risko** – mourned the loss of his crew and became part of several other crews. He completed all his missions and returned to Detroit afterward. His parents bought him a red Pontiac with white wall tires, and his girlfriend Jean was sitting in it when he returned. They married and had two children. He was saddened that none of his crew could be at his wedding and chose not to have a best man. Interested in electrical work, he joined the Public Lighting Commission of Detroit where he rose to senior lineman. At the age of thirty-seven he volunteered to fill in for a man who had called in sick and left for the U.S. Army Nike Base on the west side of Detroit. He visited his parents during his lunch hour to make sure they were alright. Although dressed in protective clothing for the icy, windy, weather that day and equipped with all his safety gear, a live wire of 4700 volts lashed across his face in the wind, killing him. He left a wife, son and daughter, Robert and Sharon, and was buried December 23rd, 1960. After Christmas the family found the hidden gifts he had bought and wrapped for them.

**Jerry Sage** - After the war, the colonel became an instructor at West Point, and wrote a book of his war experiences, entitled, "Sage." Although the character of Hilts, the "Cooler King," in "The Great Escape" is an amalgamation, many believe Sage to be the model.

**Moose Stillman** – who sat so proudly beside Albert Clark on the tank on liberation day at Moosburg, became the first Commandant of Cadets at the United States Air Force Academy in 1954, and retired as a major general. During the war, he commanded the 322nd Bomb Group in England and was shot down on his second low-level bombing mission. In 1959, he was named to Sports Illustrated's Silver Anniversary All-American

Football team. He died May 22, 1991, at the age of eighty and is buried at Ft. Sam Houston in San Antonio, Texas.

**Hanns Joachim Scharff** – Master Interrogator at Dulag Luft was ordered to the United States by the Department of Justice to testify in the trial of an American defector and other planned trials of United States servicemen accused of collaborating with the Germans. Many came to naught for lack of any incriminating evidence and objection by Hanns. Living in the United States, Hanns made mosaic tables for Nieman Marcus in his New York studio after the war. He became a world-known figure in mosaic artistry producing the five mosaic Cinderella murals of the Magic Castle at Disney World in Orlando, Florida, and the restoration of the Senate floor for the Capitol Building in Sacramento, California. In addition, he created the mosaic adorning the entry ramp to the Land Kraft pavilion at the EPCOT Center, as well as other beautiful murals and fountains. One of his creations was a one-hundred-twenty-foot mural at Dixie College in St. George, Utah, co-pilot, Dee Butler's home, where the crewman returned to live after the war. After a painful divorce from Margaret, Scharff later married Baroness Sabine von Danckelman, a direct descendant of the Minister of Finance of Prussia under Frederick the Great. Eventually, Hanns was joined in the United States by his four adult children, Hanns-Felix, Hanns-Christian Gloria Rydell (Della) and Hanns-Claudius. He was made an "Honorary Chief" of the Kawaiisu Indian Tribe in 1987 and one year later he was elected "Grand Officer of the Order of Good Hope" (Spei Bona), regarded as South Africa's premier order which is awarded to individuals who have earned the respect and gratitude of the Republic of South Africa. Scharff died in California at the age of eighty-four having passed on his artful mosaic skills to his daughter-in-law, Monika Scharff, who helped him with all his stunning projects. His style of interrogation became legendary.

**Stalag Luft III** – was converted to a headquarters that provides military training for the Polish Army. The Russians had used the museum building where the camp's artifacts are held for military training until the fall of Communism. The entrance to tunnel Dick is still in Sagan concealed in a drain on the floor of the shower room in Hut 122. When closed and sealed, it was under several feet of water. The Germans never found it, and recent excavators have found it contains much contraband and escape material. It was assumed that no Poles ever worked at the camp or aided prisoners, but in 2003 excavations unearthed the trapdoor that hid the mouth of the Dick tunnel, which turned out to be made from crash debris of an aircraft flown by members of the Polish resistance movement. No one knows how that material got into the camp and to the tunnel's entrance.

**Villa in Greiz** – for so many generations the home of the Scharff family was known as Villa Jahn. It was taken by the Russians at the end of the war. After departing with the bronze figurine at the end of the war, Hanns Scharff never saw the villa again. It was renamed "The Soviet Pioneers Clubhouse."

✵✵✵

*"Take these men as your example, like them remember that posterity can only be for the free: that freedom is the sure possession of those alone who have the courage to defend it."* Pericles 431B.C.

Courtesy of the Collings Found

# Appendix

Letters from Thomas Jeffers to Phyllis Jeffers 1944 from Sagan Germany, Prisoner of War Camp – Stalag Luft III Shot down June 18, 1944 Kriegsgefangenpost – U.S. censored Mit Luftpost Par Avion

### June 30, 1944

Dearest Wife,

I am now at a permanent prison camp & wish you would write to me here. Dee and I are together here. Both okay. The Red Cross is doing a wonderful job here and is taking good care of us supplying us with clothes and food parcels. I love you very much, Honey. Hope to see you soon.

Jeff

### July 2, 1944

Dearest Phil,

Hope you and Scrubby are doing fine. He ought to be coming along fine now, Honey, and should really be a big boy by this time. When you send a parcel Honey, please include some spices etc. as we do our own cooking here and can use them. I hope I'm not here to receive the parcel, but it won't hurt to send it.

All my love, Jeff

## July 6, 1944

Dearest Phil,

I sure hope that you and Scrubby are doing fine and are both getting fat. I am feeling fine and hope to be able to see you real soon. As yet, Dee hasn't heard whether it's a boy or a girl, and I'm sure Miriam has had the baby now. I hope that the apartment is coming along okay and that you intend to hang onto it till I get home. You won't have any monetary worries since your allotment checks will still come regularly every month. I imagine that you and Mom are keeping in contact now. I hope so. If Scrubby is giving you any trouble, give him a couple of spankings for his pop, honey. We had a big July 4th celebration here in camp today. It was pretty nice. Music and everything. Dee and I are planning a vacation in Yellowstone sometime after we get home. How would you like that? Say hello to folks.

All my love, Jeff

## July 30, 1944

Dearest Phil,

I hope by this time that you will already have been notified by the War Department that I am alive and well although unfortunately a prisoner. I hope also that you and Mom did not take too badly the news that I was missing. Your allotment will continue for the duration so keep your apartment and continue to prepare for the baby's arrival. Keep in touch with Miriam and compare notes with each other when either of you receives a letter. Also keep in touch with the Red Cross and find out from them how to send parcels to me.

I pray for the war's end soon so that you and the baby and I and all the other couples in the world can enjoy a happy home life again. I'll write as often as I can, but you won't receive more than one letter a month usually, so don't worry about me at all. Write to me often.

Love, Jeff

## August 11, 1944

My Darling Wife,

By the time this letter reaches you, I imagine that Junior will be just about ready to announce his squalling presence to the world. I wish that I could be with you then Honey, and I still have hopes of being able to do so. If I can't, I've asked Mom to be there and help you out as much as she can. Also, I've asked her to help you with the procedure of having the baby baptized as soon as possible. I hope that your allotment money is coming through all right. If it's not, inquire at the finance department at Patterson Field how to check on it. I hope to receive some mail from you soon, with plenty of pictures. I hope that you are still writing to me as often as you used to before I landed in Germany. The postal regulations are the same only delivery is not as fast. If you send a parcel, I need some socks, underwear, candy etc. I have hopes of seeing you before you receive this.

All my love, Jeff

## August 22, 1944

My Darling Wife,

I hope you and the baby are feeling fine now. I am doing pretty well and am feeling swell. I expect that very soon now I will be receiving letters and parcels from you. It seems like forever since I had my last letter from you. It has been about two and one half months. I miss you terribly, Honey, but I guess I'm no worse off than all the others here in that respect. We all have someone that we miss very much. It won't be too long now before we will all be home with those we love. I expect that you and I and Junior will be able to have Christmas dinner together. Honey, from time to time, I'll mention in my letters things that I need here, and you can include them in parcels. I need some underwear & a pair of old shoes, a set of collar brass and wings in addition to what I've already mentioned in my other letters. Honey, don't buy anything new in the way of clothes to send, because I may not receive the apparel and old things would be a small loss.

All my love to you and baby.

Jeff

## September 10, 1944

Dearest Phil,

In a little over two months from today we'll be proud parents. I still have hopes of being there with you when the time comes. If not, we should surely be able to have Christmas dinner together. In any event Honey, this war should be over very soon. The news is good and shows every evidence of continuing to be so. I hope that your allotment is reaching you all right every month then I can be sure that you don't have any financial worries. I hope by this time that my clothes have arrived home. Take good care of them, I'll be using them again soon. Dave's pilot and co-pilot are here now, but I haven't been able to talk to them yet, so don't know whether he's still alive. I hope that he is okay. He is a swell guy. Also Chris' co-pilot is here too. The place is beginning to be populated by our good buddies. There isn't much I can write Honey except that I miss you and hope to see you soon. . .

All my love, Jeff

## September 30, 1944

My Darling Wife,

In a few more days, our second wedding anniversary will have come and gone. I hope that it will be the last we will have under wartime conditions. I am sure that our next will be an event worth remembering. These that we have away from each other will soon be just a memory. Next year, we should be able to have a regular family gathering and have lots of fun. The weather here is beginning to turn cool, and we are all following the fighting results very closely. We have high hopes of eating Christmas dinner at home. I imagine that you and Junior will be home and doing fine when this letter arrives. I hope, Honey, that you won't have had too bad a time. Mom should be able to help you quite a bit. . . . I hope to see you very soon, Honey.

All my love, Jeff

## October 11, 1944

My Darling Wife,

I hope that you and baby are both doing well now. I have been worrying about you quite a bit these past few weeks and hope that you aren't having too bad a time. There are a lot of personal parcels from the states here in camp now, and I hope when they are distributed that I'll have one from you. It all depends upon whether the government was able to send you a mailing slip before the mailing period was up. I hope so, as I am getting short of socks and underwear. I'd like to have a few pair of heavy wool socks right now. There are quite a few Ohio boys here and we are forming an Ohio P.O.W. Club. There is a boy from Springfield over in the west camp. I believe his name is C.F. Kouse. Also, one from Findlay, his name is D.P. Fuller. . . . . Dee still doesn't know if his baby is a boy or girl.

All my love, Jeff

## October 19, 1944

My Darling Wife,

I received my first letter on October 12, one from you dated September 11 and one from Lorraine dated September 12, in which she told me about her coming event. Seems to be quite an epidemic of births in the states. I also received mail on the 13th and 14th from you, two from Mom, and one from Lorraine. You can't imagine how happy and relieved I am to know that you are okay. The letters were full of news and leave none of the questions in my mind unanswered. I'm glad you are going to Patterson as I know you will receive the best of care there. Honey, I'd like for you to buy yourself that Chesterfield coat as a Christmas present, you certainly deserve it, and I want you to look sharp when I come home. I told Dee about Julie Ann as he hadn't received any mail then. He has had several now though.

All my love to you Honey, Jeff

## November 6, 1944

My Darling Phil,

Received four more of your letters yesterday and am glad to hear that you and Scrubby are still doing fine. Also happy to know that you are fixed up okay at the Field. I would have had a little trouble signing that application at this time.

I was sorry to learn that Mr. Flaugher's son is dead and happy that no one else was injured. I'm sure that they are all okay now. Send me any further news you may get. Please give his parents my sincerest condolences. He was one of the finest men I have ever known.

Honey, whatever you may be told to the contrary, your letters as you are writing them in August are spaced just about right. In fact, I could stand having you write much more often. Also, send more pictures. Glad to hear that you met and like all the folks up in Massachusetts. I intend to take you there for a visit when I get home.

I love you very much, Honey and hope to see you soon.

Love, Jeff

## November 14, 1944

My Darling Wife,

Today, Sunday is your big day. Honey, you can't realize how badly I feel that I can't be there with you today holding your hand as I'd promised I would. I hope that someday soon I'll be able to make it up to you some how. I'm doing lots of pacing up and down in true husbandly fashion, and I'm sure that the folks at home are doing some for me too. I hope that Mom was able to get there and be of some help to you. I got a big kick out of your story about Scrub and the cereal he didn't like. Your parcel hasn't arrived yet. I sure hope there are some heavy socks in it, as I've just about had my socks. The pictures you sent are swell, but they aren't anywhere near enough. Let's be sending lots more, huh? Keep writing as often as you do Honey and get the others to write too if they'd like….. I love you very much, Honey and am lonesome for you too. Hope to be home real soon.

All my love, Jeff

# End Notes

[1] Cardenas Carranza, Alejndro, *Un Lagunero en La Guerra*, 2005.

[2] Cardenas Carranza, Alejndro, *Un Lagunero en La Guerra*, 2005.

[3] Granholm, Jackson, *The Day We Bombed Switzerland*, 2000, Airlife Publishing Ltd. Printed with permission.

[4] Pearson, Kevin, *The Combined Bomber Offensive—A Historic Perspective of the Strategic Bombing of Germany (1939-1945)*.

[5] Slane, Robert M., *Journey to Freedom and Beyond*. St. Victoria, B.C., Canada: Trafford Publishing, 2004.

[6] Durand, Arthur, *Stalag Luft III: The Secret Story*. Baton Rouge, Louisiana: Louisiana State University Press, 1988.

[7] Durand, Arthur – conversation March 20, 2006.

[8] Chiesl, Oliver M., *Clipped Wings*. Seattle: Robert W. Kimball, privately published, 1948, unpaged.

[9] Rennell, Tony, Nichol, John, *The Last Escape--The Untold Story of Allied Prisoners of War in Europe 1944-45*. New York: Viking Press, 2003.

[10] Durand, Arthur, *Stalag Luft III: The Secret Story*. Baton Rouge, Louisiana: Louisiana State University Press, 1988.

[11] Clark, Albert P., *33 Months as a POW in Stalag Luft III, A World War II Airman Tells His Story*. Golden, Colorado: Fulcrum Publishing, 2004.

[12] Chiesl, Oliver M., *Clipped Wings*. Seattle: Robert W. Kimball, privately published, 1948, unpaged - Evacuation Chapter.

[13] Reed, Duane J., former archivist, U.S.A. F. Academy, conversation June 22, 2006.

[14] Slane, Robert M., conversation, February 2, 2006, *Journey to Freedom and Beyond*. St. Victoria, B.C., Canada: Trafford Publishing, 2004.

[15] Durand, Arthur, *Stalag Luft III: The Secret Story*. Baton Rouge, Louisiana: Louisiana State University Press, 1988.

[16] *Goodrich, Charles G. History of the USAAF POW of South Compound, Stalag Luft III*. 1945. Albert F. Simpson Historical Research Center, Maxwell AFB, Alabama.

[17] Clark, Albert P., *33 Months as a POW in Stalag Luft III, A World War II Airman Tells His Story*. Golden, Colorado: Fulcrum Publishing, 2004.

[18] Albert F. Simpson Historical Research Center, Maxwell AFB, Alabama. *Goodrich, Charles G. History of the USAAF POW of South Compound, Stalag Luft III*. 1945.

[19] Foster, Renita, Lt. Col., USA, *He Signaled Freedom with Old Glory*, to Moosburg Online, December 2000.

[20] Toliver, Raymond F., *The Interrogator, The Story of Hanns Scharff Luftwaffe's Master Interrogator*, Fallbrook, California: Aero Publishers, Inc., 1978.

[21] Stalag Luft III 50th Reunion, Former Prisoners of War brochure, 1995, Cincinnati, *Combat, Evasion and Capture by World War II Airmen*. Published by Stalag Luft III Former Prisoners of War, 1992, Ohio.

[22] Consolmagno, Joe, *Through the Eye of the Needle, 68 First Person Accounts of Combat, Evasion and Capture by World War II Airmen*. Published by Stalag Luft III Former Prisoners of War, 1992.

# Sources

### Internet

www.b24.net/pow/Dulag.htm.

www.458bg.com

www.merkki.com

www.wpafb.af.mil/museum/history/ww1/ww1-22.htm

www.axpow.org/pow_link.htm

www.archives.gov/research/ww2/electronic-records.html

www.wwiimemorial.com

www.armyairforces.com

www.accident-report.com

www.aviationarcheology.com

air@aviationarcheology.com

www.armyairforces.com/dbmacr.asp. - MACRS

www.b24.mach3ww.com

www.2ndair.org.uk

afhso.research@pentagon.af.mil

www.8thairforce.com

www.elsham.pwp.blueyonder.co.uk/gt_esc/

freepages.military.rootsweb.com/~hfhm/index.html

www.B24bestweb.com

www.zenoswarbirdvideos.com

www.web-birds.com

aad.archives.gov/aad/title_list.jsp

Norfrec@norfolk.gov.uk

archives.norfolk.gov.uk

eafa@uea.ac.uk

www.pro.gov.uk

www.uea.ac.uk/eafa

www.moosburg.org

www.luftwaffe.cz/greiner.html.

www.vetrecsarchives.gov

www.skylighters.org/special/cigcamps/cigmas.html

## Public Records

National Personnel Record Center – St Louis, MO
Public Records Office, Kew, London, England
National Archives and Records Administration. Center for Electronic Records. World War II POW Reports.
U.S. War Department. Military Intelligence Service. American Prisoners of War in Germany. Dulag Luft and Stalag Luft IV and Stalag Luft III.
Landeshauptstadt Kiel, Stadtarchiv, Rathaus, Fleethörn 9 – 17, 24103 Kiel, Germany.

# Books

Ash, William, *Under the Wire, The World War II Adventures of a Legendary Escape Artist and "Cooler King"* New York: Thomas Dunne Books, St. Martin's Press, 2005.
Bartel, Gretchen, *Zur Geschichte der Gemeinde*, Wagersrott, Germany, 1993.
Beltrone, Art and Lee, *A Wartime Log.* Charlottesville, VA: Hopewell Press, 1994.
Bowman, Martin, W., *Fields of Little America, An Illustrated History of the $8^{th}$ Air Force, $2^{nd}$ Air Division 1942-45.* Cambridge, England: Patrick Stephens Limited, 1977, 1983.
Brickhill, Paul, *Reach for the Sky, The Story of Douglas Bader, Legless Ace of the Battle of Britain.* New York: W.W. Norton Company, Inc., 1954.
Brickhill, Paul, *The Great Escape.* New York: W.W. Norton & Company, Inc., 1954.
Burt, Kendal, Leasor, James, *The One that Got Away.* London: 1956.
Cardenas, Alejandro Cardenas Carranza, *Un Lagunero en La Guerra.* Torreon, Mexico: Direccion Municipal de Cultura, Coleccion Centenario TOMO XXVIII, 2004.
Chiesl, Oliver M., *Clipped Wings.* Seattle: Robert W. Kimball, privately published, 1948.
Childers, Thomas, *In the Shadows of War.* New York: Henry Holt & Company, 2003.
Childers, Thomas, *Wings of Morning.* New York: Addison-Wesley Publishing Company, 1995.
Clark, Albert P., *33 Months as a POW in Stalag Luft III, A World War II Airman Tells His Story.* Golden, Colorado: Fulcrum Publishing, 2004.
Consolmagno, Joe, *Through the Eye of the Needle, 68 First Person Accounts of Combat, Evasion and Capture by World War II Airmen.* Published by Stalag Luft III Former Prisoners of War, 1992.
Crawley, Aidan, *Escape from Germany.* New York: Dorset Press, 1985.
Currier, Donald R., *Fifty Mission Crush.* New York: Pocket Books, 1992.
Daniel, Eugene, *In the Presence of Mine Enemies: Memories of German Prisoner of War Life. Feb 16, 1943 to April 29, 1945* Attleboro Mass: 1985.
Davies-Scourfield, Gris, *In the Presence of My Foes,* South Yorkshire, England, Pen and Sword Books Limited, 1991.
Dolibois, John E., *Pattern of Circles, An Ambassador's Story,* Kent, Ohio: Kent State University Press, 1989.
Durand, Arthur, *Stalag Luft III: The Secret Story.* Baton Rouge, Louisiana: Louisiana State University Press, 1988.
Galland, Adolf, *The First and the Last. The Rise and Fall of the German Fighter Forces 1938-1945.* Great Britain, Methuen & Co., Ltd., 1955.
Granholm, Jackson, *The Day We Bombed Switzerland.* England: Airlife, 2000.
Holmstrom, Carl, *Kriegie Life.* Published by Carl Holstrom, 1946.
Hopewell, Clifford, *Combine 13.* Dallas, TX: Merrimore Press, 1990.

Jablonski, Edward, *Flying Fortress*. Garden City, New York: Doubleday, 1965.

James, B.A., *Moonless Night, The World War II Escape Epic*. Oxford, England: ISIS Publishing Ltd.: 7 Centremead, Osney Mead, 2001.

Kaplan, Philip and Smith, Rex, *One Last Look—A Sentimental Journey to the Eighth Air Force Heavy Bomber Bases of World War II in England*, New York, Abbeville Press, 1983.

Klaas, Joe, *Maybe I'm Dead*. New York, 1955.

Laffin, John, *The Man the Nazis Couldn't Catch*. Phoenix Mill-Thrupp-Stroud-Gloucestershire, England: Sutton Publishing, 2004.

Martensen, Matthias, *Stenner 2003/04, Gymnasium An der Stenner, Stennerstrabe*Iserlohn, Iserlohn, Germany: Aufarbeiten von Kriegserlebnissen hautnah miterlebtt, 2004.

Mazer, Harry, *The Last Mission*. New York: Laurel Leaf; Reissue edition, 1981.

McCright, Ewell Ross. *Behind the Wire: Stalag Luft III, South Compound*. Benton, AK: Arnold Wright, 1993.

McGuire, William C. II, *After the Liberators: A Father's Last Mission, A Son's Lifelong Journey*. Parkway Publishers, Inc.: Boone, North Carolina, 1999. New York: ibooks, 2000.

McLachlan, Ian, *Night of the Intruders*. Patrick Stephens Ltd., 1994.

Miller, Donald L., *Masters of the Air—America's Bomber Boys Who Fought the Air War Against Nazi Germany*. New York, Simon & Schuster, 2006.

Newcomb, Alan, *Vacation With Pay*. The Record Publishing Company: Haverhill, MA, 1947.

Philpot, Oliver, *Stolen Journey*. New York, Dutton, 1952.

Rennell, Tony, Nichol, John, *The Last Escape-- The Untold Story of Allied Prisoners of War in Europe 1944-45*. New York: Viking Press, 2003.

Reynolds, George A., The *History of the 458$t^h$ Bomb Group. The 458th Bombardment Group (Heavy)*. Birmingham, Alabama, 1974.

Richard, Oscar G., *Kriegie, An American POW in Germany*. Baton Rouge, Louisiana: Louisiana State University Press June, 2000.

Sage, Jerry, *Sage*. Wayne, Pennsylvania: Miles Standish Press, 1985.

Samuel, Wolfgang, *German Boy*. Jackson, MS: University Press of Mississippi, 2000.

Simmons, Kenneth W., *Kriegie*. NY: Nelson Publishers, 1960.

Slane, Robert M., *Journey to Freedom and Beyond*. St. Victoria, B.C., Canada: Trafford Publishing, 2004.

Smith, Sydney, *Mission Escape*. New York: 2005, Popular Library, 1968.

Smith, Sydney, *Wings Day: The Man Who Led the RAF's Epic Battle in German Captivity*. London: Collins, 1968.

Spivey, Delmar T., *POW Odyssey, Recollections of Center Compound, Stalag Luft III and the Secret German Peace Mission in WW II*. Attleboro, MA: Printed by Colonial Lithograph, Inc., 1984.

Stiles, Bert, *Serenade to the Big Bird*. New York: W.W. Norton & Co., Inc., 1947.

Toland, John, *The Last 100 Days: The Tumultuous and Controversial Story of the*

*Final Days of World War II in Europe.* New York: Random House, 1966.
Toliver, Raymond F., *The Interrogator, The Story of Hanns Scharff Luftwaffe's Master Interrogator.* Fallbrook, California: Aero Publishers, Inc., 1978.
Vance, Jonathan F., *A Gallant Company, The True Story of The Great Escape.* New York, ibooks ,2000.
Von Luck, Hans, *Panzer Commander.* New York, New York: Dell Publishing, 1989.
Westheimer, David, *Song of the Young Sentry.* Canada: Little Brown and Company, 1968.
Westheimer, David, *Sitting It Out.* Houston, Texas: Rice University Press, 1992.
Williams, Eric, *The Wooden Horse.* New York: Pen and Sword Publishers, 1949.
Wolter, Tim, *POW Baseball in World War II, The National Pastime Behind Barbed Wire.* North Carolina: McFarland Company, Inc., Publishers, 1957.

## Manuscripts

*The Longest Mission.* – Published for the 50th POW Reunion of Stalag Luft III, Cincinnati, Ohio, 1995.
Eighth Air Force Historical Society, *458th Bombardment Group*, www.8thafhs.org 2005.
Gamble, Kay, *Memoirs of Dee Butler*, Preston, ID.
Risko, Robert, *Unpublished Journal of Joe Risko*, Farmington Hills, Michigan.
Hale, Blare, *Sharing Memories of WWII 1944-45.* Logan, UT.

## Articles

Science News. *Seeing Past the Dirt*, July 20, 2005.

## Interviews

### United States

Armes, Christine
Beatty, Robert and Sara Beatty
Brodek, Jean
Burgess, Val
Cardenas, Alex and Estela
Cardenas, Angelita
Clark, General Albert P.
Cole, Sam
Dean, Lawrence

Deimel, Frank and Marian
Flaugher, Max
Flaugher, Tracy
Foster, Renita
Flynn, Sam
Gamble, Kay
Gonzales, Marie
Gonzales, Jack
Gribi, Charles
Haag, Maria
Hargrove, Mary
Haygood, Tamara
Hewitt, Trevor
Hewitt, Derek
Hill, Blaine
Jeffers, Thomas F.
Leverette, Cliff
Martensen, Claudia and Gerhard
McDarby, Dennis and Julie
Mitchell, Heike
Morea, Brenda
Northrop, Michael
Petty, Greg
Petty, Katharine
Petty, Mike
Reed, Duane
Robert Risko, Jr.
Scharff, Claudius and Monika
Schwartz, Jennifer
Slane, Robert
Stout, Don and Ercellmae
Taylor, Anna
Tribbett, Everette
Waddington, Linda
Weinberg, Bob

## Canada

Wanless, Wilkie
Watts, Tom and Bernice

## The Netherlands

van Drogenbroek, Ben

## Belgium

Reniere, Ed

## Germany

Bartel, Juergen and Gretchen
Briel, Jutta
Glienke, Peter
Gotzke, Angela and Manfred
Klaws, Katie and Wolfgang
Kuhl, Claus
Martensen, Hartwig
Mueller, Horst

## Poland

Jakubiak, Jacek

## References

Air Force Museum, WPAFB, Stalag Luft III file Prisoners of war drawer, research division.
Albert F. Simpson Historical Research Center, Maxwell AFB, Alabama.
Goodrich, Charles G. History of the USAAF POW of South Compound, Stalag Luft III. 1945.
USAF AF Academy, Albert P. Clark Collection 1942-1975. Special Collections Room. Delmar T. Spivey Collection Spec. Collections.

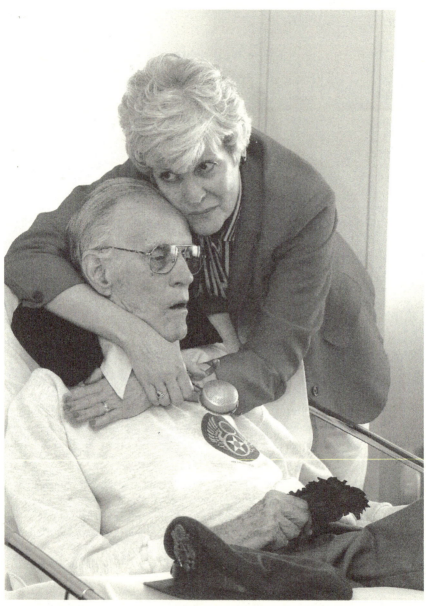

Lt. Colonel Thomas F. Jeffers and his daughter, Marilyn, examine the pieces of his plane brought from the crash site in Germany.

## About the Author

Marilyn Walton. is a graduate of The Ohio State University. She has written six books for children, including the successful Celebration Series for Raintree-Steck-Vaughn. Her book, *Chameleons' Rainbow*, won a Children's Choice award in 1986. She and her husband, a retired Miami University marketing professor, raised three sons in Oxford, Ohio, where they currently reside. After locating her father's crew and their relatives, she was instrumental in finding the crew families of the B-24, "Belle of Boston," that crashed in England in 1944. She currently conducts World War II research to assist other families in learning the history of their fathers' war experiences and in finding relatives of the crews. With 78,000 American World War II men missing in action, of which 38,000 are considered recoverable, she works with other researchers trying to locate the remains of these men so that they can finally be brought home.